Lena Mirošević, Gregory Zaro, Mario Katić,
Danijela Birt (eds.)

Landscape in Southeastern Europe

Studies on South East Europe

edited by
Prof. Dr. Karl Kaser
(Graz)

vol. 21

LIT

Lena Mirošević, Gregory Zaro, Mario Katić,
Danijela Birt (eds.)

Landscape in Southeastern Europe

LIT

Knjižnica Državnog arhiva u Zadru, sign.: 5247, Rkp-3412
Marko Lauro RUIC (karta Like i Krbive), Dette riftessioni l'antico storiche: sopra sfafo civile ed eccles iastico detta cittd ed isota di pago o'sia dell'antica Gissa faffe a diversi autori, diptomi, privilegi ed atire cafte p;ubbliche e private/raccolte con ta possibite esatezza e ditigenza da Marcilauro Rujch, Pag, 1780., str. Ga

The volume was published within the project titled: *Cultural Landscape as a Source of Knowledge about the Organization of Space,* financed by the University of Zadar.

This book is printed on acid-free paper.

Bibliographic information published by the Deutsche Nationalbibliothek
The Deutsche Nationalbibliothek lists this publication in the Deutsche Nationalbibliografie; detailed bibliographic data are available on the Internet at http://dnb.d-nb.de.

ISBN 978-3-643-80283-5 (pb)
ISBN 978-3-643-85283-0 (PDF)

A catalogue record for this book is available from the British Library

© LIT VERLAG GmbH & Co. KG Wien,
Zweigniederlassung Zürich 2018
Klosbachstr. 107
CH-8032 Zürich
Tel. +41 (0) 44-251 75 05
E-Mail: zuerich@lit-verlag.ch   http://www.lit-verlag.ch
Distribution:
In the UK: Global Book Marketing, e-mail: mo@centralbooks.com
In North America: International Specialized Book Services, e-mail: orders@isbs.com
In Germany: LIT Verlag Fresnostr. 2, D-48159 Münster
Tel. +49 (0) 2 51-620 32 22, Fax +49 (0) 2 51-922 60 99, e-mail: vertrieb@lit-verlag.de
e-books are available at www.litwebshop.de

CONTENT

Chapter 1
INTRODUCTION TO LANDSCAPES IN SOUTHEASTERN EUROPE; Mario Katić, Lena Mirošević, Danijela Birt 9

Chapter 2
THE LEGENDS OF ROCK: STORIES, LANDSCAPE, AND BOUNDARIES IN THE CENTRAL VELEBIT MOUNTAIN; Vedrana Glavaš 15

Chapter 3
LANDSCAPE ARCHAEOLOGY AND SOCIAL INEQUALITY IN NORTHERN ALBANIA: RESULTS OF THE 2014 FIELD SEASON OF THE PROJEKTI ARKEOLOGJIK I SHKODRËS (PASH); Michael Galaty, Lorenc Bejko, Sylvia Deskaj, Richard Yerkes, Susan Allen, and Rachelanne Bolus 35

Chapter 4
LANDSCAPE AS LEGACY IN NORTHERN DALMATIA; Gregory Zaro, Martina Čelhar 49

Chapter 5
LANDSCAPE AND SETTLEMENTS OF SOUTHEAST EUROPE: PREMODERN BOSNIA AND SERBIA; Jelena Mrgić 69

Chapter 6
DEATH PROXIMITY, GROUP COHESION & MOUNTAINOUS PILGRIMAGE IN ALBANIA; Konstantinos Giakoumis, Christopher Lockwood 89

Chapter 7
RELIGIOUS LANDSCAPES AT THE BORDER: THE CASE OF THE BORDER REGIONS OF PETRICH, BULGARIA AND STRUMICA, MACEDONIA; Violeta Periklieva 129

Chapter 8
SITES OF MEMORY AND SOCIAL CHANGE IN CROATIA: A CASE STUDY OF THE SEAGULL'S WINGS MONUMENT; Marko Mustapić, Benjamin Perasović 147

Chapter 9
CONCLUDING THOUGHTS: (CULTURAL) LANDSCAPES IN SOUTHEASTERN EUROPE; Gregory Zaro 165

LIST OF FIGURES AND TABLES

Chapter 2
Figure 1: Study area 17
Figure 2: Dolabella's boundary wall 20
Figure 3: The "Pisani kamen" boundary inscription 21
Figure 4: Boundary wall and wall line in relation to the 500 paces buffer zone 26
Figure 5: Reconstructed civitates territories in the Central Velebit area 29

Chapter 3
Figure 1. Map of the PASH study region showing sites identified and documented. Shefqet Lulja 37
Figure 2. Photograph and drawing of the east profile of Unit 3 at Gajtan. Michael L. Galaty 40, 41
Figure 3. Distribution of faunal remains from Tumulus 52, 88, and 99 by species. Richard Yerkes 44
Table 1. List of AMS radiocarbon dates from northern Albania generated by PASH and Beta Analytic, Miami, Florida, USA 42

Chapter 4
Figure 1. Geographic location of the study 53
Figure 2. Oblique aerial photo of Nadin-Gradina. The tree line reflects the shape of the megalithic fortification wall (photo courtesy of Vedrana Glavaš) 54
Figure 3. Probe B after excavation in 2015, showing the complexity of a settlement history that includes Iron Age (IA), Classical Antiquity (CA), and Late Antiquity (LA). Bedrock (BR) is also noted 56
Figure 4. A repurposed Roman capital (spolia) is visible in a Late Antique wall.
Figure 5. A paved road leading up to the north gate through the megalithic wall (note the post holes associated with the gate) 59

Chapter 5
Table 1: Distances between the 'core area' centers – capital cities in Bosnia and Serbia - and other central places of these polities and international maritime trade centers 77
Figure 1: The Monastery of Djurdjevi Stupovi near Ras (Novi Pazar) 79

Chapter 6
Graph 1: A flowchart of the chapter's thesis 90
Table 1: The methodological roles of the researcher 99
Table 2: Table of the types of Communitas encountered in each Pilgrimage Site 121
Figure 1: Cave Hermitage of Saint Nicholas, southern view, 16th century, stone and mortar, Tranosisht, Lunxhëri - Gjirokastër, Southern Albania 97

Figure 2: Cave Hermitage, 14th century, Kosharisht, Librazhd, central Albania 97
Figure 3: Cave Hermitage of Saint George, western view, 12th century, stone and mortar, Dhivër, Saranda, Southern Albania 98
Figure 4: The steep pathway from Laç city to the convent of Shna Ndout ... 100
Figure 5: Cave Hermitage of Saint Blaise, North-eastern view, Shna Ndou Convent, Laç, Northern Albania 101
Figure 6: On the way to the convent of Shna Ndou in Laç, hordes of pilgrims climb up the stony path and light candles in the slope's cavities 102
Figure 7: The Teke of Sarı Saltık, Lodge's Exterior, 1992, stone with mortar and lime, Kruja, Central Albania 107
Figure 8: The Teke of Sarı Saltık, Lodge's Interior, 1992, stone with mortar and lime, Kruja, Central Albania 107
Figure 9: The Teke of Sarı Saltık, Kurban place, 1991, Kruja, Central Albania ... 108
Figure 10: The Teke of Sarı Saltık, the Funerary Cave, 1991, Kruja, Central Albania 108
Figure 11: The Shrine of Sarı Saltık's Footstep, Kruja, Central Albania 110
Figure 12: The Shrine of Abbas Ali's Footstep, Mount Tomorr, Southern Albania 112
Figure 13: The Sacrificial Place, Teke of Abbas Ali at Kulmak, Mount Tomorr, Southern Albania 113
Figure 14: Tombs of Deceased Dervishes, Teke of Abbas Ali at Kulmak, 1924 (reconstructed in 1994), Mount Tomorr, Southern Albania 113
Figure 15: Lodge for the guardians and the Teke Community, Teke of Abbas Ali at Kulmak, Mount Tomorr, Southern Albania 114
Figure 16: The Türbe of Abbas Ali on the top of Kulmak, Mount Tomorr, Southern Albania 114
Figure 17: Capital of a Funerary Stele from the Türbe of Abbas Ali with a photograph underneath. Top of Kulmak, Mount Tomorr, Southern Albania 116
Map 1: The location of the Holy Trinity Monastery at Pepel, Dropull, Gjirokastër, Southern Albania 104

Chapter 7
Map 1: Petrich – Strumica map 134

Chapter 8
Figure 1: The Seagull's Wings Monument, dedicated to the Establishment of the Yugoslav Navy in Podgora, 1942 148
Figure 2: Map of the Makarska Riviera 153
Figure 3: Posters; 40th anniversary of the Establishment of the Yugoslav Navy (1982); the first celebration of the Day of the Croatian Navy (1993); concert and the celebration of Torcida Podgora (2013) 157

INTRODUCTION TO LANDSCAPES IN SOUTHEASTERN EUROPE

Mario Katić[1], Lena Mirošević[2], and Danijela Birt[3]
[1] University of Zadar, Department of Ethnology and Anthropology
[2] University of Zadar, Department of Geography
[3] University of Zadar, Department of Ethnology and Anthropology

Definitions of landscape vary widely among (and within) disciplines. There are political landscapes (Christie, Bogdanovic and Guzman 2016), religious landscapes (Kong 2004), contested landscapes (Bender and Winer 2001), and inscribed landscapes (David and Wilson 2002). There are phenomenological approaches to landscapes (Tilley 1997), material approaches to landscapes (Tilley and Cameron-Daum 2017), landscapes beyond land (Arnason, et al. 2012), invisible landscapes (Ryden 1993), emotional landscapes (Feld and Basso 1996), landscapes of tourism (Ringer 1998), and conversations with landscapes (Benediktsson and Lund 2010). And, there are temporalities of landscapes (Ingold 1993) and socio-ecological landscapes (Balée 2006), just to mention a few.

Landscape is no longer conceptualized as a passive background but as an active foreground that is created by and creative of life-worlds (Bender 1993, 1996: 323; Tilley 1994: 233). This conceptualization has paved a broad spectrum of theoretical and methodological approaches which can be coarsely divided into four different interrelated approaches (Katić, Gregorič Bon, Eade 2017): 1) Representational (Cosgrove & Daniels 1988), 2) archaeological and geographical (Olwig 1996, 2002; Jones & Olwig 2008; Bender 1996), 3) experiential and phenomenological (Ingold 1993, 2000; Tilley 1994; Hirsch & O'Hanlon 1995; Basso 1996; Árnason, Ellison, Vergunst & Whitehouse 2012; Telban 2016), and 4) ontological and environmental (Descola 2016; Tsing 2017; Virtanen, Lundell, Honkasalo 2017).

In the opening sentence of their book, Christopher Tilley and Kate Cameron-Daum emphasize that landscape is a subject that belongs to no one, and to research and interpret various elements of a landscape means that one enters a field populated by different theoretical and methodological approaches (Tilley and Cameron-Daum 2017: 1). They write that landscapes encompass "topographies, geologies, plants and animals, persons and their biographies, social and political relationships, material things and monuments, dreams and emotions, discourses and representations and academic disciplines through which they are studied. So landscapes are mutable, holistic in character, ever-changing, always in the process of being and becoming" (2017: 20). Yet, it is this vast array of theoretical and methodological approaches infused in landscape studies that suggest just the opposite to us: landscapes belong, at once, to everyone. In this manner, along with material features, human values with subjective and spiritual experiences in the physical world also come into focus in landscape studies. A landscape, therefore, becomes a medium that reflects material, spiritual, and cultural activities of communities in the past, present and future.

The European continent is a mosaic of different landscapes created through thousands of years of interactions among communities, and between communities and the physical world. Each landscape constituent has its properties permeated by numerous perceptions and memories. In this manner, the identity of a community, through various human activities, is embedded in the landscape. In this context, special importance is placed on everyday landscapes from the past to the present. Understanding landscapes in the context of space and time necessarily demands the conceptual approaches of different scientific and expert fields of study.

The purpose of this volume is to explore, through a variety of case studies, the concept of landscape from multiple fields of study in order to gain insight into how such disciplines (e.g., archaeology, ethnology, folklore, sociology, history) define and approach the concept of landscape. What similarities are shared among disciplines? What differences are apparent? Can we use one another's research, interpretations, and results effectively in a comparative manner? For this reason, we offered no specific definition or charge to our cohort of authors and the onset of this exercise beyond simply an exploration of "landscape" in Southeastern Europe. Rather than provide a definitional stance to our approach, we thought to do the opposite by drawing conclusions from the drafted papers of this volume with respect to the main concepts, elements, and approaches to landscape research in the context of Southeastern Europe.

The kind of interdisciplinary, holistic, and varied conceptual and methodological approaches to landscape noted above is evoked in the first set of papers of the volume, which stem from the field of archaeology. In their contribution, Michael Galaty and colleagues address prehistoric social change in the Shkodër province of northern Albania. Following Hirsch and O'Hanlon (1995), the authors refer to landscapes as containers that are bounded by geographical features but also enable human perceptions and behaviours. They realize that archaeological excavations alone are insufficient if the aim is to explain long-term socio-dynamic and human-nature interactions. In the subsequent chapter, Vedrana Glavaš demonstrates the utility of geographic information systems (GIS) in landscape research, but moreover, how oral traditions are becoming a valuable source of information for archaeological landscape studies. Oral traditions contain local collective memories and can thus provide useful input into local landscape meanings and interpretations. Gregory Zaro and Martina Čelhar utilize the archaeological record at Nadin-Gradina, Croatia, as a single case study to explore urban and landscape changes more broadly over time. They view modern landscapes to be cumulative expressions of long-term interactions between humans and non-human agents of change. Their work is thus centered on the historical role humans play in shaping modern landscapes and how such information may benefit contemporary societies facing issues of sustainable development, environmental policy, and other twentieth century challenges.

Elsewhere in the volume, Jelena Mrgić reminds us that beyond the physical nature of the built environment, there is a symbolic and religious aspect to the "experience" of landscape. Moreover, as Mrgić effectively shows, societies are composed of a myriad of social groupings, each of which possesses its own particular perspective, relationship, and engagement with landscape, and often reflected in various and ambiguous meanings. This is also exemplified in the chapter by Konstantinos Giakoumis and Christopher Lockwood and their characterization of mountainous landscapes, pilgrimage, and religious beliefs in Albania. Likewise, Violeta Periklieva further develops the interrelationship between belief systems, institutions, objects, and religious landscapes in border region between Bulgaria and Macedonia. Facing again the problem of definitions, Periklieva defines the religious landscape as a social and cultural space constructed from interactions with specific religious models. She argues that there is visible - material - expression of religiosity in the landscape, but also an intangible element that includes beliefs and discourses that are associated with material. She concludes that religious landscapes can serve as a map to aid in the decipherment of religious processes at local and national levels. Finally, using a fixed place in the landscape as an interpretational point, Marko Mustapić and Benjamin Perasović, analyze discourses and practices connected to one particular monument to interpret social changes in broader Croatian society. Their work reminds us of the importance of memory (individual, local, or collective) in the landscape research.

Based on the papers presented in this volume, it seems that landscape research in Southeastern Europe still holds a predominantly representational perspective, while phenomenological (Tilley 1997), or more-than-representational (Maddrell et al 2015), approaches remain absent.

As the conceptual ways of framing the landscape differ, so do the particular analyses and methods to landscape studies. In this volume, authors are most focused on the traditional approach to studying material changes in landscapes. This approach has been modernized since the second half of the 20th century by the introduction of digital technology into scientific disciplines. Along with indispensable cadastral data (i.e., cadastral plans and cartographic material), aerial photos, satellite imagery, and GIS are becoming increasingly more prevalent and reliable tools. Such spatial analyses provide a way to monitor changes in land use due to different economic activities (agriculture, industrialization, urbanization, etc.). Consequently, landscapes become a common framework for research of different expert fields and scientific disciplines from a historical perspective, but also from the perspective of regional planning. Such methodologies are directed at collecting data, reconstructing a landscape's past, and defining cultural areas.

The basic object of observation in all chapters is the notion of a cultural landscape formed by the Presence of humans and shaped by their activities. In this manner, a connection with the physical world is created through symbolic meaning. Such observation of the landscape includes landscape morphology (i.e., observing changes in the process of landscape creation), but also incorporated symbols and meanings common to particular social groups. Landscapes in this volume are not observed solely through material marks imprinted on physical spaces, but also through the complexity of landscape interpretation. Therefore, cultural landscapes may be interpreted as an announcement, declaration, and exposure of data on social groups that inhabit a specific area. In short, landscapes are necessarily anthropogenic and contain layers of information about the value systems, inclinations, beliefs, fears, and truths of their "creators".

REFERENCES

Arnasson, Arnar Nicolas Ellison, Jo Vergunst and Andrew Whitehouse, eds. 2012. *Landscape Beyond Land; Routes, Aesthetics, Narratives.* Berghahn Books: New York and Oxford.

Balée, William. 2006. The research program of historical ecology. *Annual Review of Anthropology* 35: 75-98.

Bender, Barbara (ed.). 1993. Landscape: Politics and Perspectives. Oxford: Berg.

Bender, Barbara. 1996. Landscape. In: Barnard, Alan & Jonathan Spencer (eds.), Encyclopedia of Social and Cultural Anthropology. London & New York: Routledge, pp. 323-324.

Bender, Barbara and Margot Winer, eds. 2001. *Contested Landscapes: Movement, Exile and Place.* Berg: Oxford and New York.

Benediktsson, Karl and Katrin Anna Lund. 2010. *Conversations with Landscape.* Routledge: London and New York.

Christie, Jessica, Jelena Bogdanovic and Eulogio Guzman, eds. 2016. *Political Landscapes of Capital Cities.* University Press of Colorado: Boulder and Logan.

Cosgrove, Denis & Stephen Daniels (eds.). 1988. The Iconography of Landscape: Essays on the Symbolic Representation, Design and Use of Past Environments. Cambridge: Cambridge University Press.

David, Bruno and Meredith Wilson, eds. 2002. *Inscribed Landscapes: Marking and Making Places.* University of Hawai`i Press: Honolulu.

Descola, Philippe. 2016. Landscape as Transfiguration. Edward Westermarck Memorial Lecture, October 2015. *Suomen Antropologi* 41(1): 3-14.

Feld, Steven and Keith Basso, eds. 1996. *Senses of Place.* School of American Research Press: Santa Fe.

Hirsch, Eric and Michael O'Hanlon, eds. 1995. *The Anthropology of Landscape: Perspectives on Place and Space*. Clarendon Press: Oxford.

Ingold, Tim. 1993. The temporality of the landscape. *World Archaeology* 25(2): 152-174.

Ingold, Tim. 2000. The Perception of the Environment: Essays on Livelihood, Dwelling and Skill. London & New York: Routledge.

Jones, Michael & Kenneth R. Olwig (eds.). 2008. Nordic Landscapes. Region and Belonging on the Northern Edges of Europe. Minneapolis & London: University of Minnesota Press.

Katić, Mario, Nataša Gregorič Bon, and John Eade. 2017. Landscape and Heritage Interplay: Spatial and Temporal Explorations. *Anthropological Notebooks* 23: 5-19.

Kong, Lily. 2004. Religious Landscapes. In, *A Companion to Cultural Geography*, Duncan, James, Nuala Johnson, and Richard Schein, eds. Blackwell Publishing: Hoboken.

Maddrell, Avril, Veronica della Dora, Alessandro Scafi, Heather Walton, eds. 2015. *Christian Pilgrimage, Landscape and Heritage: Journeying to the Sacred*. Routledge: London and New York.

Olwig, Kenneth R. 1996. Recovering the Substantive Nature of Landscape. *Annals of the Association of American Geographers* 86 (4): 630-653.

Olwig, Kenneth R. 2002. Landscape, Nature and the Body Politic: From Britain's Renaisance to America's New World. Madison: University Wisconsin Press.

Ringer, Greg. ed. 1998. *Cultural Landscapes of Tourism*. Routledge: London and New York.

Ryden, Kent. 1993. *Mapping the Invisible Landscape: Folklore, Writing, and the Sense of Place*. University of Iowa Press: Iowa.

Telban, Borut. 2016. Kraji in časi v novogvinejski pokrajini (Zbirka Prostor, kraj, čas). Ljubljana: Založba ZRC.

Tilley, Christopher. 1994. A Phenomenology of Landscape. Oxford: Berg.

Tilley, Christopher. 1997. *A Phenomenology of Landscape: Place, Paths and Monuments*. Bloomsbury: London.

Tilley, Christopher and Kate Cameron-Daum. 2017. *An Anthropology of Landscape*. UCL Press: London.

Tsing, Anna. 2017. The Buck, the Bull, and the Dream of the Stag: Some Unexpected Weeds of the Anthropocene. *Suomen Antropologi* 42 (1): 3-21.

Virtanen, Pirjo Kristiina, Elenoora L. Lundell, Marja-Liisa Honkasalo. 2017. Introduction: Enquiries into Contemporary Ritual Landscapes. *Journal of Ethnology and Folkloristics* 11(1): 5-17.

THE LEGENDS OF ROCK: STORIES, LANDSCAPE, AND BOUNDARIES IN THE CENTRAL VELEBIT MOUNTAIN

Vedrana Glavaš
University of Zadar, Department of Archaeology

INTRODUCTION

Following the establishment of Roman governance in Illyricum in the early Principate, the former independent communities of the region were organized into new territorial administrative unites - *civitates* - with precisely defined territorial boundaries (Mesihović 2011, 75-76). Reconstructing their territories and identifying traces of boundaries in the landscape have been a challenge for archaeologists for a long time (Glavičić 1997; Čače 2006; Dubolnić 2007). Reconstruction of community territories is a difficult and complex issue due to the absence of literary sources, material evidence of demarcation, and archaeological field surveys. Therefore, the majority of reconstructed Roman *civitates* territories in the area of former Illyricum is a result of spatial analysis of site distribution and sparse material evidence (Glavičić 1997; Čače 2006; Dubolnić 2007).

In the area of the Central Velebit Mountain, *civitates* territories have not been systematically examined thus far. Previous researchers placed communities in the landscape of Velebit in the same way as in the other areas of the former Illyricum province. These territory boundaries are questionable as they were reconstructed mostly on the basis of poor literary sources and limited material traces (Zaninović 1984; Glavičić 1997).

New approaches to territoriality and cultural landscape research were initiated by the development of geographic information systems (GIS) and its application in archaeology (Novaković 1998; Ducke, Kroefges 2007; Glavaš 2015). Oral tradition became increasingly used as a valuable source of information in archaeological landscape research (David et al. 2004; Sheppard, Walter, Aswani 2004; Hrobat 2007; Boeyens 2012; Katić 2014).

Oral traditions are preserved in the collective memory of local people and therefore can be used for interpretation and understanding of the local landscape. Accordingly, oral traditions and a contextual understanding of them is an important source of information in archaeology comparable to other available sources (David et al. 2004; Sheppard, Walter, Aswani 2004; Hrobat 2007; Boeyens 2012; Katić 2014).

Velebit Mountain was mostly populated with pastoralists due to its specific geomorphologic and climatologic features, and seasonal pastoralism was a dominant economic pattern on Velebit Mountain from prehistory to the middle of the 20th century. The area remained mostly isolated from outer influences because of its inert karst landscape that restricted greater transformations, as well as due to a closed economic pattern of exploiting modest karst resources.

Many stories and narratives about places such as Velebit have been preserved (Dronjić 2008, 241-256; 2009, 245-274; 2012, 133-154). Use of oral traditions as a relevant source of information in cultural landscape research confirms its value, as many of these stories are related to old dry stone walls and prehistoric hill forts (Dronjić 2008, 241-256). One such story is related to a Roman boundary wall built in the 1st century AD in the Central Velebit area. Another story recorded in this area mentions an inscription called *Mali pisani kamen* (eng. Small written stone) that was lost a long time ago. However, both stories are related to a well-known Roman inscription referred to by local people as *Pisani kamen* (eng. Written stone), which provides a clue about territorial demarcation between indigenous *civitates* in the Central Velebit area.

The main aim of this paper is to reinterpret the *Pisani kamen* boundary inscription and reconstruct Roman *civitates* territories in the area of the Central Velebit. We employ an interdisciplinary approach that includes epigraphic analysis of inscription, field survey, aerial photography, use of geographic information systems (GIS) and oral traditions. The study area encompasses a segment of Central Velebit from the wider maritime Jablanac to Begovača area in the hinterland (Figure 1).

REGIONAL CONTEXT OF THE LANDSCAPE

The research area is located on the border between Northern and Central Velebit Mountain (Figure 1). The low relief along the mountain alan pass (1340 m.a.s.l.) is a natural divide between both sections of the mountain. Typical karst landscape characterizes the whole mountain range, which is reflected in a lack of surface streams and a lack of soil cover. A range of karst geomorphic features is well represented, from small rillenkarrens and grikes to larger features such as dolines and other joint induced karst depressions. In the upper sections of the Velebit Mountain, between karst depressions, there is a number of conical hills and steep peaks that are formed from massive limestone breccia (Bognar 1994, 3-4).

Figure 1: Study area

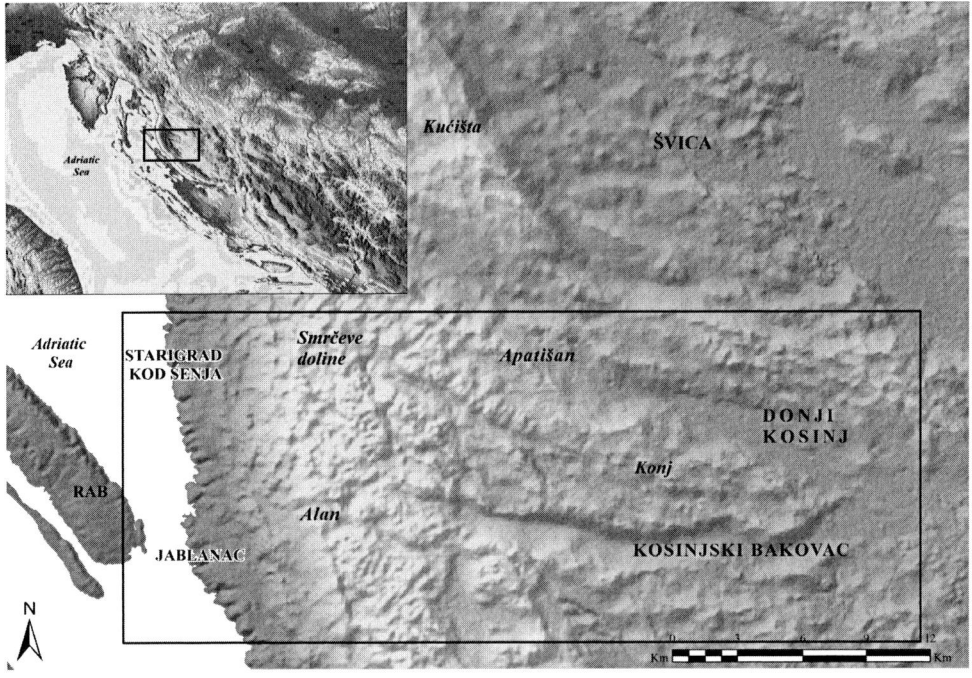

The Velebit area is characterized by great variation at small distances, including sub-Mediterranean climate in the Velebit channel, Alpine climate above the tree line, and humid continental climate on the inner mountain slope. Higher areas on Velebit are not as dry as the littoral slope during summer due to the effect of katabatic winds. The highest areas of the mountain are characterized by Mediterranean-Alpine humid climates with great amplitudes of daily temperature (Rogić 1957, 92). The inner slope and higher Velebit areas are also characterized by greater precipitation, which is more typical for colder periods of the year. Lower slopes display far less precipitation, which is a result of the lack of orographic effect in lower littoral areas (Perica-Orešić 1999, 15-30).

Natural factors such as sea proximity, Mediterranean climate, carbonate bedrock, karst and altitude have the greatest effect on formations and spread of Velebit vegetation. The vegetation is thus adapted to a dry environment. The vegetation spread is greatly affected by temperature variation, which can be quite substantial within small distances. Barren and rocky landscape prevails on Velebit littoral slopes. Bushy vegetation typical for karst landscapes dominates plant life (Rogić 1957, 97-8; Forenbacher 1990, 324, 439, 493, 665). The higher zones include numerous meadows and pastures composed of different types of grass. These grasses contain higher calorie values and are better suited for livestock grazing than the vegetation on the Velebit littoral side (Forenbacher 1990, 43-5, 59-63).

Morphology, climate and vegetation are factors that framed human adaptation to topo-climatic characteristics of Velebit. The primary economic activity has always been animal husbandry. Arable land on Velebit is scarce on its littoral slopes, and opportunities for practicing agriculture are few. However, seasonal pastoralism was dominant on Velebit as well as on other Dinaric mountains in Bosnia and Herzegovina and Montenegro (Marković 2003, 33-75). Mountain pastures and the quality of grass produced specific land use patterns. Littoral communities were situated into permanent settlements along the coast but owned a portion of territories in the higher zones of the mountain where they spent spring, summer, and early autumn months. Such a subsistence pattern and seasonal pastoralism was preserved on Velebit until the middle of the 20th century (Marković 1980, 7).

The boundary wall built in the time of Dolabella (14.-20. AD) is situated in the vicinity of Jablanac. It was built on extremely karstified terrain of the littoral slope of Velebit where permanent *civitates* settlements were positioned. The littoral part of the mountain has always lacked a quality grass that would be adequate to sustain livestock breeding. In such circumstances, people moved their herds to the higher altitudes as early as spring months. Dundović pod (600-800 m.a.s.l.), positioned to the east of Dundović kosa, is a spacious depression where the inhabitants from the littoral Velebit had their shepherd's compounds and permanent settlements. The largest part of Dundović pod is nowadays covered by deciduous forest and maquis vegetation. However, at the time when this area was at the peak of exploitation for the purposes of animal husbandry, the forests and maquis were mostly absent (Rukavina 1990, 281-290).

Mountain pastures such as Mirovo, Tudorevo, Bilenski and Šegotski padež, along with numerous others, are positioned at altitudes higher than 1200 m.a.s.l. east of Dundović pod. Remains of shepherd's compounds are still visible in some of these places. The pastures were exploited in summer periods when the grass at the lower altitudes was dry and of poor quality. The terrain descends to the east of these pastures towards Begovača, and the vegetation changes as well. Forests start to appear, but pastures are still present in the landscape. Begovača was one such pasture, which is currently overgrown in thick forest due to lack of exploitation. Begovača is an elongated lowland region positioned at an elevation of 820 m.a.s.l. It is separated from Kosinjski Bakovac to the south-east by Gavranuša ridge and its extension. Poljes in Donji Kosinj and Lipovo Polje are positioned to the north-east of Begovača. Kosinjski Bakovac, Donji Kosinj and Lipovo Polje abound with water. The Lika River flows through Donji Kosinj and Lipovo Polje, while several springs as well as the Bakovac stream can be found in the Kosinjski Bakovac area. The Begovača area was extremely significant for summer grazing because it had a perennial water source - a rare occasion on Velebit.

CENTRAL VELEBIT: HISTORY, ARCHAEOLOGY AND ORAL TRADITIONS

HISTORICAL AND ARCHAEOLOGICAL CONTEXT

Following the formation of the Illiyricum province in the early Principate, Roman authorities continued the process of administering the province initiated by Caesar. The hitherto autonomous indigenous communities become peregrine or dependent. Peregrine communities (*civitates peregrinae*) are formed as Roman administrative units, which was also the first step toward their integration into the Roman state (Mesihović 2011, 75-76). Accordingly, it was necessary to determine precise territories of indigenous communities in Liburnia, and the Velebit region was no exception.

The constitution of the Roman province commenced following the cessation of hostilities during Bato's war in 9 AD. Administering the province was a significant endeavor for Rome. Demarcation issues were entrusted with the *legatus Augusti pro praetore provinciae Dalmatiae*, which testifies to the importance of such affairs for Rome. The mandate of legate included implementation of imperial policies, and they answered directly to the Emperor (Glavičić 2014, 42). Apparently, this is the reason they were entrusted with the task of territorial demarcation. The first legate to begin the demarcation of Liburnian territorial communities was *Publius Cornelius Dolabella* (14-20 AD), as documented by contemporary inscriptions (Wilkes 1974, 258-68). The demarcation of territorial communities was featured in a great number of boundary inscriptions (Wilkes 1974, 258-68; Zaninović 1984, 38; Babić 1996, 57-69; Čače 2003, 7-43; Catani 2008, 75-86), testifying to the efforts to regulate relations within the Illyricum province (Mesihović 2010, 57-90). The stability of the province, and consequently its development, efficient management, and exploitation was facilitated by the demarcation process. Exploitation was manifested in the use of natural resources, conscription of the local population, and numerous other obligations. But the biggest change imposed by the authorities on local people was taxation.

All boundaries were mapped onto the Dolabella map (*forma Dolabelliana*), whose existence is confirmed by an inscription from the Archaeological Museum in Split (*ILJUG* 874). *Forma Dolabelliana* contained records of demarcation. The Roman authorities referred to it when the boundaries were renewed, and forma constituted the first provincial cadaster. This official document was archived in *porticus Vipsania* in Rome built by Agripa (Suić 2003, 161-62).

The demarcation of the territory is attested in two instances in Central Velebit area. The first is the boundary wall from Jablanac in conjunction with the boundary inscription (*ILJUG* 02, 00919), and the second is the boundary inscription in Begovača (*CIL* III, 15053). The first territorial demarcation was discovered by archaeologists in the year 1900 in the vicinity of Jablanac (Figure 2). The wall stretches from the coast and Panos area in the west to the Dundović kosa in the east (Brunšmid 1900, 231). The wall width ranges from 1,20 to 1,50 m, and its greatest preserved height is 0,5 m. The wall stretches in a straight line (*rigor*) from the coastline to an elevation of 350 m. It crosses the Mujić glava hill, thereby maintaining the *rigor* and finally ends below the peaks of Dundović kosa. This dry stone wall boundary is categorized as *limites montani* or "limits facing mountains" (Campbell, 245-6, *Nomina Limitvm* L 248.6, 13). Thus far, this is the only proof of such territory demarcation between peregrine communities in the study area. The boundary inscription was found *in situ* in the Panos area. It was part of the dry stone wall boundary itself. This find confirms that the wall is indeed a boundary wall (Rendić-Miočević 1968, 63-74). The reading of the inscription is as follows: *Ex dec[r(eto)] / P (ubli) Cornel[i] / Do⟨l⟩label⟨l⟩ae / leg(ati) pr(o) pra[et(ore)] ⁵ [[////////////////]] int(er) Beg(i?)os et Ortopli[n(os)]* (eng. According to Publius Corenlius Dolabella propretorian legate's decree [[////////////////]] between Beci and Ortoplini). The fifth line, which apparently clarifies the act of demarcation, is missing. According to Rendić-Miočević, the line contained a short formula. The purpose of this formula was to describe the occasion in which the inscription was erected without actually naming the *iudex* or the person responsible (Rendić - Miočević 1968, 68). What may have happened was that one of the sides in the boundary dispute was disappointed with the outcome and removed the formula (*termini positi?*) that defines the boundary between two communities. This probably took place somewhat later, during the time of Dolabella's successors, in an effort to alter the past state of affairs in a more favorable manner for the aggrieved party.

Figure 2: Dolabella's boundary wall (Photo: V. Glavaš)

Other evidence of territorial demarcation is found higher up the mountain in the Begovača area (Figure 3). Another boundary inscription, known by local people as *Pisani kamen*, is carved into an enormous carbonate rock (*montibus lapides naturales*) and often elaborated upon in literature. The inscription is almost completely preserved with only minor damage. The inscription reads: 1. *Ex conventione finis inter Ortoplinos et Parentinos.* "As negotiated, the boundary between *Ortoplini* and *Parentini*." 2. *Aditus ad aqvam vivam Ortoplinis passus D latus I.* "Spring access - 500 paces (long) and 1 pace wide." (Ilakovac 1978, 375). The first part of the text is quite clear and is undisputed by scholars. However, the second part of the text was interpreted differently by different scholars. The portion of the inscription over which scholars disagree is the interpretation of rights to spring access. Some of the authors accept the interpretation of the pace wide access allowed by *Parentini* to *Ortoplini* (Patch 1990, 29-31; Rendić-Miočević 1968, 63-73; Ilakovac 1978, 375; Glavičić 2003, 86). Brunšmid formed the second interpretation of the text by omitting the number *I* at the end of the inscription, suggesting it is a later intervention (Brunšmid 1901, 100-1). If that were the case, the inscription would say that the *Ortoplini* are allowed spring access 500 paces wide (740m).

Figure 3: The "Pisani kamen" boundary inscription (Photo: V. Glavaš)

Although the inscription text is legible and the formulas rather clear, it seems that the interpretation of the text is not completely adequate. What is possible to interpret from this text is that the boundary was placed on this location between *Ortoplini* and *Parentini*. It can also be understood that *Ortoplini* were allowed spring access in the length of 500 paces and 1 pace width. Previous authors writing about this inscription believed it was about the spring in Begovača. The spring is located on a meadow in Begovača and never dries in the summer months. And while authors concentrated mostly on the problem of the *Ortoplini* spring access width, they ignored the actual distance between the Begovača spring and the *Pisani kamen* inscription. The spring distance from the boundary stone doesn't fit the measures mentioned on the stone. The spring is 1200 meters away from the inscription that mentions the passage in the length of 500 paces (which is 740m) to the spring. This is precisely why it would appear that the *Pisani kamen* inscription does not refer to Begovača spring, which will be demonstrated in this paper.

Apart from evidencing demarcation, these inscriptions are significant in a sense that they name Roman *civitates Ortoplini*, *Beci*, and *Parentini*, which inhabited the Velebit region. Some communities are mentioned by Roman literary sources (Matijević-Sokol 1994.), but the *Parentini* community is known only through the Begovača boundary inscription. *Ortoplini* inhabited the areas of Stinica (Zaninović 1984, 38) and Starigrad kod Senja. Their territory stretched deeper inland, as suggested on the *Pisani kamen* inscription. The *Beci* lived south of the *Ortoplini* and their center is commonly placed at contemporary Karlobag - Roman *Vegium* (Rendić-Miočević 1968, 70). Unlike *Ortoplini* and *Beci*, the *Parentini* community is known only through the *Pisani kamen* boundary inscription. The discovery of the boundary inscription facilitated the reconstruction of their hypothetical territory. Scholars have commonly placed them in the area of Gornji Kosinj and Perušić (Patch 1990, 31; Brunšmid 1898, 174-76; Brunšmid 1901, 101). However, the reconstruction of Velebit *civitates* might suggest a different solution to the problem of the *Parentini* core territory. The different interpretation is based on the reinterpretation of the *Pisani kamen* inscription and the use of the oral traditions collected during the course of research.

ORAL TRADITIONS

Rich oral traditions within the Velebit area are quoted many times in the literature (Dronjić 2008, 2009, 2012). Locals from the Velebit Mountain are curious about prehistoric hill forts, old settlements, shepherds houses, old cemeteries and pounds, which are reflected in oral traditions.

During our field studies on Velebit Mountain, local people often narrated the local history and stories they have heard from their ancestors. These stories have been repeated for generations. Even though our work in the area is not focused explicitly on the local oral tradition, we did encounter two stories of potential importance for boundary interpretations. Consequently, we investigated the two narratives that we heard in the local villages of Jablanac, Donji Kosinj and Kosinjski Bakovac.

The first of these oral traditions refers to the Jablanac boundary wall.

According to the informants' stories, the wall stretches to the area beyond Dundović kosa in the direction of Begovača where *Pisani kamen* was found. Moreover, according to the sayings, the inhabitants of the sub-Velebit littoral followed the wall to Begovača themselves, or some of their ancestors did. There is also another version of this story, which states that a wall stretches up to Apatišan. Both stories were also stated in older literature (Brunšmid 1900, 231). However, the second version of the story was never mentioned by our informants. They persistently repeated the information about a wall built in direction of Begovača.

Apart from the story of the wall stretching to Begovača, there is another story connected to this area. On the Gavranuša ridge west of Begovača, people from Kosinjski Bakovac and Donji Kosinj area tell a story of the existence of an inscription called *Mali pisani kamen* (eng. Small written stone). The story states that one peasant was collecting mistletoe in the area of Gavranuša. When he became tired, he laid down on a stone, which appeared flat as a board. When he took a closer look, he saw an inscription on it that he could not read because it was written in a language unknown to him. When this person wished to return to his place of discovery, he could not find it anymore.

In the late 19th and early 20th century, more stories about the existence of older inscriptions were recorded in the area of Velebit (Brunšmid 1901, 101). Reports about the existence of these types of monuments are related to the area of Švica and Smrčeve doline. However, the inscription from Smrčeve doline is from the modern era and doesn't belong to the group of boundary inscriptions. The inscription that was mentioned by Cvjetko Vurster to be placed above the Švica water spring (Ljubić 1880, 231) has not been found. Brunšmid also mentioned information about the inscription in the area of Kućišta (Brunšmid, 1901, 101). However, he says he didn't have time to find it. In this context, one interesting element could be the oral tradition about a buried treasure connected to Kućišta (Dronjić 2008, 243). However, we did not receive any information about inscriptions in the area of Švica and Kućišta. Nevertheless, S. Glumac from Lipovo Polje told us a story about the search for a lost inscription in the area of Konj. About 50 years ago, a number of forestry workers were hired by "some museum people" to find the inscription but they were unsuccessful.

Based on the information presented above, it is clear that stories about old inscriptions can be of great interest to those archaeologists searching for them. Due to fairly impassable terrain on Velebit, information from local people about inscriptions was sometimes the only way to find them. Furthermore, the *Pisani kamen* inscription was found in this manner. Even though there is little possibility of discovering new inscriptions, such oral traditions must be incorporated into local cultural landscape research. They assign meaning to locations, which must then be evaluated in the context of the wider cultural landscape.

RESEARCH METHODS

This project utilizes archaeological, inscriptive, historical and oral, and landscape data to reconstruct the territories of indigenous *civitates*. We utilize topographic maps (TK1:25,000 and TK 1:5,000), historical maps of the Habsburg Empire from the 19th century, aerial oblique photographs, orthophotographs, a digital elevation model (DEM) and GIS. Contemporary topographic maps and orthophotographs were used from the online service Geoportal.dgu.hr. Historical maps of the Habsburg Empire were examined through service mapire.eu. A digital elevation model (DEM) was created using the Ordinary Kriging interpolation method in ESRI ArcGIS 10.1 from elevation point data and used for data visualization.

The starting point of the research was the epigraphic analysis of the *Pisani kamen* inscription, since this boundary inscription is the physical basis for reconstructing territories. The inscription was geolocated in detail, and the text was re-examined and clarified.

Contemporary topographic maps (TK1:25,000 and TK 1:5,000) and Austrian military maps from 19th century (the first and second military survey 1:28,800 scale and third military survey 1:75,000 scale) were studied based on conclusions derived from the analysis of the inscriptions. Maps were used for locating and mapping of old shepherd paths that are overgrown with vegetation and barely visible. They were also used for organizing field reconnaissance.

Archaeological aerial reconnaissance in Europe is usually carried out using high-wing light aircraft from which an archaeologist examines photographs for ground features that are of interest (Renfrew, Bahn 2016, 80-93). The resulting oblique images are geolocated using data from continuous GPS placed in the aircraft. Selected images can then be transformed to provide accurate plan views. Such aerial reconnaissance as a method of research enables prospection of the terrain and provides important information about the landscape as a whole. This is the main reason why this particular method was applied. Through a series of flights, our survey attempted to establish whether the boundary wall continues as stated in the oral tradition as well as in the literature.

Field reconnaissance was carried out in those areas that are related to the oral tradition where material demarcation traces were expected. For the purpose of directing field reconnaissance, we used ESRI ArcGIS 10.1. Preserved remains of the wall were mapped from aerial photographs by using GIS. Presumed continuation of the wall as suggested by the oral tradition was extrapolated in the direction of Begovača. Additionally, positions of the *Pisani kamen*, the Begovača spring and positions of other water springs were geolocated as well as old pedestrian and livestock tracks in the study area. After that, a 500-Roman paces buffer zone from the *Pisani kamen* boundary inscription was calculated in GIS. All these data were imported into GPS for the purpose of field inspection.

The area from Dundović kosa towards Begovača, presumably a boundary wall line, was particularly scrutinized to determine if the remains of the wall are still visible, as suggested by oral tradition. Field inspection was aimed towards the areas of the possible wall extension and delineated by GPS in the direction of its presumed continuation. The field inspection was conducted in the area of Begovača in order to find traces of former streams, which could be related to the *Pisani kamen* context. The research was conducted within a buffer zone of 500 Roman paces of the *Pisani kamen* inscription. The area of Gavranuša, which is connected to the story of *Mali pisani kamen*, was also inspected in order to try to find the location to which the story is connected.

RESULTS AND DISCUSSION

Since the oral tradition suggests that the boundary wall from Jablanac stretches to the other side of Dundović kosa in the direction of Begovača towards Kosinj, the decision was made to test this claim in the field. Field survey and aerial reconnaissance of that area did not identify any remains of a wall that would extend in that direction. Nevertheless, information from the oral narratives was critically evaluated and taken into consideration for further reconstruction of the *Ortoplini* territory. If the geomorphology of the area where the wall is preserved is considered, one can determine that this is the typical karst terrain where geomorphological slope processes that could destroy the wall are not in operation. In addition, vegetation is poor and all structures that were not mechanically removed from the littoral side of Velebit are preserved *in situ* as small or large collapsed walls. Similarly, the Dolabella's boundary wall was preserved. It is lower today than in the past due to the secondary use of its stones for building new dry stone walls. On the other side of the Dundović kosa and further in Velebit, the geomorphology of the terrain changes. Slopes are much steeper, and as elevation increases, the vegetation and precipitation change. On the steep slope below Alan, such as Balenske brižine and Butković plan, the wall could have been built, but its structure would not likely be preserved because of slope processes. We should expect a preserved boundary wall structure on the flat pastures of Mirovo and Tudorevo, but surprisingly, no remains were found there either. Most of the other areas, where traces of the boundary wall should be present, are covered by lush forests that make field survey difficult. Furthermore, there are some areas like Panoga and southern parts of Gavranuša that are totally inaccessible due to very steep terrain and huge grikes, rendering it extremely difficult or impossible for the wall to have been built. Nevertheless, the information about the wall originated from the early 20th century. Since that period, vegetation has changed due to a reduction in livestock breeding, which should be taken into consideration. Many former pastures are today overgrown with dense forest, such as the Begovača area. Therefore, the information about the wall stretching further into Velebit should not be ignored. If it did not exist physically, the assumption that the story about the wall refers to an old boundary between Jablanac and Stinica area and their pastures seems plausible. For that reason, the existence of the boundary preserved in local stories was taken into consideration, which is the reason why we extended the line of the wall due to its bearing in the direction of the *Pisani kamen* inscription (Figure 4).

Figure 4: Boundary wall and wall line in relation to the 500 paces buffer zone (Author: V. Glavaš)

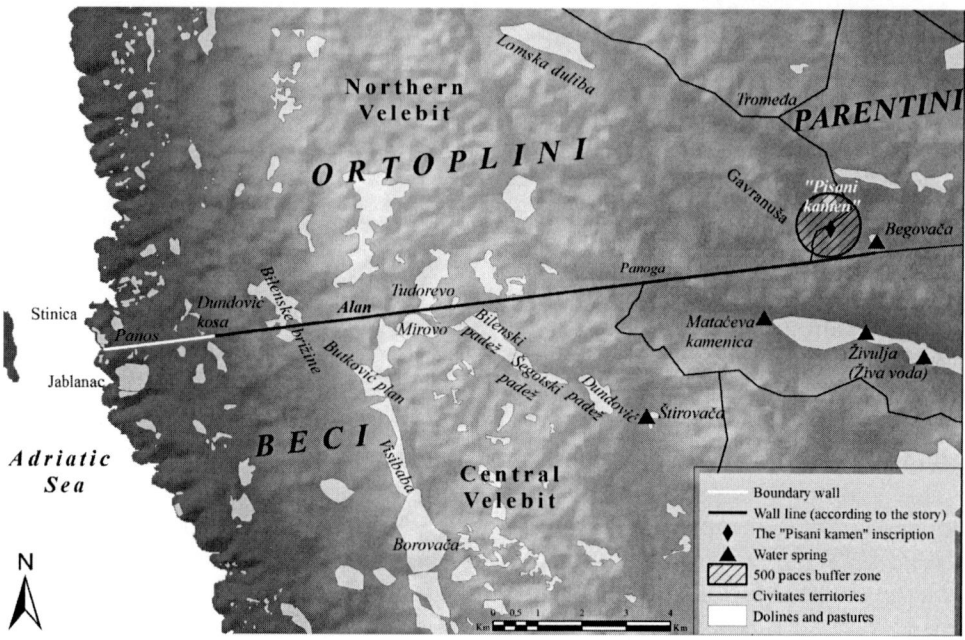

The examination of the *Pisani kamen* boundary inscription established that the depth and curving pattern are identical on the entire inscription. Therefore, the Roman numeral *I* at the end of the text that caused much dispute among the scholars is, in fact, part of the original content. The numeral is slanted in relation to other characters. However, the entire final line of the inscription is not curved in a straight line. Rather this line appears uneven in comparison to the rest of the text. Therefore, the reading of Ilakovac (Ilakovac 1978, 375) seems to be correct. The point of disagreement with other scholars is that the inscription refers to the Begovača spring. The problem is that the actual distance between the *Pisani kamen* inscription and the Begovača spring is 1200m when in fact the inscription merely states that the water access is 500 Roman paces (740m) long and one pace wide. Although the inscription was erected according to the agreement between two communities, the appearance of the text clearly shows that its template was written by an official. It is also evident that the measurements engraved in the stone were defined by the Roman division of the territory. So it is hard to doubt that a mistake was made by an amateur land survey. Moreover, if *Ortoplini* did indeed have an access of 500 paces wide, it would mean that they were allowed passage through the *Parentini* territory – that is, through the entire valley. In that sense, they would have been allowed to exploit *Parentini* pastures and water, which was likely not an option. If we take into consideration the fact of how precisely the contemporary wall is aligned, the possibility that such a great error in precise measurement could have been made seems implausible.

On the basis of these facts, the first assumption we explored was the existence of an older spring at a distance of 500 Roman paces from the inscription – possibly one that has since dried. There are numerous reasons for springs drying out in karst landscapes, and they can be related to human or natural factors. However, during our field inspection, we didn't come across any appropriate deposits or bedrock types that might allow a presence of any kind of springs in the past. Another possibility is that passage was allowed through the *Parentini* territory on a path 500 paces long to the spring in Kosinjski Bakovac. There is a track and a natural passage above the *Pisani kamen*, connecting Begovača and contemporary Kosinjski Bakovac. This track is the only possible way to pass Gavranuša, and it ends near a spring called Živulja in the Bakovac area (Figure 5). On older Habsburg Empire maps, Živulja is mapped as Živa voda which, if translated directly, matches the text *Aqua viva* from the boundary inscription in Begovača.

A boundary wall line from Jablanac seems to confirm this interpretation, which, if we extend it to Gavranuša, passes 765m from the *Pisani kamen* stone, or about 25m beyond the 500-paces buffer zone (740m). In this case, *Ortoplini* would have been allowed water access through the territory of *Parentini* only through the 500 paces long and 1 pace wide track. The water was situated on the community territory in Kosinjski Bakovac. This interpretation appears far more plausible because the distance of 500 paces stated in the text almost completely corresponds to the direction of the Dolabella wall (+-1,03%) (Figure 4). This interpretation makes much more sense than the previous interpretation referring to Begovača spring, which is located 1200m from the inscription.

The oral tradition on *Mali pisani kamen* is connected to Gavranuša ridge, the area where the wall line adjoins the buffer zone defined at 500 paces around the *Pisani kamen* inscription. Neither the *Mali pisani kamen* nor the continuation of the wall was found in the field. It is reasonable to assume, though, that the tradition of its existence could refer to an old boundary place. In the future, it is necessary to further inspect the entire area to Begovača, beyond the termination of the Dolabella wall because it is quite possible that the boundaries were marked differently in the high area of Velebit. Therefore, the manners of boundary demarcation likely varied and were not strictly limited to walls.

The weakness of this idea could be the distance of the Živulja spring in Kosinjski Bakovac and whether or not *Ortoplini* actually walked 2,5 km from the inscription to the spring. However, if we keep in mind that they moved together with their livestock over Legenac and Begovača during summer months when they used ponds for watering their livestock, it seems reasonable to conclude that they descended from the mountain after summer grazing through

Kosinjski Bakovac. This is where they would have had access to spring water, after which they could have continued through Krčevine and Bovan back to their territory. On the one hand, *Parentini* surely would not have allowed the exploitation of the only spring they owned on Begovača to be polluted by livestock. The spring at Begovača as we know it today was reconstructed during the 1990s. Brunšmid describes it as a powerful spring that is often muddy and easily polluted (Brunšmid 1901, 101). Perhaps that is the reason why *Parentini* would not allow water access to *Ortoplini*. On the other hand, there are several springs in Kosinjski Bakovac, which could be the reason why the community that lived there didn't have a problem allowing watering livestock to *Ortoplini*.

Following this logic, the *Ortoplini* boundary would have included the area from *Pisani kamen* through Begovača towards the northeast to the highest peak above Legenac (881 m.a.s.l.). The boundary can further be assumed to have extended to Ledena draga ridge, Bijeli grič peaks (1051 m.a.s.l.) through Bijeli vršak to Tromeđa. *Ortoplini* thus had in their possession the pastures at Lomska duliba through which they could reach Begovača. This is probably where they would stop before moving to the littoral area in late summer months.

Scholars have commonly claimed that *Parentini* inhabited the area of Gornji Kosinj and Perušić (Patch 1990, 31; Brunšmid 1898, 174-176; Brunšmid 1901, 101). However, this work has reached a different conclusion on the *Parentini* core territory. There are arguments that suggest that *municipium Tesleum* in the 2nd and 3rd century should be located in Donji Kosinj area. Horvat was the first that mentioned this municipium in literature when publishing his discovery of a Latin inscription where the text *municipium Tesleum* was engraved (Horvat 1993, 58). Today the inscription is lost. However, confirmation of the existence of a *municipium* in the Donji Kosinj area comes from urns with inscriptions that mention decurions (Glavičić 2008). Accordingly, *Tesli?* is assumed to be the name of the community that inhabited the area of Donji Kosinj (Glavičić 2008, 154-155). Therefore, this area should be excluded as the possible *Parentini* territory (Glavičić 2008, 154-155). The karst polje in Donji Kosinj area is divided by the Lika River into the northeastern part of Donji Kosinj and the southwestern part of Lipovo Polje. The entire polje covers an area of 14 km^2, and it is separated by a ridge from the Gornji Kosinj polje. The area where the Lika river cuts into it is 1,4 km long. Despite the fact that poljes in Gornji Kosinj and Kosinjski Bakovac are two different features, geomorphologically they are connected by Bakovac stream, which empties into the Lika River in Gornji Kosinj. Fresh water and fertile lands are abundant in the whole area and provide normal functioning for several communities. Since we took into consideration the possibility of the boundary between *Ortoplini* and *Beci* stretching further into the mountain according to the direction of boundary wall, the *Parentini* territory was reconstructed considering the direction of that particular wall. Despite the fact that the territory was reconstructed according to the direction of the wall, it is difficult to assume that the wall was indeed built along the whole stretch. Geomorphological characteristics of the terrain simply wouldn't allow it. The intersection of boundaries between *Ortoplini*, *Parentini*, and an unknown community is located at Gavranuša. From that position, the boundary extends over the higher peaks (872 m.a.s.l. and 864 m.a.s.l.) in the direction of Begovača. The boundary stretches further from Paljevina to Mali konj where it turns east towards Prteni konj (826 m.a.s.l.) and Crkvica (831 m.a.s.l.) extending to Škarina kosa (826 m.a.s.l.) all the way to contemporary Kosinj bridge. The bridge is a natural divide between Donji Kosinj and the Lipovo Polje area and Gornji Kosinj. These peaks are geographically associated with the Lipovo Polje area, and they naturally divide Lipovo Polje from Kosinjski Bakovac. The Lika River is assumed to be a boundary between the *Parentini* and *Tesli?* communities. Since the Roman land surveyors stated that a river was often utilized as a natural boundary, it could have been the case in this area as well. Although geomorphologically this polje is a single feature, traditionally the area is separated into two. Different names for the northeastern and southwestern part of the polje testify to this. Furthermore, both poljes feature a strong hill fort, which could have functioned as the central settlement. The *Parentini* central settlement could have been located at Prespa hillfort in Lipovo Polje, a prominent hill rising above the Lika River. The Lipovo Polje area is naturally connected to Begovača. Numerous paths, only a few hours walk from the mountain pastures and Begovača spring, confirm the homogeneity of this area. In this particular case, it is necessary to point out another component of the division between Donji Kosinj and Lipovo Polje. Even today, these two cadaster municipalities are divided by the Lika River, which could reflect a traditional boundary along its course. From the Lika River ponor, the *Parentini* and *Tesli?* boundary was assumed to pass over Bujednik through Goljak and Gizdin vrh (879 m.a.s.l.) to Risovac (932 m.a.s.l.) (Figure 5).

Figure 5: Reconstructed civitates territories in the Central Velebit area (Author: V. Glavaš)

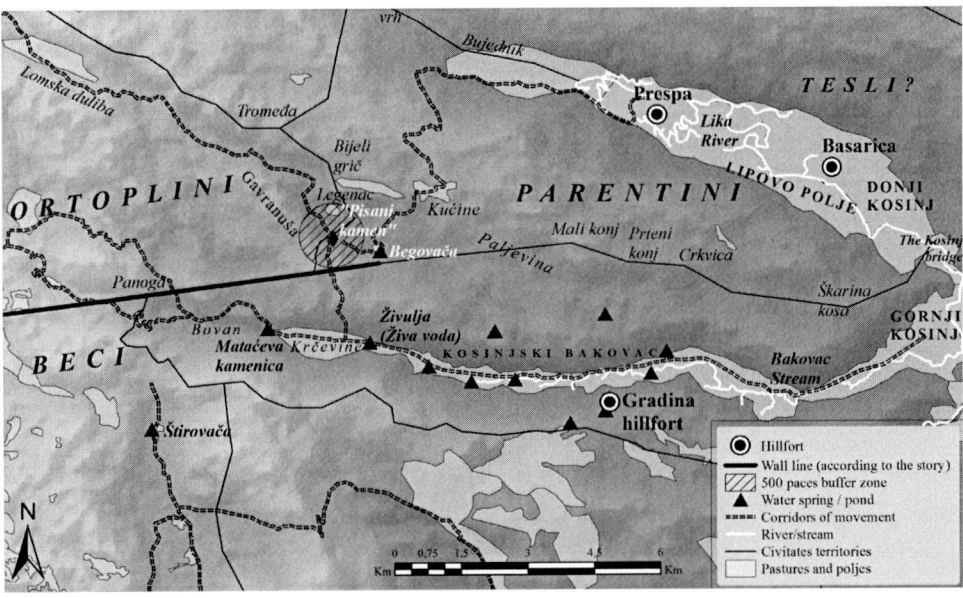

CONCLUSION

This paper investigates the territorial organization of indigenous *civitates* in the area of Central Velebit in the period of the constitution of Roman authority in Liburnia. The analysis of data acquired by field survey, aerial reconnaissance, epigraphic analysis, the application of GIS, and use of oral tradition were used to reconstruct the territories of Roman communities. The main goal of this paper was to reinterpret the meaning of the boundary inscription of *Pisani kamen* and demonstrate the usefulness of stories and oral tradition in cultural landscape research and the territorial reconstruction of indigenous communities.

Although the content of the collected oral tradition probably eroded over time while transferring through generations, they still represent valuable source of information for cultural landscapes research. Our research indicates that oral tradition could contain historically relevant information. We believe that the legends about the boundary wall and *Mali pisani kamen* that were utilized in this paper to reconstruct territories reflect a tradition of the existence of older boundary traces that were preserved in the memory of a place and people who passed it on from one generation to another. Since the majority of the Velebit area remained isolated from significant outside influence, numerous legends of places were preserved and available for research. Talks with local residents that we conducted during our research of this mountain show that there is a story about each place on Velebit. Archaeologists must take these stories into consideration in the same manner that we use material remains to reconstruct past lives. This is the main reason why we used different methods of boundaries research. But final reconstruction of territories would not be possible by using only one of these research methods. Consequently, it is necessary to point out the meaning of the interdisciplinary research of the cultural landscape by utilizing various archaeological methods as well as local stories. Through stories, some landscape features become recognizable and important to archaeologists. They also gave the landscape its spatial and physical identity, which helps preserve traditions (in this case boundary traditions) for the present and the future.

REFERENCES

Babić, Ivo. 1996. "Dva međašna natpisa namjesnika Publija Kornelija Dolabele iz Trogirske zagore." *Arheološki radovi i rasprave* 12: 57-69.

Boeyens, C. A. Jan. 2012. "The intersection of archaeology, oral tradition and history in the South African interior." *New contree: a journal of historical and human sciences for Southern Africa* 64. 1-30.

Bognar, Andrija. 1994. "Temeljna skica geoekoloških osobina Velebita." *Senjski*

zbornik 21. 1-8.
Brunšmid, Josip. 1898. "Arheološke bilješke iz Dalmacija i Panonije II." *Vjesnik za arheologiju i historiju dalmatinsku* n. s. 3. 149-190.
Brunšmid, Josip. 1900. "Izvještaji muzejskih povjerenika i prijatelja, književne vijesti." *Vjesnik za arheologiju i historiju dalmatinsku* 4. 218-240.
Brunšmid, Josip. 1901. "Arheološke bilješke iz Dalmacije i Panonije IV." *Vjesnik za arheologiju i historiju dalmatinsku* n. s. 3. 87-168.
Campbell, Brian. 2000. "*The writing of the Roman land surveyors. Introduction, text, translation and commentary.*" Society for the promotion of Roman studies. Journal of Roman studies and monograph no. 9.
Catani, Enzo. 2008. "Arheološko-povijesne bilješke o *Castellum Tariona* u rimsko doba." *Vjesnik za arheologiju i povijest dalmatinsku* 101: 75–86.
CIL. 1873. "*Corpus Inscriptionum Latinarum III.*" Suppl., Berlin, 1902.
Čače, Slobodan. 2003. "Aserija u antičkim pisanim izvorima." *ASSERIA* 1. 7-43.
Čače, Slobodan. 2006. "South Liburnia at the Beginning of the Principate: Jurisdiction and Territorial Organization." In: *Les routes de l'Adriatique antique: Géographie et économie - Putovi antičkog Jadrana: geografija i gospodarstvo. Bordeaux- Zadar, Ausonius Mémoire*: 65-79.
David, Bruno, McNiven, Ian, Manas, Louise, Manas, John, Savage, Saila, Crousch, Joe, Neliman, Guy, Brady, Liam. 2004. "Goba of Mua: archaeology working with oral tradition."*Antiquity* 78(299). 158-72.
Dronjić, Matija. 2008. "Zakopano blago u usmenoj predaji Podgoraca." *Senjski zbornik* 35: 241-56.
Dronjić, Matija. 2009. "Usmene predaje velebitskog Podgorja." *Senjski zbornik* 36: 245-74.
Dronjić, Matija. 2012. "Prilog istraživanju predaja o *starom narodu* na području Like i Podgorja." *Senjski zbornik* 39: 133-54.
Ducke, Benjamin, Kroefges, C. Peter. 2007. "From Points to Areas: Constructing Territories from Archaeological Site Patterns Using an Encanched Xtent Model." In Posluschny, A., Lambers, K., Herzog, I. (eds.) *Layers of perception. Proceedings of the 35th International Conference of Computer Applications and Quantitative Methods in Archaeology (CAA). Berlin, Germany, April 2-6, 2007*: 245-51.
Dubolnić, Martina. 2007. Argyruntum i njegov teritorij u antici." *Radovi Zavoda za povijesne znanosti HAZU u Zadru* 49: 1-58.
Forenbacher, Sergej. 1990. *Velebit i njegov biljni svijet.* Zagreb: Školska knjiga.
Glavaš, Vedrana. 2015. "Romanizacija autohtonih *civitates* na prostoru sjevernog i srednjeg Velebita." PhD diss., University of Zadar.
Glavičić, Miroslav. 1997. "*Civitas - municipium Lopsica.*" *Radovi Filozofskog fakulteta u Zadru* 35(22), Zadar. 45-70.
Glavičić, Miroslav. 2008. "Dvije četverokutne kamene urne s natpisom iz Donjeg Kosinja." In *Arheološka istraživanja u Lici, Izdanja Hrvatskog arheološkog društva* 23, edited by Tatjana Kolak, 251-257. Zagreb: Hrvatsko arheološko društvo - Muzej Like Gospić.
Glavičić, Miroslav. 2014. "Organizacija uprave rimske provincije Dalmacije

prema natpisnoj građi." *Klasični Rim na tlu Hrvatske. Arhitektura, urbanizam i skulptura.* 41-51

Ilakovac, Boris. 1978. "Pisani kamen." *Živa antika* 28. 373-376.

Katić, Mario. 2015. "Oral Tradition Emplaced in the Landscape: The Skakava Monastery in Bosnia." *Folklore* 126: 1. 20-36.

Ljubić, Šime. 1880. "Razne viesti." *Vjesnik Arheološkog muzeja u Zagrebu* 2. 123-8.

Marković, Mirko. 1980. *Zbornik za narodni život i običaje južnih Slavena.* Knjiga 48. Zagreb.

Marković, Mirko. 2003. *Stočarska kretanja na Dinarskim planinama.* Zagreb: Naklada Jesenski i Turk.

Matijević-Sokol, Mirjana. 1994. "Povijesna svjedočanstva o Senju i okolici." *Senjski zbornik* 21. 25-40.

Mesihović, Salmedin, 2010. *AEVVM DOLABELLAEA - Dolabelino doba.* Centar za balkanološka ispitivanja, Akademija nauka i umjetnosti: knjiga XXXIX. 99-123

Mesihović, Salmedin. 2011. *Rimski vuk i ilirska zmija. Posljednja borba.* Sarajevo: Filozofski fakultet u Sarajevu. http://www.ff-eizdavastvo.ba/books/sm-rimski_vuk_i_ilirska_zmija.posljednja_borba.pdf

Novaković, Predrag. 1998. "Detecting Territoriality and Social Structure in the Bronze and Iron Ages. GIS and the hillforts in the Kras region. Ancient Landscapes and Rural Structures." In: B. Slapšak (ed.) *On the good use of geographic information systems in archaeological landscape studies. Proceedings of the COST G2 WG2 round table. Ljubljana, 18 to 20 December.* 101-15

Palavestra, Vlajko. 1966. "Narodna predaja o starom stanovništvu u dinarskim krajevima." *Glasnik Zemaljskog muzeja Bosne i Hercegovine* 20/21: 5-86.

Palavestra, Vlajko. 2004. *Historijska usmena predanja iz Bosne i Hercegovine.* Sarajevo - Zemun: MostArt.

Patch, Karl. 1990. *Lika u rimsko doba.* Gospić: Biblioteka Ličke župe.

Perica, Dražen and Orešić, Danijel. 1999. "Klimatska obilježja Velebita." *Senjski zbornik* 26. 1-50.

Rendić-Miočević, Duje. 1968. "Novi Dolabelin "terminacijski" natpis iz okolice Jablanca." *Vjesnik Arheološkog muzeja u Zagrebu* s. 3, 3. 63-73.

Renfrew, Colin, Bahn, Paul. 2016. "*Archaeology: Theories, Methods, and Practice.*" (7th edition). Thames and Hudson: London.

Rogić, Veljko. 1957. "Velebitska primorska padina." *Hrvatski geografski glasnik* 19. 61-100.

Rukavina, Ante. 1990. "Još žive velebitske šume." *Senjski zbornik* 17. 281-90.

Sheppard, Peter, Walter, Richard, Aswani, Shankar. 2004. "Oral Tradition and the Creation of Late Prehistory in Roviana Lagoon, Solomon Islands." In: *Pacific Odyssey: Archaeology and Anthropology in the Western Pacific. Papers in Honour of Jim Specht. Records of the Australian Museum.* 29. 123-32.

Suić, Mate. 2003. *Antički grad na istočnom Jadranu.* Zagreb: Golden marketing - Tehnička knjiga.

Šašel, Jaroslav, Šašel, Ana. 1978. "Inscriptiones Latinae quae in Iugoslavia inter annos MCMLX et MCMLXX repertae et editae sunt." *Situla* 19. Ljubljana (ILJUG 02)

Wilkes John J. 1974. "Boundary stones in Roman Dalmatia." *Arheološki vestnik* 25. 258-271.

Zaninović Marin. 1984. "Stanovništvo velebitskog Podgorja u antici." *Senjski zbornik* 10-11. 29-40.

LANDSCAPE ARCHAEOLOGY AND SOCIAL INEQUALITY IN NORTHERN ALBANIA: RESULTS OF THE 2014 FIELD SEASON OF THE PROJEKTI ARKEOLOGJIK I SHKODRËS (PASH)

Michael Galaty[1], Lorenc Bejko[2], Sylvia Deskaj[1], Richard Yerkes[3], Susan Allen[4] and Rachelanne Bolus[4]

[1]University of Michigan
[2]University of Tirana
[3]The Ohio State University
[4]University of Cincinnati

INTRODUCTION

PASH was designed to study prehistoric social change, such as the appearance of social inequality, in the Shkodër province of northern Albania, as reflected in a diverse, regional landscape (for a review of regional approaches to European archaeology generally, see Galaty 2005). As with much of the rest of Europe, the transition to the Bronze Age in northern Albania was marked by burial of important individuals in earthen mounds (tumuli) and the construction of fortified settlements (hill forts) (see Borgna and Müller-Celka 2011, for mounds; Parkinson and Duffy 2007, for fortifications). These monuments seem to have appeared suddenly in Shkodër during the Early Bronze Age (beginning about 3100 B.C.; Prendi and Bunguri 2008), but their origins have remained unclear. Were forts and mounds, and therefore social inequality, local inventions, or were they introduced from the outside, through migration for example? Might a regional approach, grounded in holistic, interdisciplinary analysis of the landscape, help clarify the timing of their appearance and source, with lessons for the study of such issues elsewhere in the western Balkans?

Our approach to regional archaeology is explicitly grounded in landscape studies. Following Hirsch and O'Hanlon (1995), our definition of "landscape" is an expansive one. Landscapes are containers. They hold and are bounded by geographical features, such as mountains, lakes, plains, and rivers, but also enable and limit human perceptions and behaviors. As such, we addressed seven factors, linked to, and by, Shkodër's landscape, which might have contributed to social change during the course of the Bronze Age: 1) settlement shifts, e.g. from small villages to defensible fortresses, 2) rising inequality, as indicated by mound burial, 3) conflict, 4) economy and diet, 5) trade, 6) migration, and 7) environmental changes. To collect our data, we conducted archaeological and geological surveys in the plains and hills around Shkodra, excavations at three hill forts and three mounds, and scientific analysis of artifacts, environmental samples, and human remains.

The results of our research, while preliminary, are interesting. As described in more detail below, we determined that the first hill forts in northern Albania were in fact occupied prior to the Early Bronze Age, perhaps as early as the Late Neolithic (4800-4500 BC). The social changes that came with the start of the Bronze Age and the appearance of hill forts may well have been local phenomena, at least in part. Burial in mounds seems to have begun somewhat later, during the late Early Bronze Age or at the start of the Middle Bronze Age (2000-1600 BC). This mortuary practice may have been introduced from the outside, perhaps during the so-called Cetina expansion (beginning about 2100 BC; Tomas 2009); at least one individual buried in a mound was a foreigner, based on Strontium-isotope analysis of a tooth (see below). Interestingly, mounds appear to have connected communities not divided them, so that despite the fact that people were living in defensible forts, intra-regional conflicts may have been limited (Deskaj in press). Likewise, diet across communities was similar, focused on farming and herding (see below). Short-distance transhumance may have linked the Shkodra region to other adjacent regions and facilitated trade, in pottery for example (Galaty et al. 2013). Finally, changes in the size and nature of Shkodra Lake and surrounding rivers likely also shaped social changes in the region through time. For example, prior to about 1200 years ago, the lake was a large marshland, which would have limited agricultural activities and, perhaps, encouraged settlement in the hills (Mazzini et al. 2016). Likewise, the Kir River appears to have shifted it course sometime in antiquity, prior to the Roman conquest (Galicki et al. in press). We therefore conclude that key social changes in Shkodra were outcomes of both local invention and regional diffusion, and that this give and take, between innovation and sharing, likely characterizes human history generally. Furthermore, these conclusions could not and would not have been reached without the critical input of regional-scale data and a landscape approach.

RESULTS

The Projekti Arkeologjik i Shkodrës (PASH), the Shkodër Archaeological Project, is an international, collaborative, regional research project, directed by Drs. Michael Galaty and Lorenc Bejko, of University of Michigan and the

University of Tirana respectively.[1] PASH is focused on the Shkodër province of northern Albania, a strategically important region located in the western Balkans along the Adriatic coast (Figure 1). We conducted five years of interdisciplinary archaeological field research, from 2010 to 2014, during which time 2518 tracts covering 16 sq km and 175 tumuli were surveyed.[2] Our study region encompasses the Shkodra Plain and surrounding hills, and is situated along the eastern shore of Shkodra Lake, the largest freshwater lake in the Balkans. This paper reports preliminary project results. Our aim is to situate the results of excavations conducted in 2014 within a larger regional framework, as established through archaeological and environmental surveys.

Figure 1: Map of the PASH study region showing sites identified and documented. Shefqet Lulja.

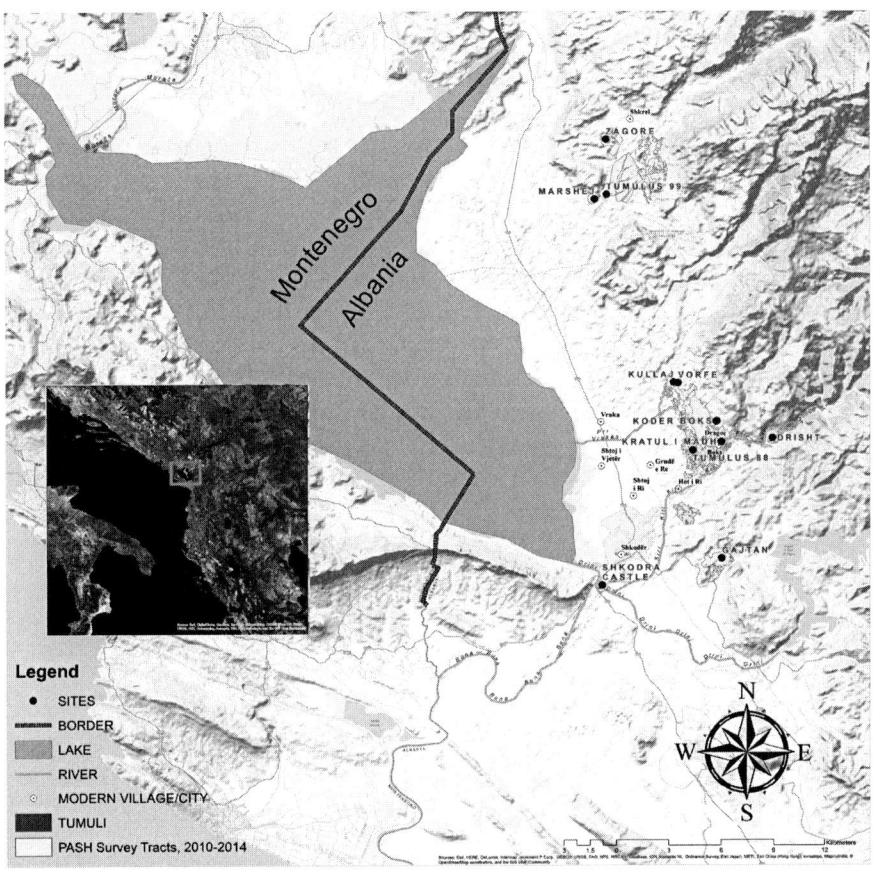

---

[1] The PASH website is available at: http://shkodraarchaeologicalproject.weebly.com/.
[2] This chapter is based upon work supported by the National Science Foundation under Grant No. BCS1220016. Any opinions, findings, and conclusions or recommendations expressed in this material are those of the author(s) and do not necessarily reflect the views of the National Science Foundation.

PASH survey data are still being processed, but we can draw some initial interpretations. Despite evidence for a robust human presence in Shkodër during the late Upper Paleolithic and, perhaps, the Mesolithic, the region was not occupied during the earlier phases of the Neolithic. When humans did return to Shkodër, during the Late Neolithic, settlement was confined to the hills, and remained so (literally) through the Medieval period, demonstrating remarkable continuity. Tumuli were built on the plains, beneath hill forts, overlooking the lake. It may be the case, therefore, that the plains were the abode of the dead and the hills the lands of the living (Deskaj in press).

During the summer of 2014 PASH conducted excavations at three prehistoric settlements – Kodër Boks, Zagorë, and the large hill fort at Gajtan – and at two burial mounds, Tumulus 88 in Shtoj and Tumulus 99 in Shkrel (see again, Figure 1). Another mound, Tumulus 52, was excavated in 2013, but was largely a modern construction (see below). In all cases, units were excavated in 10-centimeter arbitrary levels or, where possible, following natural stratigraphy. All dirt was screened through quarter-inch mesh. An approximately one-liter soil sample was collected from each level, using the pinch sampling method, and processed using bucket flotation. The recovered archaeobotanical samples were analyzed by Dr. Susan Allen, of the University of Cincinnati, and her student, Ms. Rachelanne Bolus. All excavated bone was kept, including that from flotation, and analyzed by Dr. Richard Yerkes, of the Ohio State University.

Kodër Boks

The site of Kodër Boks was discovered in 2012 in the course of field survey. It was targeted for test excavation due to its unusual location – in an upland valley – and the large number of prehistoric artifacts found on the surface and throughout the region. The site is covered with dense vegetation and could not be gridded and systematically surface collected. Consequently, 1x1 meter units were opened adjacent to a modern field road. The site clearly spans the transition from late prehistory to the early historic periods, but in all units deposits were mixed. As a result, float samples from the site were not analyzed. Faunal analysis indicates equal numbers of sheep and/or goats and cattle, very few pigs, and no wild species.

Zagorë

Zagorë was first excavated by the Albanian Institute of Archaeology in 1986 under the direction of Zhaneta Andrea (Andrea 1996). She describes two uninterrupted phases of prehistoric occupation: one Middle Bronze Age, and the other Late Bronze Age and transitional to the Early Iron Age (beginning about 1100 BC). Like Kodër Boks, Zagorë is covered with dense vegetation and could not be gridded and systematically surface collected. Moreover, the previous excavations were extensive, covering 206 square meters, so our seven 1x1 meter test pits were limited to the site's edges. Deposits at Zagorë were also relatively mixed. The vast majority of prehistoric pottery dates to the Late Bronze Age, as also documented by Andrea. Very little Iron Age material was recovered and we question whether the settlement remained occupied into the Iron Age. We also identified Copper and Early Bronze Age components, which were not documented by Andrea. Botanical remains from Zagorë have not yet been analyzed, but faunal analysis points to a reliance on sheep and/or goats, with some cattle and pig, and, with the exception of two bird bones and one fish vertebra, no wild species.

Unit 4 at Zagorë was excavated within the confines of a small bedrock feature that had clearly been used as some kind of structure. A floor feature and wall trench were identified at 20 centimeters below surface. A horn core resting on the floor returned an AMS radiocarbon date of 1425-1265 BC calibrated, i.e. the Late Bronze Age.

Gajtan

Gajtan is an extremely large hill fort settlement. It was the location of the Albanian Institute of Archaeology's first large-scale prehistoric excavations, conducted in 1961-1962 (Islami and Ceka 1965). These excavations revealed that Gajtan had been constructed during the Bronze Age, perhaps as early as the Early Bronze Age. We surveyed the site in 2012 and conducted systematic surface collections in areas with good visibility and dense prehistoric artifact scatters. In 2014 three deep 1x1 meter soundings were excavated in areas near the 1961-1962 excavation trenches. The upper portions of these units (levels 1-4; see Figure 2 and Table 1) had been disturbed and the deposits were mixed, but lower levels were intact. AMS radiocarbon dating of seeds from Unit 3, levels 4, 6, and 10 returned Late and Middle Bronze Age dates. AMS radiocarbon dating of charcoal from level 13 returned a date of 3765-3645 BC calibrated, i.e. the Copper Age. Finally, AMS radiocarbon dating of soil organics and charcoal from levels 15-18 returned dates spanning the Late Neolithic. These are the first absolute dates for the Late Neolithic from north Albania and they point to an unexpectedly early founding of what would become in the Bronze Age one of Albania's largest hill forts.

Archaeobotanical analysis of the float samples from Gajtan indicates that a wide variety of domesticated plant species were grown, including several types of wheat, millet, lentil, bitter vetch, and barley. Importantly, it appears that by level 8 (which dates to the Middle to Late Bronze Age), if not sooner, there existed a well-established dependence on cultivated legumes and cereals. This may indicate permanent settlement at Gajtan as early as the Copper to Early Bronze Age, perhaps combined with some animal transhumance. Unfortunately, no botanical remains were recovered from Late Neolithic levels. Analysis of faunal remains from Gajtan revealed dependence on sheep and/or goats, cattle, and pigs in frequencies that were similar to Zagorë. Previous work by Galaty and colleagues, including Allen and Yerkes, at Grunas, a prehistoric (Late Bronze Age-Early Iron Age) hill fort located to the north of Gajtan in the high mountain valley of Shala, indicated that the site was occupied during the summer and that sheep and/or goats may have been pastured there (Galaty et al. 2013). That being the case, it is likely that the occupants of Grunas came from settlements in the vicinity of Shkodër. In fact, Gajtan and Grunas bear a striking resemblance to one another: at both sites, gullies were blocked by large retaining walls and terraced, creating large defensible living spaces.

Figure 2: Photograph and drawing of the east profile of Unit 3 at Gajtan. Michael L. Galaty.

PASH
Gajtan Unit 003
East Profile
20 cm
SURFACE
#sherds
0
10
20
30
40
1505-1220 BC
50
60
1260-1055 BC
70
80
90
100
1880-1690 BC
110
120
3765-3645 BC
130
140
5055-4930 BC
150
5215-5025 BC
160
170
4585-4455 BC
180
4545-4450 BC
190
200
210
220
230
001 7YR 3/2 65
0
002 10YR 4/2 55
003 7.5YR 3/4 53
004 10YR 4/4 80
005 10YR 4/3 42
006 10YR 4/3 10
007 2.5YR 3/3 8
008 2.5YR 3/3 8
009 7.5YR 3/3 6
010 10YR 3/3 5
011 10YR 3/3 4
012 10YR 3/3 13
013 2.5YR 4/6 2
014 2.5YR 4/6 1
015 10R 4/6 122
016 10R 4/6 83
017 10R 4/6 61
018 10R 4/6 39
2.5YR 4/6
SONDAGE
019
0
Rock
Burned Soil
Daub
Gravel

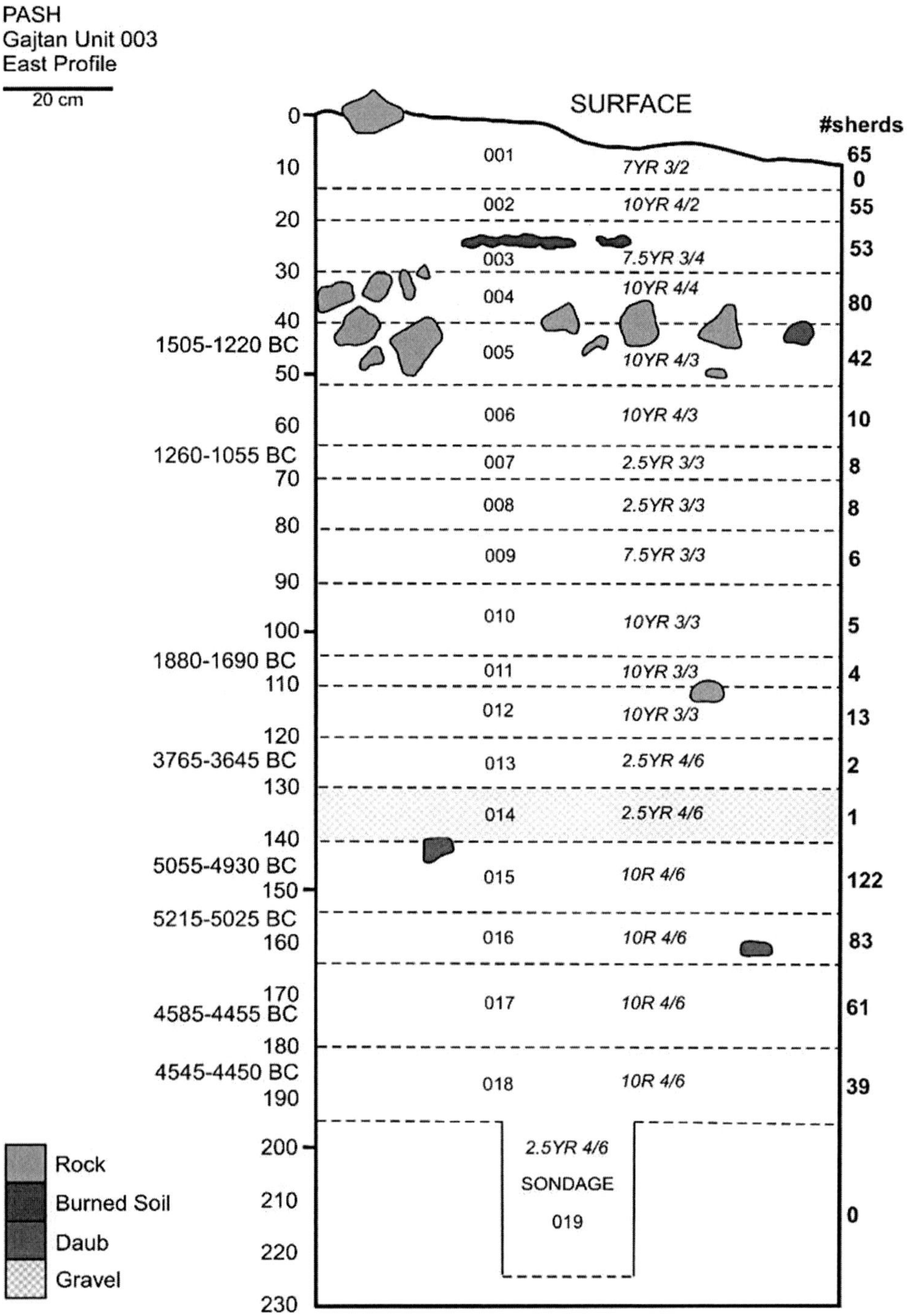

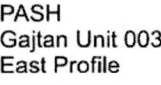

Table 1: List of AMS radiocarbon dates from northern Albania (PASH and Beta Analytic)
Note: dates on soil organics likely overestimate age.

Description	Small Find No.	Year	Additional description	Date (2 sigma cal.)	
TUMULI					
Human tooth, T99-001-002, MIT#: SD 002	GT-2811	2014	adult canine; Sr local	1740-1610 BC cal.	MBA
Human tooth, T99-001-001, MIT#: SD 005	GT-2840	2014	adult canine; Sr non-local	1885-1690 BC cal.	MBA
Human tooth, T127 (Shkrel)		2013		1310-1120 BC cal.	LBA
MARSHEJ					
Human tooth, surface	GT-2636	2013		AD 600-660 cal.	Early Medieval
ZAGORËS					
Horn core, S015 Unit 004 Level 003	GT-2699	2014		1425-1265 BC cal.	LBA
Charcoal, S015 Unit 004 Level 004	GT-2718	2014	Feature 1, wall trench	AD 1450-1640 cal.	Late Medieval
GAJTAN					
Charcoal, S011 Unit 001 Level 013	GT-2878	2014		4690-4520 BC cal.	Late Neolithic
Seed, S011 Unit 003 Level 004		2014	indet. seed	1405-1220 BC cal.	LBA

Seed, S011 Unit 003 Level 004		2014	Triticum	1505-1410 BC cal.	LBA
Seed, S011 Unit 003 Level 006		2014	V. ervilia	1260-1055 BC cal.	LBA
Seed, S011 Unit 003 Level 010		2014	Lens culinaris	1880-1690 BC cal.	MBA
Charcoal, S011 Unit 003 Level 012	GT-2819	2014		3765-3645 BC cal.	Eneolithic
Soil, S011 Unit 003 Level 015		2017		5055-4930 BC cal.	Late Neolithic
Soil, S011 Unit 003 Level 016		2017		5215-5025 BC cal.	Late Neolithic
Charcoal, S011 Unit 003 Level 017		2017		4585-4455 BC cal.	Late Neolithic
Charcoal, S011 Unit 003 Level 018		2017		4545-4450 BC cal.	Late Neolithic

Tumuli

Like Gajtan, Kodër Boks and Zagorë also experienced growth during the Bronze Age. Unlike Gajtan, both are associated with large fields of tumuli, at Shtoj and Shkrel respectively. Excavation of a large, damaged tumulus at Shkrel, Tumulus 99, directed by Ms. Sylvia Deskaj, an archaeologist with the Museum of Anthropological Archaeology at the University of Michigan, produced remains of at least three individuals buried together in a central grave, one of whom was a juvenile. AMS radiocarbon dating of two adult molars produced dates of 1740-1610 BC calibrated and 1885-1690 BC calibrated (Table 1). Diagnostic pottery sherds from the tumulus fill generally support this Middle Bronze Age date. Strontium isotope analysis of the latter molar, conducted by Deskaj, indicates a non-local origin. Its strontium 86/87 ratio is .709653, which fits an inland signal, as established by previous analysis of modern land snails. One of the individuals buried in the Shkrel tumulus appears to have been born on the interior, perhaps in the neighborhood of Kosovo, and moved to the Shkodër region later in life. During prehistory, trade routes through the mountains connected the Shkodër region to Kosovo via sites like Grunas in Shala. It is not surprising, therefore, that prehistoric individuals may have migrated from inland to coast, and vice versa, perhaps through marriage exchange networks, as was also the case in historic times. Unfortunately, the skeletal remains from Tumulus 99 are too fragmentary to be sexed, but we can speculate that the individual who moved to Shkrel was a female.

Deskaj also excavated a mound at Shtoj, Tumulus 88. Unlike Tumulus 99, which was artifact poor, Tumulus 88 generated a remarkably rich array of artifacts dating from the Copper Age through the Late Roman period (i.e. deposited over the course of 4000 years), including pottery, coins, and beads, and thousands of tiles, but no human remains. It may have served as some kind of long-term ritual installation. However, there is good evidence from the Lofkënd tumulus in south Albania that mounds were sometimes constructed from fill obtained from distant, possibly ancestral, village sites (Papadopoulos et al. 2014). Thus, the Lofkënd tumulus contained artifacts dating from the Middle Paleolithic through Modern times. A similar kind of long-term "collective memory" behavior may explain the Shtoj tumulus.

Archaeozoological analysis of faunal remains from the mounds, one used for burial and the other used for ritual, generated very different profiles (Figure 3). The Shtoj mound produced equid and cattle remains, whereas the Shkrel mound did not. This difference may reflect the fact that the Shtoj mound was used for a longer period of time and for a different purpose. Another mound, Tumulus 52, excavated in 2013, turned out to be a mostly modern construction. Its faunal profile was completely different from the other two mounds.

Figure 3: Distribution of faunal remains from Tumulus 52, 88, and 99 by species. Richard Yerkes.

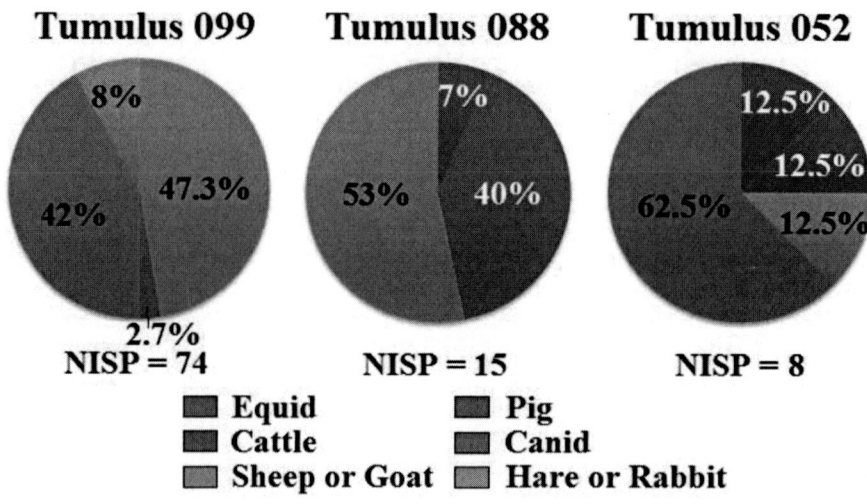

DISCUSSION

In summary, PASH's preliminary results point to a dynamic prehistoric landscape in Shkodër, one with Late Neolithic roots, a Bronze Age expansion, and complex patterns of economy, interaction (including migration), and ritual. Together, these led to remarkable changes in social complexity, marked by hill fort construction and mound building. Our work thus far allows a few tentative conclusions.

We *cannot* yet explain the sudden appearance of hill top settlements in Shkodër during the Late Neolithic. We *can* say that there is no evidence for a preceding Middle (and Early) Neolithic occupation of the region, unless it is now under Shkodra Lake. This is in contrast to nearby Kosovo, where a rich Middle (and Late) Neolithic occupation can be documented (Berisha 2012). There was a Mesolithic occupation of Shkodër – PASH surveyors collected numerous Late Glacial and Mesolithic stone tools – and Mesolithic hunter-collectors may have inhibited settlement of the region by farmers. However, we might also propose an environmental explanation for the delayed, yet sudden, Late Neolithic settlement of Shkodër. Collaborative research between PASH and a Swiss-Italian team, which is studying several deep cores from the lake, indicates that during the Mesolithic, the Shkodra Lake basin was occupied by a braided river system (Mazzini et al. 2016: 8). After about 6000 BC, a large wetland with peat bogs formed (Mazzini et al. 2016: 8). It may be that the wetland's appearance and expansion attracted agricultural settlers, who occupied upland sites and, later, buried their dead down below, on the plain. Whatever the case, those who lived at Kodër Boks and Zagorë during the subsequent Bronze Age were in fact wealthy enough to build and maintain hundreds of mounds, whether for burial or for ritual purposes. The expansion of settlement and mound construction in Shkodër, which appears to date to the late Middle Bronze Age or early Late Bronze Age may coincide with a cool period identified in the Shkodra Lake cores which lasts from 2547 to 2459 BC calibrated (Mazzini et al. 2016: 8). This cooling event matches the so-called 4400 BP climate event that affected the whole Eastern Mediterranean. It also precedes the so-called Cetina expansion, which derived from regions just to the north of Shkodër, in southern Croatia. Cetina pottery has been found throughout the Adriatic and as far south as Greece (Tomas 2009). Participation in the Cetina interaction sphere may well have given impetus to Shkodër's Bronze Age expansion, leading to the movement of people, such as the non-local individual interred in the Shkrel tumulus.

CONCLUSION

In conclusion, while interesting, our results from Shkodër may yet be found to match trends being slowly identified elsewhere in Albania. While southern

Albanian hill top settlements have not yet been subjected to systematic test excavation and radiocarbon dating, they may well have been occupied initially in the Late Neolithic, like Gajtan. As such, the Late and Final Neolithic take on added archaeological importance in Albania, as they have throughout the Balkans, including Greece. We simply cannot understand the foundations of Bronze Age society, including profound changes in social complexity and inequality, without also documenting and understanding these preceding periods.

Likewise, exploring the origins of social complexity and inequality requires regional data, drawn from interdisciplinary landscape studies. Excavation alone is not sufficient if one of our aims as archaeologists is to explain long-term socio-dynamics and human-nature interactions, whether in Albania, elsewhere in the Balkans, or anywhere in the world. PASH provides a valuable case in point. Systematic, intensive, regional survey, of the kind commonly practiced throughout the Mediterranean (Alcock and Cherry 2004), but still rare in the Balkans, provided the background data necessary to place the results of excavations in context. One of our goals was to determine when hill forts were settled, and why, and how many tumuli were out there. To meet this goal, we needed to know whether settlement in the region preceded hill fort construction, and what factors, such as changes to the regional environment, might have encouraged occupation in the hills as opposed to on the plains. Our conclusions regarding prehistoric settlement in Shkodër, as described in preliminary fashion above, are, not surprisingly, very complex. Perhaps most interesting is in fact the social dimension. During the Bronze Age, people may well have lived in the hills surrounding Shkodra Lake because, just like today, the lake varied in size, from quite large during flood stage, to non-existent in drought (Galicki et al. in press). But they also maintained belief systems that enabled and reinforced a new social order, one linked to changes in economy and, consequently, inequality. Given their number and omnipresence, as determined by survey, tumuli – whether as places of burial or sites of ritual expression – reinforced social divisions between families and, we might expect, tribal segments, signalling the potential for conflict. And yet, they also served to connect hill forts: one could not walk from Kodër Boks to Zagorë without passing through their respective fields of tumuli, and being reminded of the ancestors who, similarly, once walked there as well (Deskaj in press). Hill forts and tumuli together, therefore, compose the social landscape of Shkodër and served to channel and define human occupation and land use there, together with, not in spite of, the natural landscape of lake, rivers, hills, and plains.

REFERENCES

Alcock, Susan E., and John F. Cherry. 2004. Introduction. In *Side-by-Side Survey: Comparative Regional Studies in the Mediterranean World*, edited by Susan E. Alcock and John F. Cherry, pp. 1-9. Oxford: Oxbow Books.

Andrea, Zhaneta. 1996. Venbanimi i Zagorës. *Iliria* 26(1-2): 21-55.

Berisha, Milot. 2012. *Archaeological Guide of Kosovo*. Ministry of Culture, Youth and Sport, Institute of Archaeology. Prishtina.

Borgna, Elisabetta, and Sylvie Müller-Celka (eds.). 2011. *Ancestral Landscapes. Burial Mounds in the Copper and Bronze Ages. Central and Eastern Europe - Balkans - Adriatic - Aegean, 4th-2nd Millennium BC.* Travaux de la Maison de l'Orient et de la Méditerranée, No. 58. Lyon: Maison de l'Orient et de la Méditerranée.

Deskaj, Sylvia N.D. Living among the Dead : Establishing and Maintaining Community in Northern Albania. In *The Bioarchaeology of Community*, edited by Sara Juengst and Sarah K. Becker. Archaeological Papers of the American Anthropology Association, Vol. 28. Washington D.C.

Galaty, Michael L. 2005. European Regional Studies: A Coming of Age? *Journal of Archaeological Research* 13(4): 291-336.

Galaty, Michael L. Ols Lafe, Wayne E. Lee, and Zamir Tafilica. 2013. *Light and Shadow: Isolation and Interaction in the Shala Valley of Northern Albania.* Monumenta Archaeologica 28. Los Angeles: UCLA Cotsen Institute of Archaeology Press.

Galicki, Stan, Catherine E. Henry, Michael L. Galaty, and Lorenc Bejko. N.D. Medieval Anthropogenic Nonpoint Source Sediment Runoff in the Wetland Fringe of Lake Shkodra, Albania. Submitted to the *Geomorphology*.

Hirsch, Eric, and Michael O'Hanlon (eds.). 1995. *The Archaeology of Landscape: Perspectives on Place and Space*. Oxford: Clarendon Press.

Islami, Selim and Hasan Ceka. 1965. Të dhëna të reja mbi lashtësinë iliret ë territorin e Shqipërisë. *Konferenca e I e studimeve albanologjike*, pp. 449-452. Tiranë.

Ilaria Mazzini, Elsa Gliozzi, Michael L. Galaty, Lorenc Bejko, Laura Sadori, Ingeborg Soulié-Märche, Rexhep Koçi, Aurelien Van Welden, and Salvatore Bushati. 2016. Holocene Evolution of Lake Shkodra: Multidisciplinary Evidence for Forgotten Landscapes in Northern Albania. *Quaternary Science Reviews* 30: 1-11.

Papadopoulos, John K., Sarah P. Morris, Lorenc Bejko, and Lynne A. Schepartz. 2014. *The Excavation of the Prehistoric Burial Tumulus at Lofkënd, Albania*. Monumenta Archaeologica 34. Los Angeles: UCLA Cotsen Institute of Archaeology Press.

Parkinson, William A., and Paul R. Duffy. 2007. Fortifications and Enclosures in European Prehistory: A Cross-Cultural Perspective. *Journal of Archaeological Research* 15: 97-141.

Prendi, Frano, and Adem Bunguri. 2008. *Bronzi i Hershëm në Shiqipëri* [The Early Bronze Age in Albania]. Prishtinë: Archaeological Institute of Kosova.

Tomas, Helena. 2009. The World Beyond the Northern Margin: The Bronze Age Aegean and the East Adriatic Coast. In *Archaic State Interaction: The Eastern Mediterranean in the Bronze Age*, edited by William A. Parkinson and Michael L. Galaty, pp. 3-28. Santa Fe, NM: School for Advanced Research Press.

LANDSCAPE AS LEGACY IN NORTHERN DALMATIA

Gregory Zaro[1,2] and Martina Čelhar[3]

[1] University of Maine, Department of Anthropology
[2] University of Maine, Climate Change Institute
[3] University of Zadar, Department of Archaeology

INTRODUCTION

Human impacts on Earth's biosphere since the industrial revolution are widely recognized, but significant, long-lasting, and pervasive human impacts on the environment have a much longer history in the Holocene that include, among others, the onset of farming, sedentary life, and the emergence of cities. Importantly, the rise of urbanism further catalyzed agricultural intensification, socioeconomic stratification, and transformation of habitats within urban settings and the rural hinterlands on which they rely. As a long-term process, urbanization has shaped socio-environmental change over the course of at least the past three to five thousand years globally. Consequently, contemporary societies inherit local and regional environments that are already characterized as "anthropogenic," reflecting land use legacies that stretch deep into the past. Delineating such legacies is crucial for current decision-making processes that seek to understand environmental baselines and project future challenges in the context of both human- and climate-induced changes in the environment. This paper suggests opportunities for archaeology to contribute to a more robust understanding of long-term urban-ecological relationships centered on northern Dalmatia, and particularly the Croatian port city of Zadar and the surrounding Ravni Kotari, as reflective of a millennial-scale process of urbanization. The nearby archaeological site of Nadin-Gradina, centrally positioned in the Ravni Kotari, is proposed as a proxy measurement of urban and landscape change through time. Although the archaeological component of this project is still in its early stages at the time of writing, its potential as a registry of landscape change can nevertheless be outlined.

Our approach utilizes the concept of landscape as a key focal point between humans and the broader physical environment, and it is designed to showcase how the delineation of long-term landscape change can help reveal the historical role humans have played in shaping the contemporary world. We use the term "landscape" broadly, but recognize it to mean the cumulative impacts of human and non-human agents on the physical world. Hence, landscapes reflect human engagement with the environment (and with each other) and link the social and physical worlds into a dynamic mold.

LANDSCAPE AS LEGACY

In recent decades, assessments of human-environment dynamics indicate that most of Earth's ecosystems have been either directly or indirectly influenced by human activities (Costanza et al. 2007; Fisher et al. 2009; Kirch 2005; Redman 1999; Redman et al. 2004; Vitousek et al. 1997). While errors may be large, some estimates suggest that roughly 16-23% of Earth's terrestrial ecosystems have been directly transformed by humans via row crop agriculture, pastureland, or urban-industrial areas (Vitousek et al. 1997). In other estimates, all contemporary cultivated landscapes combined are said to encompass roughly 16 million square kilometers, or about 11% of Earth's land mass (Vitousek et al. 1986). These kinds of work have prompted the proposed naming of a new geologic era in the Anthropocene. However, there is much debate over the types of material indicators that should be used in assessing such an epoch (Certini and Scalenghe 2011; Ellis et al. 2013; Kaplan et al. 2009), and the asynchronous onset, regionally and globally, of its indicators also presents challenges to its applicability. Despite this asynchrony, on-the-ground recognition of the cultural and historical nature of landscapes becomes critical for managing a sustainable relationship between humans and the environment. As a growing field of study, historical ecology provides one perspective to investigate the fluid relationship between people and their physical world because it treats them as a richly interconnected analytical unit, where modern landscapes are viewed to be the cumulative expression of long-term interactions between human (e.g., cultural) and non-human (e.g., biological, climatic, geophysical) processes (Balée 2006; Balée and Erickson 2006; Crumley 1994; Hayashida 2005). Coming from forestry, David Foster and colleagues (2003) have referred to these human imprints on the landscape as "land use legacies," a term that underscores the pervasive and long-lasting effects of human activities on the physical world, whether intentional or unintentional. Past human-environment dynamics are therefore embedded in landscapes, providing a historical context in which contemporary peoples and places are situated (see also Erickson 2010).

Cities represent concentrated centers of resources that are often key drivers of landscape change through production, consumption, and waste disposal (Grimm et al. 2008:759). Their margins extend into the surrounding rural countryside, amplifying changes in soils, vegetation, human settlements, and the emergence of secondary urban centers. As Grimm and colleagues note, these hinterland settings can be characterized as extended urbanized regions (2008:757). Adding time depth to the study of these landscapes can reveal changes in resource management strategies, while also serving to detail the complexity of relationships among variables like population growth or decline, resource distribution, agricultural potential, technological innovation, civic construction, climate, and other factors shaping urbanization over the course of several thousand years. Long-term landscape studies are also pivotal to understanding the ecological relationships that societies today hold with their physical environment. One critique of many studies of socio-environmental dynamics is that they often overemphasize contemporary or very recent biophysical conditions and therefore only consider the latest component of long, complex sequences of change (van der Leeuw and Redman 2002:599). Urban planning, development, and resource management in the modern world would therefore be better contextualized within a long-term process of change in the historical and more ancient past.

For the first time in human history, more than half of humanity now resides within cities (United Nations 2014). As cities expand and more and more people flock to urban centers around the world, predicting future challenges poses many difficulties. However, landscapes accumulate the impacts of human dynamics from thousands of years into the past. A deep look into antiquity provides insight into how relationships between human groups evolved, and their impact on and responses to changing environments and climate. Landscapes thus offer a reservoir of information that reflects past responses to change and the historical, cultural, and ecological connections between peoples and landscapes through time (Athanassopoulos and Wandsnider 2004; Costanza et al. 2007; Galaty et al. 2013; Schon and Galaty 2006; van der Leeuw and Redman 2002). The remainder of this paper introduces an archaeological case study in the eastern Adriatic that is building toward a better understanding of urbanization and landscape change in order to inform on 21st century challenges facing Zadar and its hinterland. Although still in its infant stages, the project is able to demonstrate the potential for archaeological data from ancient urban centers to document changing landscapes into the present era.

URBANIZATION AND LANDSCAPE CHANGE IN NORTHERN DALMATIA

Urbanization refers to the process of a settlement performing an increasingly diverse set of functions in the context of a wider hinterland (Smith 2007), but also resulting in generally higher populations that became increasingly more nucleated (at least in this part of the world), greater concentration of goods and services, greater economic specialization, increased need for building materials such as wood, stone, and fired bricks, and the territory itself is often transformed into settlement, creating new urban ecosystems. Urbanization also involves increasing social stratification, a wider range of architectural forms, and the development of long-distance trading partners with increased reliance on non-local resources. Most cities rely on food stuffs coming from specialized hinterland producers, often improved through terrace construction, canals, and other forms of *landesque capital* (Håkansson and Widgren 2014; Smith 2014). From an ecological standpoint, urbanization leads to increased patch fragmentation and diversity, which may be reflected in more interfaces or boundaries between distinct land cover types, or smaller patch sizes like urban, residential, forest, or desert land use categories (Grimm et al. 2008:756). Ultimately, this process leads to greater impact on local and regional landscapes in the form of habitat change as well as resource intensification and the development of secondary urban centers. Periods of population growth can spur major changes, usually with settlement expansion and intensification of agriculture, but the peopling of a landscape can also create stability over time in the form of field maintenance, forestry, pasture, and soil. Similarly, population decline or simply abandonment can leave significant and long-lasting effects on the environment, including impacts on soil chemistry, sedimentation, and erosion (e.g., Fisher 2005; Holliday 1992; Sandor and Eash 1991), forest regeneration (e.g., Čuka et al. 2012; Turner and Sabloff 2012), forest composition (e.g., Foster et al. 2003), and ruined relics of the recent and more ancient past (e.g., Halperin 2014), each of which may be incorporated into and recognized as part of the contemporary landscape.

Along Croatia's Adriatic coast, urbanization as a process has unfolded over the course of at least the past 3,000 years (Chapman et al. 1996; Jović Gazić 2011; Suić 2003). The ancient port city of Zadar remains an important social and economic center in the region today, but resource management, economic development, rural-to-urban migration, and environmental policy are significant issues in the 21st century, particularly in the context of projected climate change (Giorgi and Lionello 2008), sustainable development (Cavrić 2009), and a booming tourism market that peaks annually from June to August (Jordan 2000). Growth in tourism may also lead to additional pressures on water, agriculture, fishing, livestock, and other local resources, especially during summer months when population levels peak. Environmental pressures will likely be amplified over the coming century as well by predicted changes in Earth's climate, which for the Adriatic region include decreased precipitation during the summer months on the order of 20-30% by 2100, and temperature increases on the order of 2-4 degrees Celsius over the same period (Giorgi and Lionello 2008). The latest report published by the Intergovernmental Panel on Climate Change (IPCC 2013) further supports these projections, with the most significant changes occurring during summer, coinciding with high tourist season and added pressures on local resources. The relationship between urban societies and the environment is thus both of anthropological interest and a contemporary challenge concerning socio-environmental relationships that emerged millennia earlier (Balée 2006; Fisher et al. 2009; Hayashida 2005; Hughes 2005; Redman et al. 2004).

Ravni Kotari and the Nadin-Gradina Site

Croatia's coastline is a generally rugged terrain with some mountain ranges reaching elevations of 1500 m a.s.l., forming an ecotone between continental southeastern Europe and the Mediterranean climate regime of the Adriatic Sea (Roglić 1962; Walsh 2014). The Ravni Kotari, a karstic region in northern Dalmatia, is one of the few low-lying zones along the coast and a historically important region for agriculture and livestock (Čuka et al. 2012). It was the setting of numerous fortified Iron Age-to-Roman settlements (Batović 1977; Čače 2006, 2007; Chapman et al. 1996; Jović Gazić 2011; Suić 2003; Tomičić 2010), prompting Wilkes (1969) to recognize it as the most urbanized region of Dalmatia in antiquity. Because Zadar is a living city, the archaeological focus of our project centers on the nearby site of Nadin-Gradina, a hilltop settlement centrally located within the Ravni Kotari (Figure 1).

Figure 1: Geographic location of the study.

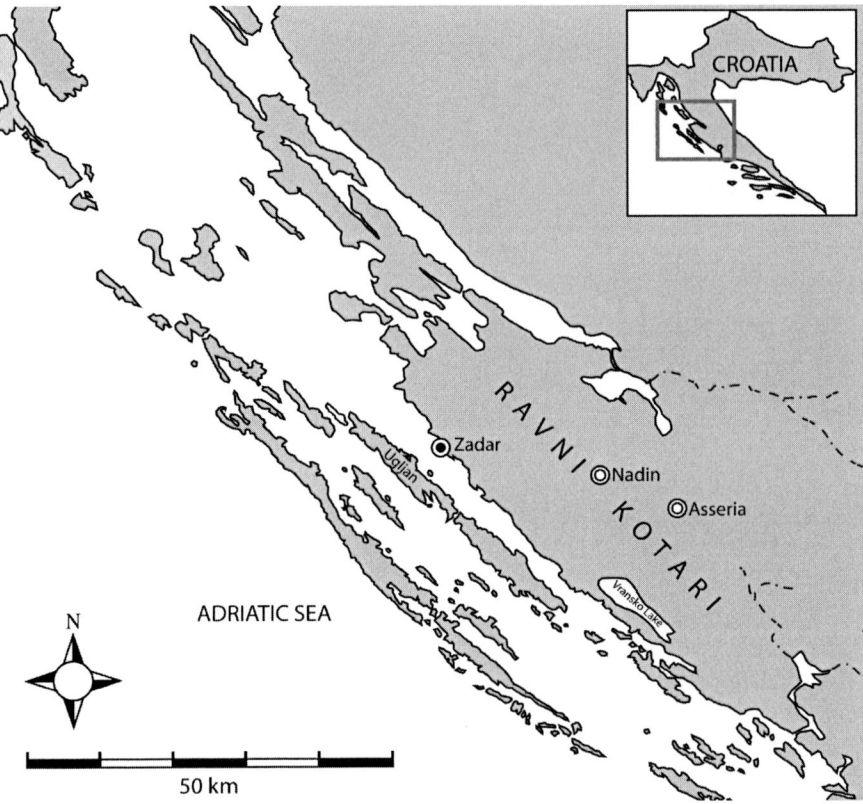

Based on early writings and inscriptions, Nadin-Gradina had already reached considerable size in the Late Iron Age and was transformed into the Roman municipium *Nedinum* in the first century CE (Wilkes 1969:212). Given their proximity, it likely held a close social and economic relationship with

Zadar, and Wilkes notes that Roman *Nedinum* was composed for the most part of native families (presumably Liburnian) with others likely being Roman colonists from Zadar (see also Kurilić 1999). The site measures 32 ha in area, about a quarter of which is enclosed by a fortification wall of megalithic limestone blocks (Figure 2).

Figure 2: Oblique aerial photo of Nadin-Gradina. The tree line reflects the shape of the megalithic fortification wall (photo courtesy of Vedrana Glavaš).

This is a pronounced topographic feature still fixed in the landscape today but one whose masonry is visible on the surface in only a few locations. Wall segments from a later Venetian, and subsequently Ottoman, fortification currently stand to heights of several meters but are now cloaked in forest. The Ottoman legacy is also reflected on a small print, which depicts a fort and small village with what is likely a mosque and minaret (see Chapman et al. 1996:125, Figure 95). Today, a mix of scrub forest, grassland, and rocky outcrops characterizes much of the site's surface, and the modern village of Nadin, which is home to approximately 400 people, lies below the western limits of the hillfort.

Archaeological investigation at Nadin-Gradina in the 1980s was part of a larger settlement survey with a principal focus on landscape change and the environment through Late Antiquity, or about the 5th century CE (Chapman et al. 1996). Limited excavation suggested a complex settlement with more than 2,000 years of possibly intermittent occupation, ranging from Iron Age settlement to the Late Middle Ages. Since 2005, the University of Zadar has conducted excavations intermittently at a cemetery on the lower western skirts of the hillfort, unearthing a rich assemblage of Liburnian Iron Age burials and artifacts, though largely disturbed by intrusive Roman cremations (Kukoč 2006, 2009; Kukoč and Batović 2006; Kukoč and Čelhar 2010, 2017).

Nadin-Gradina Archaeological Project, 2015-present
In 2015, the Nadin-Gradina Archaeological Project (NGAP), a joint venture between the University of Zadar (Croatia) and the University of Maine (USA), completed its inaugural season of fieldwork with partial support from the National Geographic Society (Čelhar and Zaro 2017; Zaro and Čelhar 2017). The intent of the project was to lay the foundation for an intensive, multi-year program of field research at Nadin-Gradina centered on long-term urbanization, landscape change, and climate in the eastern Adriatic. Several related questions help to guide the ongoing research program:

> (1) As a direct reflection of the links between humans and the environment (i.e., landscape), are there significant changes through time in subsistence and resource management at Nadin-Gradina (agriculture, herd management, processing of materials, resource specialization), and what changes are observed with respect to climate shifts like the Roman Warm Period, Medieval Warm Period, and Little Ice Age (see Buntgen et al. 2011; Mann et al. 2009)?
> (2) Are episodes of urban decline or abandonment reflected archaeologically, and how do they articulate with broader changes in landscape and environment?
> (3) Does the archaeological record reflect shifts in spatial organization and population at Nadin-Gradina, particularly from Late Iron Age through Roman, Medieval, and Ottoman eras?
> (4) How did local populations respond culturally and economically to wider pulses of globalization, foreign incursion, or environmental change?

Preliminary excavations focused on the area within the space defined by the megalithic fortification wall of the site. In 2015, an initial six units were widely spaced and excavated to bedrock, several of which reached depths of 3 m and exhibited complex cultural stratigraphy (Figure 3). Field and laboratory work during the subsequent 2016 season, partially supported by the Rust Family Foundation, were designed to further establish the occupational history/chronology of the site, with the added element of illuminating the nature of Late Medieval and/or Venetian-Ottoman era occupation at Nadin-Gradina, providing an archaeological bridge between the ancient and modern landscapes. This consisted of systematic mapping and test excavation of structures believed to be related to Ottoman occupation (principally, that of the summit fortress and presumed mosque), as well as artifact analyses of surface and immediate subsurface artifact assemblages from both 2015 and 2016 excavations.

Figure 3: Probe B after excavation in 2015, showing the complexity of a settlement history that includes Iron Age (IA), Classical Antiquity (CA), and Late Antiquity (LA). Bedrock (BR) is also noted.

Archaeological work from these initial seasons documented settlement remains across three major cultural eras, suggesting the Nadin-Gradina hilltop was intensively occupied by the 5th century BCE Iron Age, experienced a pronounced transformation during Classical Antiquity, and continued to be occupied into Late Antiquity, or about the 6th century CE, before experiencing a period of abandonment on the summit. This chronology is based primarily on a combination of fourteen radiocarbon dates, stratigraphic superpositioning of cultural deposits and features, and stylistic assessment of associated pottery and other artifact classes. Importantly, although deeply buried and partly destroyed by Roman civic transformation of the settlement, our excavations exposed a portion of a building or feature constructed of large, unmortarted stone blocks. Construction technique, associated pottery, and radiocarbon dates strongly suggest this structure/feature was built during the Late Iron Age. This appears to have been cut by a heavily mortared wall, interpreted to be of Roman construction. More expediently constructed and lightly mortared stone walls with several examples of spolia, or repurposed building material, were also exposed among the upper strata, interpreted to be of Late Antiquity in age (Figure 4).

Fifteenth century Italian imports from near-surface deposits indicate a Late Medieval re-settlement of the summit after a multi-century period of abandonment, but clear markers of "Ottoman" or "Turkish" imports have not been identified despite the presence of a presumed mosque on the summit and historic references to Ottoman control of Nadin and the surrounding area during the 16th and 17th centuries (e.g. Pitcher 1972). This is not unexpected, however, since the situation appears similarly across other parts of Ravni Kotari, like at Zemunik Donji, for example (Gusar and Vujević 2016). In any case, chronologically resolving the final centuries of occupation of the Nadin-Gradina hillfort remains a difficult challenge from an archaeological standpoint, particularly when Ottoman control of the area may have lasted little more than a century.

Figure 4: A repurposed Roman capital (spolia) is visible in a Late Antique wall.

Based on current evidence, it seems reasonable to conclude that the Nadin-Gradina hillfort site represented a primary cultural center in Zadar's extended urban hinterland for a period of about one thousand years or more before abandonment of the summit. It is also reasonable to assume that it lay visibly in ruin in the subsequent centuries, though local vegetation would have undoubtedly begun its encroachment onto the summit without human interference. Although the ruins of Late Medieval Nadin were clearly in an advanced state of decay by the 20th century, the dense overgrowth of the site today lies in striking contrast from its depiction in photos only a few decades ago, when dry-stone walls and pasture were maintained on its summit for grazing herbivores, leaving the monumental ruins of the centuries old fortress and mosque cleared of vegetation and likely visible from a distance. This swing between cultural ruin and "natural" overgrowth is indeed affected by human agency, and given the site's elevated perch on the landscape, significantly changed its symbolic character through time.

Although not a direct component of the NGAP, previous and ongoing paleoenvironmental research is helping to characterize regional environmental change into which the archaeological record can be contextualized. Pollen records from the Bokanjačko Blato sediment core, a former wetland near Zadar, indicate a decline in forest vegetation by at least the second millennium BCE (presumably forest clearance) and rising values of species like *Juniperus* that thrive in open landscapes (Grüger 1996:36-43). The record also indicates the presence of cereals, walnut, chestnut, grape, and olive, with the latter two becoming more pronounced in upper levels (Grüger 1996:36-43). This record is in general accordance with relative landscape changes interpreted from other paleoenvironmental records in the Adriatic basin (Balbo et al. 2006; Kaligaric et al. 2006; Oldfield et al. 2003; Schmidt et al. 2000), while ongoing analysis of a core recently extracted from nearby Vransko Lake should provide more localized information and hopefully with greater chronological resolution (Croatian Geological Survey 2013). Additionally, Dr. Slobodan Miko and colleagues at the Croatian Geological Survey recently secured funds to reconstruct karst lake landscapes in the context of changes in climate, environment, and human migration (https://loladria.wordpress.com/). Several of their coring sites are in Ravni Kotari, including the adjacent Nadin wetland, and the results will be instrumental to the NGAP as both projects advance.

More broadly, we also seek to address questions regarding the links between climate and urbanization at Nadin-Gradina, utilizing documented Late Holocene climate changes across Mediterranean during the Roman Warm Period (~250-400 CE), Medieval Climate Anomaly (~900-1300 CE), and the Little Ice Age (~1500-1850 CE) to identify the potential impacts of changes in temperature and precipitation on urbanized societies through time. Although not a direct correlation, past urban-climate-environment intersections can help inform and/or contextualize challenges facing contemporary residents of Zadar and northern Dalmatia.

OPPORTUNITIES AND CHALLENGES

The archaeological study of ancient urban centers provides an array of data concerning the manners in which past human societies interacted with, conceptualized, and shaped their physical world. To this end, the archaeological record at Nadin-Gradina offers a rich, 2,500-year material assemblage for study. When coupled with ongoing paleoenvironment and climate research in the eastern Adriatic, the potential runs high to characterize Ravni Kotari as a diachronic registry of human behavior with broader changes in the urban landscape through time. Although not without challenges, we describe below a number of material correlates at Nadin-Gradina that present opportunities to characterize this process as the NGAP matures over the coming years.

Urban built environment. Urban centers reflect concentrations of goods and services, surplus labor, production, the growth of non-food producing sectors of society, and broader catchments from which energy and materials come. At Nadin-Gradina, excavations have identified settlement remains (e.g., walls, structures, surfaces, building material, streets) from Iron Age, Classical Antiquity, Late Antiquity, and Late Medieval time periods, with apparent periods of abandonment of the summit following the Late Antiquity and Late Medieval settlements. Artifact assemblages include both localized and imported ceramic wares from around the Mediterranean, roofing material, mosaic tile fragments, fresco, glass, bone tools, coins and other metal objects, and stone artifacts. Such items in the archaeological record represent both a concentration of materials and labor at the site, but also the local, regional, and "international" catchment from which such materials came. Many of these objects also suggest a degree of specialized production and activity – a reflection of a growing non-food producing sector of society through time – whether those objects were manufactured at Nadin-Gradina, Zadar, elsewhere in Ravni Kotari, the Italian peninsula, or some other distant venue. The hill top settlement was also divided internally by a number of streets, while formal roads connected Nadin-Gradina to Zadar and other parts of Ravni Kotari (Figure 5). Addressing changes in the material culture spatially and diachronically, and contextualizing them within broader patterns of economy and trade (see Glicksman 2005, 2010), will offer a more complete picture of the changing landscape of the Nadin-Gradina urban center and its surroundings as the project moves forward.

Figure 5: A paved road leading up to the north gate through the megalithic wall (note the post holes associated with the gate).

As the "most urbanized region in antiquity" (Wilkes 1969), Nadin-Gradina is not an isolated case in Ravni Kotari but rather one of a number of urbanized settlements in Zadar's hinterland, which includes *Aenona, Asseria,* and *Varvaria,* among others, each with its own idiosyncratic history but part of a broader urban hinterland subject to similar geopolitical complexities as Nadin-Gradina. Citing urban planner Robert Lang, Grimm and colleagues (2008:757) write that cities today are no longer independent but rather represent nodes of urbanism with increasingly built-up intervening regions. Zadar and the Ravni Kotari may constitute a more ancient example of this, reflecting this "coalition" of urban centers with intervening landscapes altered via agriculture, animal husbandry, hunting, and other resource collection/management strategies. Ravni Kotari settlements that experience episodic periods of growth and decline like Nadin-Gradina embody a certain historic depth of place, whether as active settlements or in ruin and overgrowth, and they reflect the deep-time anthropogenic nature of landscape. As cities and towns expand and contract through time, so do the interfaces between urban-residential spaces and other intersettlement land use patches. The pronounced settlement record at Nadin-Gradina should permit characterization of this process in the coming years.

Agrarian infrastructure. Farming was first introduced to the eastern Adriatic region approximately 8,000 years ago (Forenbaher et al. 2013; Forenbaher and Miracle 2005; McClure et al. 2014). And, while significant changes in the landscape most certainly accompanied the reliance on domesticated plants and animals, these landscapes often experience rapid changes with the onset and subsequent evolution of urbanism. This often leads to agricultural intensification and an investment in landesque capital (Håkansson and Widgren 2014), with the construction of semi-permanent features such as field walls, terraces, and canals, along with other long-term investments like arboriculture and soil enhancements. These features constitute a legacy of past land use across Ravni Kotari and are common elements of the Mediterranean cultural landscape more broadly (Butzer 1996; Hughes 2005; Walsh 2014). Contemporary residents inherit these land use histories from the past, which are often reconstituted within the framework of present-day livelihoods.

Botanical and faunal collections. Because urban centers effectively represent catchments of human activity in and around such landscapes, the recovery of botanical remains in conjunction with paleoenvironmental research can help to characterize the local and regional environments from which they came. The recovery of seeds, nuts, wood, charcoal, pollen, phytoliths, starch grains, and other carbonized plant tissues present opportunities to identify patterns of exploitation, farming, deforestation, food processing, and reliance on wild vs. domesticated species (Hastorf and Popper 1988). At Nadin-Gradina, excavations employed a "pinch sampling" strategy to collect 5-10 liters of sediment from most stratigraphic units for flotation. Although analysis has only begun, this methodology has thus far proven successful in recovering botanical remains from all occupational phases represented archaeologically. The majority of extant carbon in all deposits consists of fragmentary wood charcoal, with those fragments at least 2 mm in breadth being saved for potential identification. Other remains consist of seeds and pit fragments of stone fruits. Although many specimens are poorly preserved and will not permit precise identification, a number of identifiable, economically important taxa do appear in the samples, including olive, grape, barley, and a handful of other tree crops. Seeds of wild grass and legume species are also present. These preliminary results suggest that, despite some issues of preservation, there are indeed valuable macrobotanical remains present in archaeological deposits at Nadin-Gradina that can be recovered and analyzed in the broader conceptual framework centered on landscapes (Jamie Countryman, personal communication). A historical analysis of trends will require a more intensive sampling strategy in the coming years, but the results are thus far promising.

Much like botanical collections, the recovery of fauna from urban settings may also speak to wider landscape changes with respect to animals, economy, and subsistence. Faunal analysis can reveal species presence/absence, translocation, resource depression or switching, changes in age/sex ratios and size of animals, and a changing reliance on domesticates vs. wild taxa (Amarosi et al. 1996; Reitz and Wing 1999). At Nadin-Gradina, faunal analysis is ongoing, but preliminary results indicate good preservation of domesticates like cattle, sheep, goats, pigs, and horses, as well as the presence of red deer, wild pig, and birds. Sampling will need to expand into new contexts in the coming years, but the potential is great for utilizing archaeological fauna as a reflector of changes in both subsistence and the wider landscape (Tajana Trbojević-Vukičević, personal communication).

Although the material assemblages at Nadin-Gradina offer great potential, a number of challenges remain in the path ahead that will need to be resolved as we move forward. First, like all urban settings, Zadar and the Ravni Kotari have experienced complicated histories that include an entanglement of local, regional, and broader "global" geopolitics. Situated at the cross-roads of the Mediterranean and continental southeastern Europe, Ravni Kotari landscapes have been shaped and reshaped by local processes, imperial expansion and contraction, and episodic periods of abandonment. Its complicated history, which includes the domesticated landscapes of the Neolithic era, the emergence of fully urbanized societies by the Late Iron Age and their subsequent transformation into Roman colonies and *municipia* in the first centuries CE, Slavic migration in the Middle Ages, and early modern era geopolitical reordering of the region, first among Venetian and Ottoman and subsequently by the Austro-Hungarian empires, creates a mosaic picture across the region. Consequently, the physical manifestation of that complexity in the archaeological record is palimpsestic, creating a significant challenge in the identification of patterns and trends in the archaeological record.

Chronological resolution and the comparability of data also pose significant obstacles when dealing with past records, and the resolve by which archaeologists, paleoenvironmentalists, and historians may be able to track time can vary substantially, from years to decades to centuries. Coupling various kinds of data into a single interdisciplinary framework will thus require dialogue between scholars to better understand the strengths and limitations of such data, and the ability to identify trends and patterns across millennia of landscape changes rather than specific events.

CONCLUDING THOUGHTS

Understanding past landscapes and their mechanisms of change is crucial to future projections and policies concerning the longevity of resource management and human resilience. Of paramount importance is the recognition that humans and the environment are not dichotomous entities, but rather integrated components of a complex whole. Human activities like civic construction, agricultural intensification, waste deposits, residential expansion, and long-distance trade combine with non-human biological and geophysical processes to bring about changes in the landscape. Regardless of the relative roles these variables play, landscape evolution is a historically contingent process that wholly integrates all of these biotic and abiotic elements, and although incomplete, serves as a registry of human cultural history and the arena within which the human story continues to unfold. Urbanism may dominate this relationship today, but as a long-term process, it has played a significant role in shaping our planet's landscapes and environments for millennia, effectively creating anthropogenic landscapes. Recognition of this point opens the door for archaeological research to make significant contributions to contemporary urban/ecological issues while also generating cross-cultural knowledge about urbanism in the ancient, historic, and modern worlds.

Urbanization is tightly woven into the fabric of Ravni Kotari's physical environment, leaving behind a millennial-scale landscape registry of human-environment-climate interactions accessible through the archaeological and historical records. Decision-making regarding sustainable development, conservation, and environmental policy today is a challenging task in the face of continued growth in the Zadar region and both human- and climate- induced changes to the area defined as northern Dalmatia. This necessarily requires a long-term perspective, and one that recognizes humans as active engineers in the Ravni Kotari landscape over time. Collaboration and data sharing with the general public, which includes developers, conservators, and policy makers, will ensure that the NGAP progresses in a way that provides valuable insight and context for contemporary challenges facing urban communities and their physical world. With generous support from the Croatian Science Foundation, our project can now intensify its efforts toward these ends in the coming years (2017-2020).

ACKNOWLEDGEMENTS:

This work has benefitted from the generous support of the National Geographic Society (#9647-15), the Rust Family Foundation, the University of Zadar, and the University of Maine. We also thank the Croatian Science Foundation (#IP-2016-06-5832) for its ongoing support of the NGAP.

REFERENCES

Amarosi, T., J. Woollett, S. Perdikaris, and T. McGovern. 1996. Regional zooarchaeology and global change: Problems and potentials. *World Archaeology* 28:126-157.

Athanassopoulos, E. and L. Wandsnider. 2004. *Mediterranean Archaeological Landscapes: Current Issues.* University of Pennsylvania Museum, Philadelphia.

Balbo, A.L., M. Andrić, J. Rubinić, A. Moscariello, and P.T. Miracle. 2006. Paleoenvironmental and archaeological implications of a sediment core from Polje Cepić, Istria, Croatia. *Geologia Croatica* 2006:109-124.

Balée, W. 2006. The research program of historical ecology. *Annual Review of Anthropology* 35:75-98.

Balée, W. and C. Erickson. 2006. *Time and Complexity in Historical Ecology: Studies in the Neotropical Lowlands.* Columbia University Press, New York.

Batović, Š. 1977. Caractéristiques des agglomérations fortifiées dans la region des Liburniens, *Godišnjak Centra za balkanološka ispitivanja.* 13/XV, Sarajevo, 201-225.

Büntgen, U., W. Tegel, K. Nicolussi, M. McCormick, D. Frank, V. Trouet, J.O. Kaplan, F. Herzig, K. Heussner, H. Wanner, and J. Luterbacher. 2011. 2500 years of European climate variability and human susceptibility. *Science* 331: 578 - 582.

Butzer, K. 1996. Ecology in the long view: Settlement histories, agrosystemic strategies, and ecological performance. *Journal of Field Archaeology* 23:141-150.

Čače, S. 2006. South Liburnia at the Beginning of the Principate: Jurisdiction and Territorial Organization. *Les routes de l'Adriatique antique.* Bordeaux-Zadar, 2006, 65-79.

2007. Asseria and its hinterland: Bukovica, Zrmanja River, and Southern Velebit Mountain. *Asseria* 5: 39-82.

Cavrić, B. 2009. Sustainability and its complements as the new paradigm in Croatian planning theory and practice. *Geoadria* 14:61-86.

Čelhar, M. and G. Zaro (*in press*). Nadin-Gradina: razvoj grada. Antiquitatis

sollemnia - Antidoron Mate Suić / Svečanost starine - Uzdarje Mati Suiću.
Certini, G. and R. Scalenghe. 2011. Anthropogenic soils are the golden spike for the Anthropocene. *The Holocene* 21: 1269 - 1274.
Chapman, J., R. Shiel, and Š. Batovic. 1996. *The Changing Face of Dalmatia: Archaeological and Ecological Studies in a Mediterranean Landscape.* Leicester University Press, London.
Costanza, R., L.J. Graumlich, and W. Steffen (eds) 2007. *Sustainability or Collapse? An Integrated History and Future of People on Earth.* The MIT Press, Cabridge, MA.
Croatian Geological Survey (CGS) 2013. Paleolimnological Research at Vrana Lake, Phase II. Report on File, Vransko Lake National Park, Biograd.
Crumley, C. (ed) (1994). *Historical Ecology: Cultural Knowledge and Changing Landscapes.* Santa Fe, School of American Research.
Čuka, A., and V. Graovac Matassi, and N. Lončar. 2012. Historijsko-geografske promjene u društveno-gospodarskom vrjednovanju ruralnih prostora Ravnih Kotara – Primjer Nadinskog područja (Hrvatska). *Annales Ser. Hist. Sociol.* 22: 157-170.
Denevan, W.M. 1992. The pristine myth: The landscape of the Americas in 1492. *Annals of the Association of American Geographers* 82(3): 369-385.
Ellis, E.C., D.Q. Fuller, J.O. Kaplan, and W.G. Lutters. 2013. Dating the Anthropocene: Towards an empirical global history of human transformation of the terrestrial biosphere. *Elemanta* 1:000018
Erickson, C.L. 2010. The transformation of environment into landscape: The historical ecology of monumental earthwork construction in the Bolivian Amazon. *Diversity* 2:618-652.
Fisher, C.T. 2005. Demographic and landscape change in the Lake Pátzcuaro Basin, Mexico: Abandoning the garden. *American Anthropologist* 107:87-95.
Fisher, C.T., J.B. Hill, and G. Feinman. 2009. *The Archaeology of Environmental Change.* University of Arizona Press, Tucson.
Forenbaher, S., T. Kaiser, and P.T. Miracle. 2013. Dating the East Adriatic Neolithic. *European Journal of Archaeology* 16(4): 589–609.
Forenbaher, S. and P.T. Miracle. 2005. The spread of farming in the Eastern Adriatic. *Antiquity* 79:514-528.
Foster, D., F. Swanson, J. Aber, I. Burke, N. Brokaw, D. Tilman, and A. Knapp. 2003. The importance of land-use legacies to ecology and conservation. *Bioscience* 53(1):77-88).
Galaty, M.L., O. Lafe, W.E. Lee, and Z. Tafilica (eds) 2013. *Light and Shadow: Isolation and Interaction in the Shala Valley of Northern Albania.* Monumenta Archaeologica 28, Cotsen Institute of Archaeology Press, Los Angeles.
Giorgi, F. and P. Lionello. 2008. Climate change projections for the Mediterranean region. *Global and Planetary Change* 63:90-104.

Glicksman, K. 2005. Internal and external trade in the Roman Province of Dalmatia. *OPVSCVLA ARCHAEOLOGICA* 29:189-230.
(2010) Cultural interaction and economic ambition in Roman Dalmatia. *Bollettino Di Archeologia* Volume Speciale:37-42.
Grimm, N.B., S.H. Faeth, N.E. Golubiewski, C.L. Redman, J. Wu, X. Bai, and J.M. Briggs. 2008. *Science* 319:756-760.
Grüger, E. 1996. Vegetational Change. In *The Changing Face of Dalmatia*, edited by J. Chapman, R. Shiel, and Š. Batović), pp. 33-46. Leicester University Press, London.
Gusar, K. and D. Vujević. 2016. *Utvrda u Zemuniku Donjem u srednjem i novom vijeku, Rezultati arheoloških istraživanja 2014. godine*, Zadar, 2016.
Halperin, C.T. 2014. Ruins in pre-Columbian Maya urban landscapes. *Cambridge Archaeological Journal* 24:321-344.
Håkansson, N.T. and M. Widgren (eds) 2014. *Landesque Capital: The Historical Ecology of Enduring Landscape Modifications.* Routledge, London and New York.
Hastorf, C.A. and V.S. Popper (eds) 1988. *Current Paleoethnobotany: Analytical Methods and Cultural Interpretations of Archaeological Plant Remains.* University of Chicago Press, Chicago.
Hayashida, F. M. 2005. Archaeology, ecological history, and conservation. *Annual Review of Anthropology* 34:43-65.
Head, L. 2000. *Cultural Landscapes and Environmental Change.* Oxford University Press, New York.
Holliday, V.T. (ed) 1992. *Soils in Archaeology: Landscape Evolution and Human Occupation.* Smithsonian Institution Press, Washington, D.C.
Hughes, J.D. 2005. *The Mediterranean: An Environmental History.* ABC-CLIO, Santa Barbara.
Intergovernmental Panel on Climate Change (IPCC) 2013. *Climate Change 2013: The Physical Science Basis.* IPCC Fifth Assessment Report.
Jordan, P. 2000. Restructuring Croatia's Coastal Resorts: Change, Sustainable Development and the Incorporation of Rural Hinterlands. *Journal of Sustainable Tourism*, 8:525-539.
Jović Gazić, V. 2011. Urban development from Late Antiquity to the Middle Ages: Dubrovnik, Split, Trogir, Zadar – the state of research. *Archaeologia Adriatica* V:151-196.
Kaligarić, M., M. Culiberg, and B. Kramberger. 2006. Recent vegetation history of the north Adriatic grasslands: Expansion and decay of an anthropogenic habitat. *Folia Geobotanica* 41:241-258.
Kaplan, J.O., K.M. Krumhardt, and N. Zimmermann. 2009. The prehistoric and preindustrial deforestation of Europe. *Quaternary Science Reviews* 28: 3016 - 3034.
Kirch, P. 2005. Archeology and global change: The Holocene record. *Annu. Rev. Environ. Resour.* 30:409-440.
Kukoč, S. 2006. Nadin – nekropola na SZ padini Gradine. *Hrvatski arheološki*

godišnjak 2/2005, Zagreb, 2006, 307-309.
   2009. Nadin – liburnski kult mrtvih, istraživanja 2004.-2006., 2009. god, *Asseria* 7, Zadar, 2009, 11-80.
Kukoč, S. and Š. Batović. 2006. Iskapanje nekropole na sjeverozapadnoj padini Gradine u Nadinu, *Obavijesti Hrvatskog arheološkog društva* XXXVIII, 2, Zagreb, 2006, 65-72.
Kukoč, S. and M. Čelhar. 2010. Iskapanje nekropole na sjeverozapadnoj padini Gradine u Nadinu godine 2009, *Obavijesti Hrvatskog arheološkog društva* XLII, 1, Zagreb, 2010, 34-42.
   (*in press*). Nadin (*Nedinum*): prostorna koncepcija nekropole kod Liburna. Antiquitatis sollemnia - Antidoron Mate Suić / Svečanost starine - Uzdarje Mati Suiću.
Kurilić, A. 1999. *Pučanstvo Liburnije od 1. do 3. stoljeća po Kristu: antroponimija, društveni slojevi, etničke promjene, gospodarske uloge*, Unpublished PhD, Sveučilište u Splitu, Filozofski fakultet u Zadru, 1999.
Mann, M.E., Z. Zhang, S. Rutherford, R.S. Bradley, M.K. Hughes, D. Shindell, C. Ammann, G. Faluvegi, and F. Ni. 2009. Global Signatures and Dynamical Origins of the Little Ice Age and Medieval Climate Anomaly. *Science* 326:1256-1260.
McClure, S.B., E. Podrug, A.M.T. Moore, B.J. Culleton, and D.J. Kennett. 2014. AMS C14 chronology and ceramic sequences of early farmers in the eastern Adriatic. *Radiocarbon* 56(3): 1019–1038.
Oldfield, F., A. Asioli, C.A. Accorsi, A.M. Mercuri, S. Juggins, L. Langone, T. Rolph, F. Trincardi, G. Wolff, Z. Gibbs, L. Vigliotti, M. Frignani, K. van der Post, and N. Branch. 2003. A high resolution late Holocene palaeoenvironmental record from the central Adriatic Sea. *Quaternary Science Reviews* 22:319-342.
Pitcher, D.E. 1972. *An Historical Geography of the Ottoman Empire*. Shield Press, London.
Redman, C. 1999. *Human Impacts on Ancient Environments*. University of Arizona Press, Tucson.
Redman, C.L., S.R. James, P.R. Fish, and D. Rogers, (eds) 2004. *The Archaeology of Global Change*. Smithsonian Institution, Washington D.C.
Reitz, E.J. and E.S. Wing. 1999. *Zooarchaeology*. Cambridge manuals in archaeology. Cambridge University Press, New York.
Roglić, J. 1962. Reljef naše obale. *Pomorski zbornik*, I, Zagreb, 3-16.
Sandor, J.A. and N.S. Eash. 1991. Significance of ancient agricultural soils for long-term agronomic studies and sustainable agriculture research. *Agronomy Journal* 83(1):29-37.
Schon, R. and M.L. Galaty. 2006. Diachronic Frontiers: Landscape Archaeology in Highland Albania. *Journal of World Systems Research* 12 (2): 230-262.
Schmidt, R., J. Müller, R. Drescher-Schneider, R. Krisai, K. Szeroczyńska, and A. Barić. 2000. Changes in lake level and trophy at Lake Vrana, a large karstic lake on the Island of Cres (Croatia), with respect to paleoclimate

and anthropogenic impacts during the last approx.. 16,000 years. *Journal of Limnology* 59(2): 113-130.
Smith, Michael. 2007. Form and meaning in the earliest cities: A new approach to ancient urban planning. *Journal of Architectural Planning History* 6:3-47.
Smith, Monica. 2014. The archaeology of urban landscapes. *Annual Review of Anthropology* 43:307-323.
Suić, M. 2003. *Antički Grad Na Istočnom Jadranu.* Golden Marketing, Zagreb.
Tomičić, Ž. 2010. Contribution of Asseria to the understanding of the organization of Dalmatia in the Emperor Justinian's era. *Asseria* 8:351-400.
Turner, B.L. and J.A. Sabloff. 2012. Classic Period collapse of the Central Maya Lowlands: Insights about human-environment relationships for sustainability. *PNAS* 109:13908-13914.
United Nations. 2014. *World Urbanization Prospects: The 2014 Revision, Highlights* (ST/ESA/SER.A/352), Department of Economic and Social Affairs, Population Division.
van der Leeuw, S. and C.L. Redman. 2002. Placing archaeology at the center of socio-natural studies. *American Antiquity* 67(4):597-605.
Vitousek, P.M., P.R. Ehrlich, A.H. Ehrlich, P.A. Matson. 1986. Human appropriation of the products of photosynthesis. *Bioscience* 36(6): 368-373.
Vitousek, P.M., H.A. Mooney, J. Lubchenco, and J.M. Melillo. 1997. Human domination of Earth's ecosystems. *Science* 277:494-499.
Walsh, K. 2014. *The Archaeology of Mediterranean Landscapes: Human Environment Interaction from the Neolithic to the Roman Period.* Cambridge University Press, New York.
Wilkes, J.J. 1969. *Dalmatia.* Harvard University Press, Cambridge.
Zaro, G. and M. Čelhar. 2017. The Nadin-Gradina Archaeological Project, Croatia. Final Report to the National Geographic Society's Committee for Research and Exploration (Grant Number 9647-15).

LANDSCAPES AND SETTLEMENTS OF SOUTHEAST EUROPE

– Premodern Bosnia and Serbia –

Jelena Mrgić
University of Belgrade, Faculty of Philosophy, Department of History

The absence of evidence is not, in fact, the evidence of absence.
– Vince Gaffney and Helen Gaffney (2010)

INTRODUCTION

The highly fragmented geographical space of the Southeast Europe where medieval Bosnia and Serbia were situated calls for a more flexible and sensitive approach to historical writing, being aware of the present time, which is 'rethinking the past'. Not only during the end of the last century, but studies of this region have been, and still are, rather contaminated and anachronistic. This might sound like stating the obvious, but it is a starting point to take a step forward to think and write differently. In order to do so, this text would not strive to give one, monolithic view, but to offer the possibilities for discussions on numerous issues. The inputs to challenge the old 'ideal models' and presentations come from some fresh ideas from cognitive and behavioral theories to anthropological and environmental studies. To start with, the concept of feudal 'nation-states' in medieval (or, better yet, premodern) times could be abandoned for Bosnia, with its geographical origin. Furthermore, it should not to be replaced with another rigid model that flattens space and its variety of social interactions, so it might be best to think of it as a higher ranking socio-spatial unit, an organism that saw its territory thrive in phases of expansion and growth, interspersed with the opposite – withdrawal, fragmentation and dissolution. The idea of 'border' has been examined in every field of historical studies, and it is proven to be a permeable, transitional and transitory zone 'on the edge' of the 'core area', where the central government was placed at that time (Abulafia and Berend 2002; Smith 2005, 834–835; Newman 2006, 1–19). Yet, the 'core areas' also shifted in space and it would be of interest to trace these processes. With the application of the concepts of 'heterarchy' and 'homoarchy', together with and not excluding the well known hierarchy, some new insights into relations of power and authority are possible (Crumley 1995, 1–5; Bondarenko et al. 2002, 54–79). As any other form of social interactions, these also had their spatial forms, and besides power and authority, one should look for ideology, religion, economy, and demography. By showing diversity on micro and medium levels, the overall picture of the Central Balkans should be altered. Both societies and their sociospatial structure evolved during the long period between the 'fading out' of the Roman Empire and the merging with, or inclusion into, another world empire – the Ottoman. Both Bosnia's and Serbia's royal, feudal and city archives are almost completely lost, and this great dearth of written sources (diplomatic and narrative) imposes immense troubles for unbiased research. However, as Vince and Helen Gaffney brilliantly observed *The absence of evidence is not, in fact, the evidence of absence* (ib. 2010, 79–91). Theoretical modeling, contrasting and comparing to neighboring societies (Hungary, Bulgaria, the Byzantine empire, Adriatic communes, etc.), and inclusion of the earliest Ottoman tax survey registers (*defters*) and other sources allowed, among other results, for hundreds of previously unrecorded settlements, and foremost villages, to reappear.

Populating a unit of geographical space and its demarcation is the basic expression of power that one society claims over its own space, its environment that it shapes. Spatial relations are visible results of complex interactions evolving both within a society, and between the society and its *Lebensraum* (*milieu*). From a deep historical perspective, both systems change through intricate processes of co-evolution. Every society experiences Nature through Culture: cognitive systems, ideas, preconceptions, beliefs, values, as well as more directly, through labor, tools and technology. But there is much more to this than a practical, utility-driven Man who satisfies his existential needs (*homo faber*) by shaping surrounding into built environments, making symbolic imprints, aggregating 'laboresque' and 'landesque' capital (Håkansson and Widgren 2014). Since every society is composed of different social groups (*bellatores – oratores – laboratories, cives, colones, baroni, rusaška gospoda, građani, kmeti* etc.) (Duby 1982; Ćirković 1974, 5–17; ib. 2008, 21–37), each of them has its own notion and experience of Nature (Sack 1986; Winiwarter and Knoll 2007, 115–146; Sieferle 2011, 315–324; Mrgić 2013, 32–41). Although the initial step of the *Landnahme* is to impose military and political control over the land, the process of settlement is more intricate, unfolding through more subtle norms and guidelines, such as trans-generational cultural patterns, ecological preferences, mental maps, and ideas on the order of the world and society (Gärling and Golledge 1993; Mark et al. 1999, 747–774).

The society also evaluates the environment according to norms and feelings of *homo aestheticus,* including the pleasance, familiarity, comfort and safety (Carlson 2000). A single view over a surface of land, a piece of environment that the observer frames into a unity, 'reads' its various and ambiguous meanings, regards its physical and cultural features, brings a *landscape* into life. This concept is shared by a plethora of disciplines, with their own creative agendas: landscape geography/history/ecology/archaeology, and historical geography has its own discourse (Baker 2003, 109–15). 'Hidden landscapes' (van Leusen, Pizziolo and Sarti 2011), or 'lost landscapes' (Ivanišević et al. 2015), as analytic terms, are physical realities of many archaeological sites in Bosnia and Serbia, inaccessible due to sedimentation, urbanization and agricultural changes. This should become visible, when apparent gaps in traditionally performed regional surveys and collections of written sources (ALBiH 1988, Leksikon 2010) are supplemented with data collected with new digital survey methods, GIS and geo-sciences (van Leusen 2002). What would be proposed in this chapter is a number of possible readings of archaeological remains of some examples of 'landscapes of power' and 'sacred places' in the pre-modern Bosnia and Serbia, set in the environmental, cultural and ideological context of these feudal societies with very thinly preserved written evidence, subjected to linguistic analysis. The perception of natural resources and their use would be addressed in reference to settlement spatial pattern.

THE GREEN CANVAS – MOUNTAINS HIGH AND VALLEYS LOW

In the faults of the rugged Dinaridic Alps, in the hinterland of Adriatic coast, and to the northern border – the Rivers Sava and Danube were the settings of early Slavic settlement, particularly along the valleys of the Sava's tributaries – Bosna, Drina and Morava, with their highly developed watershed systems and morphologically composite valleys. These natural corridors and a network of Roman roads facilitated the deep advancement towards the Adriatic and the Aegean Sea. Demographic decline during the 'great migrations', allowed the Slavs to choose which abandoned, yet until recently cultivated, land and settlements would be reused. According to later historical sources, two core areas emerged by the ninth century – 'chorion Bosona' and Rasa, from which the formation of Bosna and Raška/Srbija as larger social units followed. The north-south direction was of essential importance and desire for future territorial development, reaching out from the continental into the Mediterranean ecological and cultural zone, stepping out on the stage of international politics and commerce. The Neretva and Vardar river valleys were the first choices for Bosnia and Serbia, respectively, while the Roman *Via militaris* was a transregional highway reached by the Serbian polity from the end of the 12th century, and partially incorporated (Niš – Belgrade – Braničevo/Viminacium) by the end of the 13th century (Blagojević 2011; Mrgić, 2004, 43–64; Ćirković 2004, 7–9ff; Mrgić 2016, 155–170).

The Slavic structure of the world shows clear division into 'domesticated

/cultivated nature', colonized and organized, as opposed to the 'wilderness', the uncultivated and uninhibited land, and the 'desert'. Villages huddled around the arable fields and pastures, forming a basic territorial unit of medieval Bosnia and Serbia – a county (Serb./Croat. *župa*). The edge of the woodlands had to always be guarded by the axe, as in other continental parts in Europe. The tamed world enjoyed the protection of the native deities and ancestors, with clear borders toward the 'wild' and 'foreign'. Analogous to the opposition between domesticated/foreign, culture/wilderness, familiar/unfamiliar, near/far, *župa* stands opposite *gora* (*gvozd* – Lat. *mons, silva*), a densely wooded mountain (Radenković 1996, 47ff; Mrgić 2003, 163–170; Mrgić, 2010, 87–101). In line with Le Goff's remarks on forest 'wilderness' as a location of Christian monasteries, most of the Serbian Orthodox 'sacred places' were constructed into the 'wild' lands (Le Goff 1992, 47–59) and are further addressed.

The more continental zone of Bosnia and Serbia was thickly covered with lush woodland vegetation in the lowlands, as well as on the slopes of the hills and mountains, while the seasonal flooding of Sava, Bosna, Drina and Morava rivers left periodically filled channels and water-covered land, but also marshland and swamps. Unfortunately, unlike neighboring Hungary, no research of pre-modern water regulation systems in Serbia and Bosnia has been completed (Takács 2003, 289–311; Vadas 2011, 41–60). However, in Bosanska Posavina, there were traditional constructions of elongated earth mounds – *grede*, between the channels and levees – *bogazi* (Turk. gorge, narrow pass, shallow water and sluice gate), recorded in the earliest Austrian surveys and maps (Mrgić 2008, 26–28, 317–318). These testify to a more organized, communal work on water defense, and they are evidence of 'laboresque landscapes' (Håkansson and Widgren 2014). The same kind of built environments evolved in the southern parts, in the lower flow of the Neretva River, where a system of 'jendeks' (Turk. *hendek* – water-filled ditch) supplied fresh water for fields (Faričić, Šiljković and Glamuzina 2005, 193–220). The practice of irrigation is also verified by the Cyrillic documents for the medieval land estates of the monasteries of Dečani and St Archangels in the town of Prizren, but most densely in the vicinity of Skopje, as a legacy of the Byzantine Empire (Blagojević 2004, 150–155; Mišić 2007). Dalmatian craftsmen were hired to build stone water cisterns in the Bosnian interior, while the traditional use of collecting rainwater existed and is still in practice in the zone with Mediterranean climate regime, where medieval 'land' of Zahumlje/Hum (and later the Ottoman *sancak* of Herzegovina) was placed. The quantity of fresh water available for everyday consumption, food production and waterpower technology depended, not in the least instance, on climate conditions, so further regional studies on particular climate periods, such as the 'Medieval Warm Period' (MWP, from ca. 850/1000 to 1200/1300 AD) and the 'Little Ice Age' (LIA, from ca. 1550 to ca. 1850)should be included in a reconstruction of environmental conditions (Telelis 2000, 223–24; Mrgić 2011, 613–637; Vadas and Rácz 2013, 199–227).

The abundance of woody material was such that there is not a single testimony in favor of its protection against scarcity, even during the Late Middle

Ages when both Bosnia and Serbia had a highly developed mining industry and exported large quantities of metals (gold, silver, lead, copper) (Ćirković and Kovačević-Kojić and Ćuk 2002; Mrgić 2010, 87–101). Population pressure on woodland resources could be only scarcely traced through toponomy of clearings, such as locations of settlements and *župas* named after the Old Slavic verb *trebiti/trijebiti*, meaning to cut down trees and clear the land: *Trebovo, Trebetin, Trebotić* – a mountain and two counties in the interior of Bosnia (Mrgić 2008). Clearings of woodlands for making new arable fields were encouraged in both medieval polities and afterwards during Ottoman rule, because the production of food was the most essential need for every agro-ecological society. Only in the 19th century can one read about the reckless destruction of forests, as it was witnessed by Ivan Franjo Jukić in Bosnia (1843), Josif Pančić (1853) and Felix Kanitz in Serbia (1868) (Mrgić 2013, 76–79). Secondly, timber wood and charcoal were export items from Bosnia and Serbia's maritime areas to Adriatic communes, especially to Dubrovnik, which had the most developed supply network and ecological 'footprint' in the Balkan hinterlands (Mrgić 2014, 52–73). The Ottoman government organized a more complex use of wood for shipbuilding on the River Drina (Zvornik), and along the Rivers Sava and Danube, as well as in the mining industry (Handžić 1970, 141–196; ib. 1976, 7–42; Mrgić 2008, 357–363).

Legal and linguistic evidence preserved for medieval Serbia also point to well-structured agricultural activity with different levels of protection, limited access, and use. Apart from crop fields and vineyards, the most cherished were high quality pastures for horses and cattle, which were enclosed as a royal and feudal preserve – Serb. 'zabeli', though the same term denominated a densely wooded area donated for mining production, and a hunting preserve (Blagojević 1966, 1–17; Mrgić 2010, 87–101). Winegrowing, as the most intensive form of agricultural production, was also introduced from the south, likely from the Byzantine Empire and the Adriatic communes, and by the end of the 14th century, it had reached the areas near the Sava and Danube rivers (Blagojević 2004). It was certainly present in medieval Bosnia as well, since the earliest Ottoman *defter*s provide plenty of evidence for vineyards and production of grape juice and wine. Further, this indirectly points to a higher population level in winegrowing areas, since this activity was performed by skilled labourers, whose outmigration, much more than Islamic prohibition of wine as *khamr* and *haram*, and the climate deterioration during the 'Little Ice Age', led to desertification of vineyards and a shift to more climate resistant practice of plum cultivation and distilling plum brandy. This socio-climate change is verified by the change with bread grains production, where climate-sensitive wheat was being substituted with more resistant crops, such as mixed varieties of barley, rye, and millet. Times of uncertainty increased further with frequent bouts of war between the Ottoman and the Habsburg Empires from the end of the 16th to the end of the 18th century, which changed the economic structure from one based on farming to one based on cattle breading and pig rearing as a safer way of living. 'Bosnian' and 'Serbian' merchants went as far as Budapest and Vienna, and became part of the Southeast Europe urban elites (Stoianovic 1960, 234-313; Fodor 2007, 1–8; Mrgić 2011, 613–637).

FRAGMENTED SOCIAL SPACES

A more cognitive approach to the subject of social construction of space would be to observe the *local geographical consciousness* of people inhabiting and expressing their belonging to certain historical provinces – *zemlje* ('lands'). These lands – Bosnia and Serbia – were territorial units testified in medieval documents, and throughout Ottoman times, which means that they were preserved as part of *mental maps*. Their names were noted in the intitulations of the rulers in Bosnia more carefully than in Serbia, and they differed from neighboring areas by natural features, types of cultivated crops and fruits, dishes and rituals, and the mentality of people. Described by the anthropogeographers since the time of Jovan Cvijić and his disciples, these lands are clearly distinguishable even today, though with modified borders due to demographic changes and migrations. People still demarcate 'Bosnia', the 'core area' of the pre-modern state and a territorial unit, as the land/region around the upper and middle valley of the River Bosna with tributaries, surrounded on all four sides by high mountain chains to other 'lands': Podrinje to the east, Zahumlje/Herzegovina to the south, Krajina to the west, and Usora/Posavina to the north. It might be ascertained that Bosnia was originally a geographical concept that evolved into a political entity, yet the spatial denominator remained strong and persevered throughout history (Filipović 1928, 193–196; Jakobsson 1999, 91–93; Mrgic 2016, 155–170).

Leaving the more elaborated social theory aside, it seems that the concept of *heterarchy* as designator of the society as a complex network and as a multitude of parts and wholes (Crumley 1995, 1–5; Bondarenko et al. 2002, 54–79; Smith 2005, 832–849) is more adequate for understanding, studying, and interpreting socio-spatial processes in Bosnia and Serbia. For a start, strong evidence in heterogeneous authority over 'state' territory is the presence of 'co-ruled principalities' with princes (Slav. *čest*, Lat. *pars* > *česnik, česnici, participatores*) as members of the ruling families. The need to assert the highest authority over all of the parts was mirrored in the intitulation – the *Grand* Ban of Bosnia Kulin (prior to 1180 – ca. 1204) and the *Grand* Župan of Raška Stephan Nemanja (1166–1198). The participating rulers had their firm ground in the 'edge zones' where, in due course of time, local chieftains would rule as feudal lords (Usora, Soli, Donji Kraji, Zahumlje, Zeta) (Blagojević 1997, 45–62; Mrgić 2002, 33–43). The Serbian Orthodox Church organization and the sanctification of Nemanjić Dynasty members helped the social and ethnical unity in Serbia and enabled longer periods of homoarchic power (1166–1203, 1213–1282, 1316–1355), interrupted with civil wars, and the 'core area' was relocated to the South, from Ras to Prizren and Skopje, along with the conquests of the Byzantine territories. Bosnia was a different case: outside the 'land' of Bosnia, the ruler had to constantly renegotiate his authority with *barones regni* at the state assembly (*stanak*), so the other 'lands' acted as semi-autarchic regions with strong centripetal tendencies, which could and did build different relations towards the outside. Herzeg Hrvoje Vukčić (1380/1403–1416) and Herzeg Stefan Vukčić Kosača (ca. 1435–1466) stood as strong, independent rulers in opposition to the Bosnian kings, and as clear examples of religious and cultural *multiversity* (Dinić 1955; Ćirković 1964; Lovrenović 2006; Mrgić 2002, 81–108).

The concept of 'state', traditionally viewed as a flattened land with a strict hierarchical structure of central authority, could be further challenged and made more fluid when the territory is subdivided into several *varieties of zones*. For example, one can discern the zones of 'foreign influences' and overlapping cultures (Kosovo, Northern Macedonia, Northwestern Bosnia, Adriatic hinterland etc.); zones of conflicted interests over resources (Bosnia's and Serbia's struggles over the Neretva River – the salt trade, import and export, the Srebrenica silver mining region, etc.); zones of regional and international connectedness (the Rivers Sava, Danube, Drina, Cetina and Neretva, and the Adriatic coastline and communes). It should be stressed that both Sava and Danube, at least in its middle flow, deserve much more attention as huge communication lines, arterial flows for the whole of Southeastern Europe. Western Bosnia (Donji Kraji/Krajina) had gravitated towards Split and control over the ancient Salona–Servitium (Bosanska Gradiška) and Salona–Siscia (Sisak) road. Central and Eastern Bosnia (Bosna and Podrinje), as well as Southwestern and Southern Serbia belonged to the influence zone of Dubrovnik, drawing resources from great distances using *Via Narente* and *Via Drine* (Bojanovski 1974; Škrivanić 1974; McCormick, Grigoli, Zambotti et al. DARMC 2014). And on the other hand, there were 'micro zones' which were almost completely in the background, peripheral and *marginal* even during the last century and period of industrialization (Déry, Leimgruber and Zsilincsar 2012, 5–18). These areas, 'isolated pockets' of sorts, proved highly valuable for ethnographical research, such as the karstic fields of Ravno, Kupres, and Glamoč, the valleys of Rivers Janj and Žepa, the Eastern Bosnian stretch between Srebrenica and Sarajevo, or the region of Zmijanje (Skarić 1937, 37–53; GZM Etnologija 1964 – Žepa; Rakita 1979, 109–271; Ribar 2010).

THE LEOPARD SKIN – SETTLEMENTS AND THEIR ENVIRONS

The geographical distribution of pre-Ottoman settlements of Bosnia and Serbia looks similar to the leopard skin pattern, as enclaves clustered here and there, connected by a network of magisterial and capillary roads, trotted pathways over high hills and mountain passes (maps in Blagojević 1996; Leksikon

2010). The main factors shaping settlement locations were the universal ones: the composition of relief, soil and vegetation cover, the river systems and access to natural resources, the dynamics of demographic processes, and the agrarian ecological regime. With the exception of several towns, there is a general lack of archaeological reconstructions of medieval settlement layouts and regional detailed surveys with HGIS and satellite imagery, which also limits the application of new theoretical frameworks, adding to the danger of fitting the material to theory.

Starting with the legacy, archaeological sites of Roman and Romanized populations testify to their reuse and remake by the Slavic newcomers. Similar to other European regions, those locations were not 'neutral' in their meaning and appearance, and did not serve only for quarrying stones (Wickham 2001, 1–8). Among the numerous sites termed 'gradina', some of them are referenced to Roman relics, designating a possible *refugium* place, a *preserved memory of a town*, and a location of distinctive sacral meaning (Miletić 1984, 392–393). A spacious and significant Roman and Late Antiquity site near Ljubuški survived under the name of "Gračine" (Slav. augmentative of *grad, urbs, civitas*), in close proximity of the basilica in Doci (Rašić and Dziurdzik 2015). The magisterial Roman roads built by Dolabella from Salona to Siscia, to Argentaria (Srebrenica), Servitium, Sirmium (Sremska Mitrovica), and Narona (Norin/Drijeva) (Bojanovski 1974, 192–202), and the Via militaris stretch from Belgrade to Naissus (Niš) and Constantinople (Jireček 1877, Škrivanić 1974) were the directions of influences from Dalmatia, i.e. the Adriatic, and the Byzantine Empire. A more developed road network emerged with the boost of mining and metallurgy from the second half of the 13th century, with colonization of Saxon miners in Bosnia and Serbia. This also induced a new wave of urbanization, when the mining markets were transformed to urban centers with citadels or hill top castles, city councils and 'Saxon law' (Kovačević-Kojić 1978; ead. 2012).

Although 'central place theory' comes with limitations, when applied in the morphologically fragmented space of pre-Ottoman Bosnia, it does help to recognize the spatial ordering of settlements to a degree, as argued elsewhere (Mrgić 2006/7, 66–71). Proper urban centers with tributary areas were few – the government capital of Visoki, Srebrenica with the highest number of merchants from Dubrovnik and the subsidiary market center in Zvornik, the regional center of Soli (Tuzla, brine water wells), the regional capital of Jajce as the feudal residence of Herzog Hrvoje Vukčić (ca. 1380–1416), and Trebinje in the influential zone of Dubrovnik. The distance between urban spaces was quite significant, about 130–150 km (*Table 1*), or a week or so of travelling. The 'Core area' of Serbia shifted from the environs of Ras, which was well sheltered by the Ibar river valley, but also very remote from international market centers – Skopje and Dubrovnik – and from the end of the 13th century, it had its center in Prizren at *Via Zente*, and afterwards, in Skopje, at the crossroad of international communication routes.

Table 1: Distances between the 'core area' centers – capital cities in Bosnia and Serbia – and other central places of these polities and international maritime trade centers

		places' (in km)			places' (in km)			places' (in km)
Visoki	Foča	160	**Ras**	Prizren	180	**Prizren**	Ras	180
	Višegrad	160		Lipljan	130		Lipljan	60
	Blagaj	150		Zvečan	70		Zvečan	125
	Jajce	130		Skoplje	210		Skoplje	100
	Srebrenica	150		Bele Crkve (Kuršumlija)	125		Vranje	140
	Zvornik	150		Niš	180		Niš	380
	Srebrnik	130		Rudnik	150		Skadar	180
	Doboj	150		Foča	230		Kotor	245
	Livno	220		Dubrovnik	420		Dubrovnik	340
	Dubrovnik	290					Thessaloniki	350

Source: own research

One should also take into account the shared, *delegated urban functions* into a hierarchical picture of 'central places'. The generally low population density of Bosnia and Serbia, coupled with a topographically jagged and forested terrain, limited and sensitive agricultural production, underdeveloped road network, and restricted access to international trade routes – this all resulted in little economic need for a significant number of permanent market places. Instead, the cyclical periodic trade centers were more numerous, i.e. villages with weekly market day (Tornik/Tuesday at the place of the future Sarajevo, Četvrtkovište/Thursday – Bijeljina and Kladanj, etc.). Their catchment area is strongly associated with *a day-return travel* of 20 to 30 km, as evidenced elsewhere (Bintliff 2002, 209–250), and the network of regional fairs (*panadjuri* < *panagyris*) filled the economic and social space. Population increase in number and density in certain areas, with the development of mining, metallurgy and trade in precious metals from the second half of the 14th century, triggered the transformation of the former pattern. The location of the Franciscan monasteries with churches is an indicator of permanent market places, within *suburbium* of a town, or in the non-urban area in-between. Ottoman urbanization was of a different nature, 'un-organic' in character, since the foundation of towns (*kasaba*s, *şehir*s) was to secure the political, military, economic, cultural and religious dominance of the Empire (Mrgić 2006/7, 72–85).

In regard to pre-Ottoman Serbia, Carter's study still awaits a response in theoretical approach to the settlement pattern (Carter 1969, 39–56), and even if Priština was the most 'central' and accessible point, this market center lacked all the prestige, qualities, and urban infrastructure of Prizren and Skopje. The great variety of medieval settlement 'types' is, in traditional discourse, broken into only a few categories (towns, fortresses, market places, and villages), yet there were so many diverse forms of people gathering at one place. The urban centers are ranked upon the 'scale of freedom' in relation to the Serbian ruler, so that the highest degree of autonomy was enjoyed by the Adriatic communes (Kotor and Bar), and on the down scale the mining towns (Novo Brdo, Rudnik), the Byzantine towns (Prizren, Skopje), and the newly established capital cities (Belgrade, Smederevo) (Kovačević-Kojić 2012). However, numerous questions from modern urban and economic studies about the proto-urban and peri-urban centers, the 'ruralness' of towns, urban space structures (public and private; zones, sectors and nuclei) should be brought under investigation; from environmental history comes the questions of 'feeding and supplying' the cities and their ecological 'footprint', waste disposal and sanitary conditions; demographic flux, influence zones, international trade, etc. One must include also the fact that monasteries as religious centres attracted people, and they possessed spacious feudal domains that produced significant surplus. On the other hand, they had specific requirements in goods – wax, olive oil, fresh and salted fish, which were mostly imported from the coast. Therefore, a range of open market places developed as their satellites. The best known example was the monastery of Mileševa and its market place of Prijepolje, placed some ten kilometres away. Similarly, caravan posts were in the vicinity of the monastery of St Nicolas in Dabar, St Trinity near Pljevlje. Ottoman conquest did change the 'organic' functioning of urban centers with 'unfulfilled autonomy' (Ćirković 1987, 158–184), but it would be anachronistic to view it as an 'arrested development', because in most of the cases it was just the opposite during the 'Pax Ottomanica' (Kiel 1999, 195–218).

POWER IMPRESSED INTO LANDSCAPES AND SACRED GEOGRAPHY

Feudal societies in Bosnia and Serbia expressed their power and authority in physical and spatial forms. All members of the power structure, from the highest position of a ruler, his and her family members, *Männerbunds*, high nobility (*barones, velmože*) and clergy, constructed a plurality of locations of power: creating cities as *oikists*, building palaces, fortifications, churches and monasteries, crypts and tombs. Some traces of their shaping of sacred places into sacred landscapes and certain landscapes of power shall be further addressed. Only a few cases in the field of hierotopy are selected, because such studies are well advanced for Serbia as a part of the Byzantine Commonwealth, where the re-creations and translations of New Jerusalems flourished (Lidov 2004; Lidov 2015, 61–89; Erdeljan 2009, 458–474).

The monastery of Djurdjevi Stupovi is prominently situated on a hilltop, and it is a landmark of Stephen Nemanja's victory in the battle with his brothers for the supreme authority, but also over the *bogomil* heresy. The structure dominates over the whole valley with the capital of Ras, both as a *belvedere* and a Christian 'lighthouse'. In a way, it is similar to the figure of Christ at the summit of Mount Corcovado: the ruler declared that the capital city, the whole land, and the authority was his only, as the Christian ruler chosen by God and helped by St George. On another occasion, during a hunt, Stephen Nemanja discovered a place where he 'felt pleased to build here, in a deserted area, a monastery'. What was once an empty (anti-social) and wild space, roamed by the beasts, was transformed into a sacred space by building the pristine white marble monastery of Studenica dedicated to the Virgin Mary Mother of God (Erdeljan 2012, 93–101).

Figure 1: The Monastery of Djurdjevi Stupovi near Ras (Novi Pazar)

What could be further ascertained is that Nemanja, with his youngest son the first Archbishop Sava, laid the ground for a dynastic, state, and religious program of Serbia for the next four centuries, which was impressed into environments as a *spatial program*. The whole country was overlaid with a network of bishopric churches and monasteries, bringing the decisive wave of

Christianization, which aimed to reach every village and every inhabitant through the small-scale network of parishes, with churches located at the estates of the nobility.

Creating an urban space, a town as a 'living organism', required not only significant material wealth for building activity, but also 'managerial' skills of an *oikist* in attracting people, namely the merchants and artisans by granting privileges, and there were some successful and some less successful stories. The Bosnian ban and future King Stephan Tvrtko (1353–1391) failed twice, first with a shipbuilding center at the River Neretva's port of Brštanik, which was a prerequisite step for his plans of a 'Bosnian maritime fleet' and direct access to international trade. This was swiftly sabotaged by Venice and Dubrovnik, depriving him of craftsmen and skilled laborers, smothering the competition at its roots. The same reason led to failure in the case of the town of Novi, at the Gulf of Kotor, but the location was subsequently used by Herzeg Stephan Vukčić Kosača. Disregarding the protests, he established a new salt market and textile manufactures, and the town persevered until present day as Herceg Novi. More fortunate were the Serbian princes in their 'princely urbanization' – they focused on elevating the previously existing permanent market center, adding the urban structure. Prince Lazar placed his royal court in Kruševac, Despot Stephan Lazarević shaped Belgrade as the Serbian capital and international commercial center, while Despot Djuradj Branković heavily invested in fortifying Smederevo (1429–31), only to be lost in less than a decade. Soon afterwards, however, the town flourished as the seat of the Ottoman *sancak* (Kovačević-Kojić 1978; Leksikon 2010, by the register).

Reconstructing the network of sacred places in Bosnia is different from Serbia, not least because the heretical Bosnian church had no proper cult buildings, but much more due to the lack of written evidence revealing the names of the excavated remains of churches. However, one area with strong sacral meaning is at the source of the Bosna River, where the center of the county Vrhbosna was located, along with the (supposedly) erected cathedral dedicated to St Peter in the place called Brdo (1244). There are two significant sites with late Roman and early Christian remains, a smaller one in Blažuj and a larger one in Vrutci with the Romanesque Church of St Stephan. Analysis points to strong cultural and economic connections with Adriatic towns, where the skilled craftsmen and stonemasons were hired (Miletić 1984, 397–399).

Another cluster of locations of power is situated in the field of Visoko, where the ruler resided since the time of the Grand Ban Kulin, and it consists of several focal *loci* of state assembly at Mili (Arnautovići), Moštre and Zgošća. The town of Visoko dominated the area where the highest concentration of mineral wealth was placed – the mining region of Hvojnica, Kreševo, Ostružnica, Dusina, Busovača. In the 14th century, there was a shift to the other side of the Bosna River and its tributary Trstivnica, where the complex of castle and memorial church Bobovac and Kraljevska Sutjeska was erected in the Gothic style. Again, the mineral resources were placed at hand, in the region of Vareš and Olovo (Anđelić 1973).

Oral tradition in the case of Skakava village proved the value of transgenerational memory, respect and ritual usage of *sanctus locus*, and with the combined work of anthropologist Mario Katić and archaeologists, the results revealed relics of a historically documented Franciscan monastery from the end of the 14th century (Katić 2015, 20–36). Other indications could stem from two toponyms in the upper flow of the River Ljubinja – the village of Stomorine and rivulet Sutmaj, which both derive their names from *Sancta Maria*. They are located ca. 10 km upstream from the village of Gora, where the remains of a medieval church with a necropolis of *stećci* are uncovered (ALBiH 15.48; Mrgić 2016, 155–170). Quite interesting are the toponyms *Svetigora/Sveta Gora* (*mons sanctus*) in Bosnia – one is the name of the village of Sveta Gora, which pertained to the town of Ključ in 1326 and located some 17 km to the northeast. There is a hill by the same name in that area, as well as the remains of a medieval fortress Crkveni grad ('Church town', 9.108) (Mrgić 2002, 233, 239). The second, *Sveta Gora,* was recorded in the 1920's as the name for an area of arable fields in the village of Poriječani, where the local population reported that there had been "some Greek church" before. There are several necropolises of *stećci* in the close proximity of this toponym, and the relics of a fortress in Dobrinja are a few kilometers to the northwest (ALBiH 14.196, 14.71; Filipović 1928, 543; Anđelić 1984, 117, 188).

Geographical distribution of the *preserved* and recorded necropolises of *stećci* does not fit just one medieval society/state, nor one ethnicity or religion. Consequently, there cannot be one, unifying explanation for this particular burial and ritualised practice, with or without inscriptions and carvings (Bešlagić 1971; Lovrenović 2010; Erdeljan 2003, 107–119). However, there are a few general remarks, which seem indisputable: necropolises were part of the spatial structure of settlements, and they provide evidence of present or abandoned settlements in their vicinity; necropolises were also placed in prominent positions on the landscape, which were usually tabooed for further use as cemeteries or dislocation and reuse of stone; the social status of the deceased had to be indicated by the size of the monument and the level of artistic mastery of stone carvings – inscriptions with titles and with declarations of ownership over the surrounding land domain. Although *pars pro toto* conclusions are inevitably problematic, several examples warrant mention. One of the earliest crafted specimens is the stećak of the Grand Bosnian *kaznac* (*comes camerarius*) Nespina, found in the nearest surroundings of the medieval town of Goruša – Čajan grad (ALBiH 14.37, 14.250), as a part of the larger family tomb. Two other impressive tomb stones with inscriptions were also marking the power and authority of the deceased – the Grand Bosnian Counts (*palatini regni*) from the early 15th century. The first belonged to Radoje Radosalić and was placed near the relics of the Tuhelj/Toričan fortress (ALBiH 14.16, 15.389). The second was erected in the name of Batić Mirković, just a stone's throw from the medieval fortress of Dubrovnik on the Misoča River (ALBiH 15.215, 15.82). These monuments and burial rituals deserve a more modern approach and more detailed analysis that cannot, unfortunately, be presented in this text.

CONCLUSION

Inspired by fresh ideas breezing from a variety of disciplines, this paper proposes that some old concepts should be challenged, rhetoric and narratives changed, and some issues deserving of more attention and dialogue. A limited number of words imposes restriction on the width and breadth of a review, and focus is necessarily set on the most intriguing and/or pivotal processes and distinguished phenomena. Natural features and environment are viewed as even participators in historical reconstruction, and the composition of Southeast Europe requires a more fragmented approach. The space structure is further 'dissolved' into various zones of contacts, overlapping, and competition over resources, with fluid and permeable borders. The 'core areas' of two socio-spatial units, Bosnia and Serbia, are identified and further territorial outreaches could be viewed as attempts to gain access to different ecological and commercial zones, which were also culturally more diversified than the interior of these polities. However, the early and long-termed interconnectedness with Hungary and the Danubian lands to the east should not be overlooked as it has been so far. Archaeological, anthropological and visual culture studies should be combined more often, which will hopefully change the 'marginal' character of this piece of Southeastern Europe.

REFERENCES

Abulafia, David and Berend, Nora, editors. 2002. *Medieval Frontiers: Concepts and Practices.* Ashgate: Aldershot.

Anđelić, Pavo. 1973. *Bobovac i Kraljevska Sutjeska – stolna mjesta bosanskih vladara u XIV i XV stoljeću.* Sarajevo: Veselin Masleša.

Anđelić, Pavo. 1984. "Srednji vijek." In *Visoko i okolina kroz historiju 1.* 101–310. Visoko.

Arheološki Leksikon Bosne i Hercegovine I–III. 1988. Sarajevo.

Arnold, Ellen F. 2013. *Negotiating the Landscpe: Environment and Monastic Identity in hte Medieval Ardennes.* Philadelphia: University of Pennsylvania Press.

Baker, Alan R. H. 2003. *Geography and History – Bridging the Divide.* Cambridge Studies in Historical Geography 36. Cambridge: Cambridge University Press.

Bešlagić, Šefik. 1971. *Stećci – kataloško-topografski pregled.* Sarajevo: Veselin Masleša.

Bintliff, John. 2002. "Going to Market in Antiquity." In *Zu Wasser und zu Land.* Edited by Eckart Olshausenand Holger Sonnabend . 209–250. Stuttgart: Franz Steiner Verlag.

Blagojević, Miloš. 1996. *Istorijski atlas.* Editor-in-chief. Beograd: Zavod za udžbenike.
Blagojević, Miloš. 1997. "Srpske udeone kneževine."' *Zbornik Vizantološkog instituta* 36: 45–62.
Blagojević, Miloš. 2004. *Zemljoradnja u srednjovekovnoj Srbiji.* Beograd: Službeni list.
Blagojević, Miloš. 2011. *Srpska državnost u srednjem veku.* Beograd: SKZ.
Bojanovski, Ivo. 1974. *Dolabelin sistem cesta u rimskoj provinciji Dalmaciji.* Sarajevo: ANUBiH.
Bondarenko, Dmitri M., Grinin, Leonid E., and Korotayev, Andrey V. 2002. "Alternative Pathways of Social Evolution." *Social Evolution & History* 1–1: 54–79.
Carlson, Allen. 2000. *Aesthetics and the Environment: the Appreciation of Nature, Art and Architecture.* London: Routledge.
Carter, Francis W. 1969. "An Analysis of the Medieval Serbian Oecumene: A Theoretical Approach." *Geografiska Annaler. Series B, Human Geography* 51-1: 39–56.
Crumley, Carole L. 1995. "Heterarchy and the Analysis of Complex Societies." *Archeological Papers of the American Anthropological Association* 6/1:1–5. doi: 10.1525/ap3a.1995.6.1.1.
Ćirković, Sima. 1964. *Herceg Stefan Vukčić Kosača i njegovo doba.* Beograd: SANU.
Ćirković, Sima. 1974. "Rusaška gospoda." *Istorijski časopis* 21: 5–17.
Ćirković, Sima. 1987. "Unfulfilled Authonomy: Urban Society in Serbia and Bosnia." In *The Urban Society of Eastern Eruope in Premodern Times.* 158–184. Edited by Bariša Krekić. Los Angeles: Berkeley.
Ćirković, Sima. 2004. *The Serbs.* Translated into English by Vuk Tošić. London: Blackwell Publishing Ltd.
Ćirković, Sima. 2008. "Iz starog Dubrovnika: građani rođeni i građani stečeni." *Istorijski časopis* 56: 21–37.
Dinić, Mihailo. 1955. *Državni sabor srednjovekovne Bosne.* Beograd: SANU.
Déry, Steve, Walter Leimgruber, and Walter Zsilincsar. 2012. "Understanding Marginality: Recent Insights from Geographical Persepctive." *Hrvatski Geografski Glasnik* 74/1: 5–18.
Duby, Georges. 1982. *The Three Orders: Feudal Society Imagined.* Translated into English by Arthur Goldhammer. Chicago: University of Chicago Press.
Erdeljan, Jelena. 2003. "Stećci – pogled na ikonografiju narodne pogrebne umetnosti na Balkanu." *Zbornik Matice Srpske za Likovne umetnosti* 32–33: 107–119.
Erdeljan, Jelena. 2009. "New Jerusalems in the Balkans: translation of sacred space in the local context." In *Новые Иерусалимы. Иеротопия и иконография сакральных пространств.* 458–474. Edited by Alexei M. Lidov. Moskva.
Erdeljan, Jelena. 2012. "Studenica – All things Constantinopolitan." In *Symmeikta:*

zbornik radova povodom četrdeset godina Instituta za istoriju umetnosti Filozofskog fakulteta Univerziteta u Beogradu. 93–101. Edited by Ivan Stevović. Beograd.

Faričić, Josip, Šiljković, Željka, and Glamuzina, Martin. 2005. "Agrarian Changes in the Lower Neretvian Area from the Eighteenth to the Twentieth Century." *Agricultural History* 79-2: 193–220.

Filipović, Milenko S. 1928. *Visočka nahija,* Srpski Etnografski Zbornik – Naselja i poreklo stanovništva 25.

Fodor, Pál. 2007. "Trade and Traders in Hungary in the Age of the Ottoman Conquest: An Outline." *Acta Orientalia Academiae Scientiarum Hungariae* 60(1): 1–8.

Gaffney, Vince, and Gaffney, Helen. 2010. "Modelling Routes and Communications." In *Handelsgüter und Verkehrswege. Aspekte der Warenversorgung im östlichen Mittelmeerraum (4. bis 15. Jahrhundert).* Edited by Ewald Kislinger, Johannes Koder and Andreas Külzer. 79–91. Wien: Veröffentlichungen zur Byzanzforschung.

Gärling, Tommy, and Reginald Golledge, eds. 1993, *Behavior and Environment: Psychological and Geographical Approaches.* London: Elsevier Science Publishers.

Håkansson, Thomas N. and Widgren, Mats. 2014. *Landesque capital: the historical ecology of enduring landscape modification.* New frontiers in historical ecology 5. Left Coast Press: Wallnut Creek.

Handžić, Adem. 1970. "Zvornik u drugoj polovini XV i početkom XVI vijeka." *Godišnjak Društva istoričara BiH* 18: 141–196.

Handžić, Adem. 1976. "Rudnici u Bosni u drugoj polovini XV stoljeća." *Prilozi za orijentalnu filologiju* 26: 7–42.

Ivanišević, Vujadin, Veljanovski Tatjana, David Cowley, Grzegorz Kiarszys and Ivan Bugarski (editors). 2015. *Recovering Lost Landscapes.* Institute of Archaeology: Belgrade – Aerial Archaeology Research Group.

Jakobsson, Sverrir. 1999, "Defining a Nation: Popular and Public Identity in the Middle Ages." *Scandinavian Journal of History* 24–1: 91–101. doi: 10.1080/03468759950115863.

Jireček, Konstantin. 1877. *Die Heerstraße von Belgrad nach Constantinopel und die Balkanpässe.* Prag.

Katić, Mario. 2015. "Oral Tradition Emplaced in the Landscape: The Skakava Monastery in Bosnia." *Folklore* 126/1: 20–36. doi: 10.1080/ 0015587X .2014.981441.

Kiel, Machiel. 1999. "The Ottoman Imperial Registers: Central Greece and Northern Bulgaria in the 15–19th century. The Demographic Development of Two Areas Compared." In *Reconstructing Past Population Trends in Mediterranean Europe.* 195–218. Edited by John Bintliff and Kostas Sbonias. Oxford: Oxford University Press.

Kovačević-Kojić, Desanka. 1978. *Gradska naselja srednjovjekovne bosanske države.* Sarajevo: Veselin Masleša.

Kovačević-Kojić, Desanka. 2012. *La Serbie et les pays serbes : l'économie ur*

baine (XIVe-XVe siècles). Beograd: Balkanološki institut SANU.
Le Goff, Jacques. 1992. "The Wilderness in the Medieval West." In Le Goff, *The Medieval Imagination*, Translated into English by Arthur Goldhammer. Chicago: University of Chicago Press, 47–59.
Leksikon gradova i trgova srednjovekovnih srpskih zemalja: prema pisanim izvorima. 2010. Edited by S. Mišić. Beograd: Zavod za udžbenike.
Lidov, Alexei M. 2004. Editor. *Hierotopy. Studies in the Making of Sacred Spaces*. Moscow.
Lidov, Alexei M. 2015. "Creating the Sacred Space. Hierotopy as a new field of cultural history." In *Spazi e percorsi sacri: i santuari, le vie, i corpi*. 61–89. Proceedings from the conference held in Padova 17-18th December 2012. available at: http://hierotopy.ru/contents/LIDOV_ Hierotopy_ Spazi_%20sacri_2015.pdf. (March 14, 2016).
Lovrenović, Dubravko. 2006. *Na klizištu povijesti. Sveta kruna ugarska i Sveta kruna bosanska 1387–1463*. Zagreb – Sarajevo.
Lovrenović, Dubravko. 2010. *Stećci – bosansko i humsko mramorje srednjeg vijeka*. Sarajevo: Rabic.
Mark, David M., Christian Freksa, Stephen C. Hirtle, Robert Lloyd, and Barbara Tversky. 1999. "Cognitive Models of Geographical Space." *International Journal of Geographical Information Science* 13 (8):747–774.
McCormick, Michael, Leland Grigoli, Giovani Zambotti et al. 2014. *Digital Atlas of Roman and Medieval Civilizations* (DARMC), version 1.3.1., http://darmc.harvard.edu/icb/icb.do?keyword=k40248& pageid = icb.page188865 (April 18, 2016).
Miletić, Nada. 1984. "Rani srednji vijek." In *Kulturna istorija Bosne i Hercegovine*. Edited by Alojz Benac et al., Sarajevo: Veselin Masleša.
Mišić, Siniša. 2007. *Korišćenje unutrašnjih voda u srpskim zemljama srednjeg veka*. Beograd.
Mrgić, Jelena. 2002. *Donji Kraji – Krajina srednjovekovne bosanske države*. Filozofski fakultet: Beograd.
Mrgić, Jelena. 2003. "Srednjovekovni čovek i priroda." In *Privatni život u srpskim zemljama srednjeg veka*, edited by Smilja Marjanović-Dušanić and Danica Popović, 163–182. Clio: Begrad.
Mrgić, Jelena. 2004. "Rethinking the Territorial Development of the Medieval Bosnian State." *Istorijski časopis* LI: 43–64.
Mrgić, Jelena. 2006/7. "Transition and Transformation from the Late Medieval to Early Ottoman Settlement Pattern – The Case Study of Northern Bosnia." *Südost-Forschungen* 65-66: 50–86.
Mrgić, Jelena. 2008. *Severna Bosna (13–16. vek)*. Istorijski institut: Beograd.
Mrgić, Jelena. 2010. "Some Considerations on Woodland Resource in the Medieval Serbia nad Bosnia." *Beogradski istorijski glasnik* 1: 87–101.
Mrgić, Jelena. 2011. "Wine or raki – The Interplay of Climate and Society in Early Modern Ottoman Bosnia." *Environment & History* 17: 613–637.
Mrgić, Jelena. 2013. *Zemlja i ljudi – iz istorije životne sredine zapadnog Balkana*. Equilibrium: Beograd.

Mrgić, Jelena. 2014. "Rocks, Waters, and Bushes – What did the Ragusan Commune Acquire from the Bosnian King in 1399? An Environmental History Approach." In *Man, nature and environment between the northern Adriatic and the eastern Alps in premodern times*, edited by Peter Štih and Žiga Zwitter, 52–73. Ljubljana: University Press.

Mrgić, Jelena. 2016. "The Land of Bosnia in the Heart of Bosnia." In *The Balkans and the Byzantine World before and after the Captures of Constantinople, 1204 and 1453*, edited by Vlada Stanković, 155–170. Row-man & Littlefield: Lexington Books.

Newman, David. 2006. "The lines that continue to separate us: borders in our 'borderless' world." *Progress in Human Geography* 30-2, 1–19.

Radenković, Ljubinko. 1996. *Simbolika sveta u narodnoj magiji Južnih Slovena*. Narodna knjiga: Niš.

Rakita, Rade. "Privreda, ergologija i tehnologija u Janju. " *Zbornik Etnološkog insituta SANU* 9: 109–271.

Rašić, Mirko and Dziurdzik, Tomasz. 2015. *Ljubuški archaeological project 2015*. http://arheohercegovina.com/2015/10/04/ljubuski-archaeological-project-2015/ (March 20, 2016).

Ribar, Tanja. 2010. *Zapadne strane u srednjovjekovnoj bosanskoj državi*. Beograd.

Skarić, Vladislav. 1937. "Župa Zemljanik i stara nahija Zmijanje. " *Glasnik Zemaljskog muzeja u Sarajevu* 49: 37–53.

Smith, Monica L. 2005. "Networks, Territories, and the Cartography of Ancient States." *Annals of the Association of American Geographers* 95(4): 832–849.

Stoianovic, Traian. 1960. "The Conquering Balkan Orthodox Merchant." *The Journal of Economic History* 20-2: 234–313.

Škrivanić, Gavro. 1974. *Putevi u srednjovekovnoj Srbiji*. Beograd: Kultura.

Takács, Károly. 2003. "Medieval Hydraulic Systems in Hungary: Written Sources, Archaeology and Interpretation." In *People and Nature in Historical Perspective*, edited by József Laszlovszky and Péter Szabó, 289–311. CEU Department of Medieval Studies & Archaeolingua: Budapest.

Telelis, Ioannis. 2000. "Medieval Warm Period and the beginning of the Little Ice Age in Eastern Mediterranean. An approach of physical and anthropogenic evidence." 223–24. In *Byzanz als Raum. Zu Methoden und Inhalten der historischen Geographie des Östlichen Mittelmeerraumes*, eds. Belke Klaus, Friedrich Hild, Johannes Koder and Peter Soustal. Kommision für TIB: Wien, 223–243.

Vadas, András. 2011. "Late Medieval Environmental Changes on the Southern Great Hungarian Plain – A Case Study." *Annual of the Medieval Studies at CEU*, 17: 41–60.

Vadas, András and Lajos Rácz. 2013. "Climatic Changes in the Carpathian Basin during the Middle Ages: The State of Research." *Global Environment* 12: 199–22.

van Leusen, Pieter Martijn. 2002. Pattern to Proces – Methodological investigations into the formation and interpretation of spatial patterns in archaeological landscapes, PhD thesis, Rijksuniversiteit Groningen 2002, 356 p. Accessed February 5, 2016. https://www.rug.nl/research/portal/publications/pub%28fc9ead23-e2c7-40c5-942f-e06f52198222%29.html.

van Leusen, Pieter Martijn, Giovanna Pizziolo and Lucia Sarti, editors, 2011. *Hidden Landscapes of Mediterranean Europe. Cultural and Methodological Biases in Pre- and Protohistoric Landscape Studies.* Oxford: British Arcaeological Reports.

Wickham, Chris. 2001. "Introduction." in *Topographies of Power in the Early Middle Ages,* edited by Mayke de Jong and Frans Theuws with Carine van Rhijn. 1–8. Leiden: Brill.

DEATH PROXIMITY, GROUP COHESION & MOUNTAINOUS PILGRIMAGE IN ALBANIA

Konstantinos Giakoumis[1] and Christopher Lockwood[2]
[1] European University of Tirana
[2] Independent Researcher

INTRODUCTION

This chapter contributes to the understanding of the relationship between mountainous landscapes and pilgrimage. It builds upon previous research related to pilgrimage, altitude and religious rituals, as well as nearness to death, and focuses on mountainous Christian and Bektashi pilgrimage. In this chapter we contextualized five mountainous pilgrimage sites from Albania: two Orthodox Christian mountainous pilgrimage sites (the Monastery of the Holy Trinity in Pepel, Gjirokastër, and the Monastery of the Nativity of the Virgin, Ardenicë, Lushnjë); one Roman-Catholic Christian pilgrimage (Saint Anthony of Padua, Laç); one Bektashi pilgrimage site (the Tomb of Sari Satlik, Krujë); as well as another Bektashi pilgrimage site at Mount Tomorr, which attracts both Orthodox Christian (Feast of the Dormition of the Virgin, August 15) and Bektashi pilgrims (Türbe of Abbas Ali, August 20-25) throughout different days during the month of August. Utilizing historical-anthropological research methods we argue that high altitudes evoke a feeling of proximity to death, while the same feeling together with a desire to share in spiritual continuity with the past enhances in-group cohesion. This conclusion seems to support a structuralist interpretation of pilgrimage in mountainous sites, i.e. as supporting social order.

Prior to developing our discourse, it is essential to define what is meant by "pilgrimage" in this study. Pilgrimages defined as the visitation to a place where both the journey and its destination are believed to empower individuals or groups to create bonds with a higher state of being and contemplate on matters of life, death, and beyond (Morinis 1992, 1; cf. Giakoumis 2013, 268-9). Central to pilgrimage are both its 'topos' (Turner and Turner 1978: 112; Tomasi 2002: 10) and the journey to, or the movement towards it (Tomasi 2002: 10; Coleman and Eade 2004: 1-24), often purposefully long, tiring and dangerous (Preston 1992, 36) for cleansing and penitential purposes (*op. cit.*). The initiation (Turner

1969; Gennep 2004) and/or rituals performed from the outset on the way to and/or at the place of a pilgrimage (Swatos and Tomasi 2002, 207), in our definition, is a means of empowerment to create bonds with a higher state of being and contemplate matters of life, death and beyond. Moreover, in our understanding, the concept of a 'higher state of being' may also have a secular dimension.

Implied from the definition above is the idea that movement and landscape are intrinsic to pilgrimage. Landscape has been defined as "the meaning imputed by local people to their cultural and physical surroundings (i.e. how a particular landscape 'looks' to its inhabitants)" (Hirsch 1995, 1; cf. Claval 2007, 92). Thus, landscape, as a cultural product (Schama 1995) together with its constituents (wood, ground, water, and weather) can only be perceived kinaesthetically (Ingold 2011). Associating certain types of landscapes with the fear of death therefore requires experiencing the landscape that "is produced through local practice" (Hirsch 1995, 2). Such kinaesthetic experience involves walking an act which "validates the reality of the past in the present and in so doing, continually re-establishes the relation between place, story and all the beings who use the locale" (Legal 2008, 35 and Lund 2008, 101). As the pilgrimage's sacred *topos* is experienced within a context and form beyond everyday life, it is associated with concepts such as background potentiality, space, outside, and representation (Hirsch 1995, 4), to be looked at in this paper. In light of the fact that movement is embedded in landscape, one could therefore equate the pilgrimage's sacred *topos* with its particular landscape.

Having provided a definition of how religious pilgrimage is perceived and experienced in the landscape, part two of this chapter outlines the historical and textual relationship between altitude, death, and the divine or spiritual. The third part of the chapter relates fear of death and in-group solidarity with ways in which the religious centres were fully conscious and used this relation to their advantage. Finally, part four discusses the concrete case-studies of Christian and Bektashi[1] mountainous pilgrimage in Albania mentioned above. The flowchart below visualizes our thesis in this chapter.

Graph 1: A flowchart of the chapter's thesis

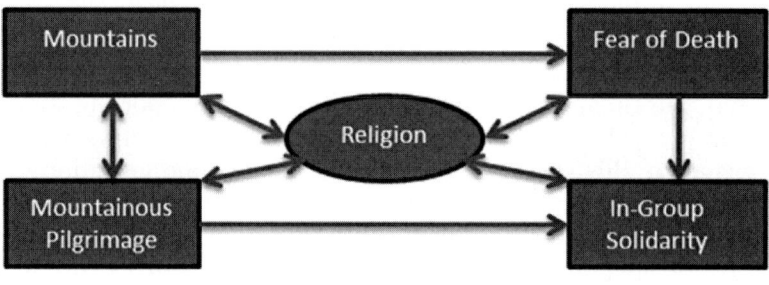

---

[1] The *BektāshīṬarīqah* (or mystical brotherhoods), comprised of various orders of dervishes, are an aspect of Islam's history in Albania. It originated from the Sufi movements in the Middle East (11th and 12th century) before settling in Anatolia and primarily Albania (Clayer 1990; Osmani 2012).

THE DIVINE AND ALTITUDE: CONTEXTUAL HISTORY AND SACRED TEXTS

The idea that elevated locations are closer to the deity, or a higher state of being, is ancient and cross-cultural. It has been influenced, above all else, by the ancient belief that god, or the gods, dwells in "high places." At some point the concept was either influenced by, or became intermingled with, a sense of divine transcendence beyond the realm of the earthly, and, by extension, the bodily or material. Thus in the Judeo-Christian tradition the same word was used for both heaven and sky (Hb. *shamayim*, Gk. οὐρανός, Lt. *caelum* [i.e., celestial]), and the modern English "heaven" itself derives from an older Germanic word for sky or firmament (*hemina*). Similarly, many ancient concepts of the soul (Hb. *nepēš*, Gk. ψυχή, Lt. *ánima*, Sk. *ātman*) or spirit (Hb. *rûaḥ*, Gk. πνεῦμα, Lt. *spiritus*, Sk. *ākāśa*) have to do with the breath or air vitalizing and animating the material body. To ascend the mountain was therefore to depart from the earth and approach or enter into the aerial and spiritual realm of god or the gods. As such the sacred space of mountains effectively "constitutes a break in the homogeneity of space... symbolized by an opening by which passage from one cosmic region to another is made possible (from heaven to earth and vice versa; from earth to the underworld)" (Eliade 1959, 37).

In this context, worship of the divine on the heights of a mountain in almost all ancient religions was accompanied by burial rituals and human or animal sacrifice. During and around the 15th century, for example, the Incas would sacrifice their unblemished children in the Andes mountains by conducting pilgrimage to the highest peaks where the person to be sacrificed would be ritually left to freeze to death in a ritual known as *capacocha* (cf. Reinhard and Ceruti 2005). Such a location, it was believed, was a highly suitable place to offer something to the gods, as this region constituted an intersection of the heavens, the divine, and the dead.

In agreement with what has been said, the perennial perception that mountains, and particularly the peaks of mountains, are the dwelling place of god or the gods is similarly widespread. In ancient Canaan the Moabites are said to have worshipped Peor (Baal-peor) on the mountain bearing his name (Num. 23:28; 25:3, 5, 18; 31:16; Deut. 3:29 ["Beth-peor"], 4:3; etc.). In ancient Greece, the pantheon of the gods was believed to have been located at the top of Mount Olympus, the second tallest mountain of the Balkans behind the comparable Mount Musala in Bulgaria. Ancient Greeks would come from all over in order to offer animal sacrifices to Zeus and his daughters at the temple of Dion located at the base of Olympus. Mythological parallels with this are of course the two Mount Idas – one the highest peak of Crete and the other in Asia Minor – together with Mount Othrys in central Greece. Much like Olympus, these three were believed to have been the dwelling places of the titans before their defeat at the hands of the gods. In Albanian folklore, Mount Tomorr itself came to be anthropomorphized into the mythical giant Baba Tomorr. This elderly bearded figure was the remnant of an ancient Illyrian deity identified directly with the mountain who, legend has it, fought jealously with Mount Shpirag for the ancient city of Berat (historically known as Belgrade) located in the valley between the two (Elsie 2001, 252-4).

Israelites of the Old Testament likewise constructed their high places (*Bamah*), or elevated altars, which served as pivotal locations for libations and ritual pilgrimages (Hirsch 1906, 388). In reality, such "high places" of religious significance were common among the Canaanite tribes before Israel's conquest of the region, and seem to have been utilized by them for the worship of tribal deities, sacred burial and ritual prostitution. Though the original use of the term was probably a reference to natural hilltops, it came to be equally applied to artificially constructed platforms of worship and sacrifice (Encyclopaedia; Carpenter and Comfort 2000, 86). As such, the construction of similar altars developed side by side with Assyrian ziggurats on platforms and initially either replaced or competed with such devotional shrines dedicated to deities venerated by the neighbouring tribes. Though officially prohibited (Deut. 7:5, 12:3), Israelite sacrifice and worship would therefore typically resume in the same location after the occupation of pagan shrines. Worship or sacrifice would in this way be conducted at the local "high place", while pilgrimage to distant or more significant shrines was also done on special occasions or in fulfilment of a vow. With the move towards strict monotheism, however, worship and animal sacrifice at such locations became effectively displaced and consolidated at Solomon's temple, which was devoted solely to Yahweh worship – itself constructed on top of the fortressed mount of Jerusalem. Prior to this, the precedent to conduct pilgrimage to various high places set by the pagan tribes was simply transposed and directed towards Yahweh. The Old Testament book of Kings therefore tells that in an earlier period the Prophet Elijah lamented the destruction of local altars that had been consecrated to Israel's God and conducted a forty day pilgrimage up into a cave on Mount Horeb – the divine mountain sometimes associated with Sinai – in order to mourn, escape the threat of death and seek consolation (1 Kings 19:7-18).

Moses is similarly said to have ascended up Mount Sinai with the whole nation of God waiting at the base of the mountain in order to meet and speak with God (Ex. 19-20). The Israelite assembly before God at Mount Sinai reveals an early association between death and sacred mountains as reflected in two separate passages. The first passage expresses a kind of divine threat of death related to the holiness of God's presence on the mountain: "*You shall set bounds for the people all around, saying, 'Take heed to yourselves that you do not go up to the mountain or touch its base. Whoever touches the mountain shall surely be put to death. Not a hand shall touch him, but he shall surely be stoned or shot with an arrow; whether man or beast, he shall not live.' When the trumpet sounds long, they shall come near the mountain.*" (Ex. 19:12-13). The second passage linking the people's assembly in the presence of the mountain with death portrays collective fear at what is being seen and heard there: "*When the people saw the thunder and lightning and heard the trumpet and saw the mountain in smoke, they trembled with fear. They stayed at a distance and said to Moses, 'Speak to us yourself and we will listen. But do not have God speak to us or we will die'.*" (Ex. 20:18-19).

In the New Testament tradition, it is Moses and Elijah who mystically appear with Jesus at the scene of the Transfiguration on the sacred mountain (Matt. 17:1-9; Mark 9:2-8; Luke 9:28-36; cf. 2 Pet. 1:16-18). Among the more common theological interpretations concerning the presence of Moses and Elijah on the mountain is a view that links their presence with their role as official representatives of the larger tradition of the law and the prophets as well as reliable witnesses of God's message concerning Jesus. Just as at Sinai, where God reveals something novel while linking himself with Israel's forefathers (Ex. 3:1, 6; 19:3), we find here again continuity with the past as well as newness and revelation. And again, just as in the divine appearance and revelation on Sinai, God manifests his presence in a tangible way. At Sinai, the scene was characterized by the presence of a thick cloud with thunder and lightning, smoke and fire, and the divine voice (Ex. 19:16-19). Similarly, here, there is divine glory and radiant light, an overshadowing cloud, and a terrifying voice from heaven (Matt. 17:2,5, etc.). It is important to note here that a connection between any particular individual and the greater concept of religious community and continuity throughout both time and space lends itself towards association with group solidarity and is stimulated in these examples by the fear of death and contact with the spiritual and divine on or near elevated topography.

A desire to connect with the spiritual realities beyond mere material or individual existence fostered ensuing imitative pilgrimage to the same or similar locations. Thus beginning with Origen (c. 185-254), subsequent Christian authors associated the site of the Transfiguration with Mount Tabor located in lower Galilee (Lee 2004, 144; Meistermann 1912). This association eventually signalled Christian pilgrimage to Tabor's summit from at least the 4th century, whereupon various churches and a monastery complex were constructed at its summit (Lee 2004, 144; Meistermann 1912). Though the site has undergone many changes throughout the centuries, it continues to host a monastery complex divided between the Orthodox and Catholic communities and functions as a popular pilgrimage destination for Christians throughout the world.

Within traditional Islam, two mountains in particular have significance while functioning as active shrines of mountainous pilgrimages. The first is a cave (*Ghar Hira*) located near Mecca on *Jabal al-Nour* (the Mountain of Light), where, according to Islamic belief, the Islamic prophet Muhammed received his initial revelation of the Quran from the angel Jibril (Gabriel). The second mountain, *Jabal Thawr* (Mount Bull), is likewise associated with a cave (similarly designated *Ghar al-Thawr* or "the Cave of the Bull") and is also linked to the life of Muhammed; this time in an episode where he and his companion Abu Bakr fled for refuge from their persecutors during their migration (*Hegira*) to Medina (Shaikh 2001, 51-2). The first is therefore directly related with contact to the divine, while the second with death and the threat of death.

In the Islamic tradition, animal sacrifice is typically associated with Abraham's attempted sacrifice of his son *on the mountain* at the command of

God. While the Judeo-Christian tradition holds that the son to be sacrificed was Isaac, Islamic tradition does not specify, leading many recent Islamic commentators to identify the son instead as Ishmael. (Gen. 22:1-19; Quran 37:99-109). This event, celebrated annually among Muslims as *Eid al-Adha,* is one of the most important dates within the Muslim calendar. On this day any Muslim who has sufficient wealth is required to sacrifice a domestic animal of high value and health so as to imitate Abraham's willingness to sacrifice his son in obedience to the will of God.

As shown above, sacred mountainous pilgrimage is associated with death in many ways, not only in terms of its rugged inhospitable and suspended terrain, but also in virtue of its proximity to the transcendent divine power and habitation located in the heavens. Such sacred journeys to "high places" serve to spiritually link the pilgrim with the past, but also the present and the future: to demonstrate continuity and newness, departure (death) and arrival, escape and refuge. As such, it naturally invokes a sense of departure from the realm of the earthly and an arrival onto a frontier beyond everyday human experience.

FEAR OF DEATH, IN-GROUP SOLIDARITY AND THE CHRISTIAN CHURCH

After demonstrating that mountains and mountainous pilgrimage enhance the feeling of proximity to death, in this section we shall demonstrate that this feeling and the very fear of death enhances in-group coherence. In doing so, we are building upon the works of cultural anthropologist Ernest Becker (1971; 1973; 1975). From the 1980s the prominent social psychologists Jeff Greenberg, Tom Pyszynski and Sheldon Solomon have developed a "Terror Management Theory" (TMT), studying "the role of the unconscious fear of death in just about everything" (Greenberg and Arndt 2012: 400). Departing from the observations that human beings have developed systems to avoid death and a cognitive ability to understand its inevitability, the theory suggests that terror produced from the confrontation of human desire to live with mortality awareness is managed through cultures as symbolic systems containing values providing meaning to human life (Greenberg, Pyszczynski, and Solomon 1986; Greenberg, Solomon, and Arndt 2008). Hence, to reduce fear of death, humans develop various mechanisms such as "self-esteem and the worldview upon which it is predicated" and "strive for and defend [them] in the service of psychological security," while they would "react negatively to anyone or anything that undermines faith in their world view" (Greenberg and Arndt 2012: 403; Greenberg et al. 1990). Since the 1980s, several scholars have tested various hypotheses stemming from TMT demonstrating – *inter alia* – that "[r]eminding people of their mortality (mortality salience…) increases positive reactions to people who validate aspects of participant's worldviews…" (Greenberg, Solomon, and Arndt 2008) Simply, fear of death or mortality salience enhances in-group solidarity (Greenberg, Koole, and Pyszczynski 2004; Kearl 2009).

There is no doubt that the Christian Church was empirically conscious of the mortality salience's property to strengthen faith in the in-group's worldviews and life attitudes. "In all you do, remember the end of your life, and then you will never sin" taught Sirach (Sir. 7:36), an admonition later taken up by the Apostle Paul in his assurance: "I protest, brethren, by my pride in you which I have in Christ Jesus our Lord, I die every day" (1 Cor. 15:31).Church services, both Orthodox and Catholic, are consequently abundant in references and symbolism of death and resurrection. In the Roman-Catholic Church calendar, Ash Wednesday rites involve the blessing of ashes which are rubbed onto the heads of the faithful as a tangible reminder of their mortality (Stravinskas 2002: 95). Furthermore, the remembrance of both spiritual and biological death was inextricably entwined in daily church practices (Zecher 2011; 2015).To quote but one example from the teachings of early desert fathers, composed in the early 7th century, St. John Climacus' *Ladder* recorded the sort of ascetic practices leading to spiritual ascent. Each of the thirty chapters ("steps") of the composition refers to a separate spiritual level. The sixth "step" referring to the remembrance of death (Zucker 2015, 182 et seqq.) provides a stunning empirical 'validation' to some of the fundamental hypotheses of TMT (St. John Climacus 1959, 35-6):

> ... 3. Fear of death is a natural instinct that comes from disobedience; but terror at death is evidence of unrepented sin. Christ fears death, but does not show terror, in order to demonstrate clearly the properties of His two natures.
>
> 4. As of all foods bread is the most essential, so the thought of death is the most necessary of all works. The remembrance of death amongst those in the midst of society gives birth to distress and frivolity, and even more—to despondency. But amongst those who are free from noise it produces the putting aside of cares, and constant prayer and guarding of the mind. But these same virtues both produce the remembrance of death and are also produced by it.

Once introduced, the dual connotation of death as involving both a spiritual and/or biological dimension has been utilized in homilies and services up to the present date (cf. Sophrony 1991, 106 and Sophrony 2006, 11-2).

The empirical understanding of the effects of fear, terror and remembrance of death by the Christian Church should not surprise us; such an understanding was inherited from much older times. In his famous Melian dialogue, Thucydides records that the brutal threat of violent death elevated by the Athenian ambassadors against the Melians in case they refused to surrender only gave the opposite effect to what was expected; the Melians enhanced their in-group solidarity and their determination to oppose the Athenians was shielded by way of moral self-assertion, a desire to remain true to the "group" values which transcended their specific existence and religious hope (Thucydides 5:84-116; Ahrensdorf 2000, 590-1). Greenberg and Arndt (2012, 400) further suggest that, as a theory, TMT can be traced as far in the past as the Sumerian epic of Gilgamesh dated in the 18th century B.C. The apprehension that remembrance and closeness to death strengthens in-group solidarity and belief systems indicates that exposure to high altitudes, where closer proximity to the deity is believed to exist, invokes fear of death and, hence, strengthens in-group solidarity. In addition to this, sacrifice, particularly involving blood, can also be reasonably viewed as a provocation of death.

Moreover, in section two above we discussed how any departure from the fleshly or material into the aerial or heavenly signalled a transition from the domain of everyday human existence into the transcendent spiritual and divine dimension (or a "higher state of being") beyond human frailty and mortality. This kind of connection with a higher spiritual reality inevitably lead to an increased sense of connection with the group or larger cultic constituency throughout, or beyond, both time and space. In relation to this, it also meant that ascent, whether spatial or spiritual, involved a move away from the "heavy" earthly and fleshly realms, towards the more ethereal realms of the air and the heavens above. Thus the process of ascending towards God on the mountain involved, for many religious pilgrims, bodily self-denial and the mortification of the flesh.

In fact, the practice of elevating oneself in an attempt to draw near to the sublime and mortify the flesh together with the mundane pre-date Christianity. Lucian of Samosata records the custom of a man mounting on a phallus-shaped Dionysian pole by the temple of the Syrian Hera at Hieropolis Bambycae (Manbij), Syria, twice a year and remaining there for a week as "people believe that the man who is aloft holds converses with the gods, and prays for good fortune for the whole of Syria, and that the gods from their neighbourhood hear his prayers" (Lucian 1913, §28, 68). Such practices are very reminiscent to those of Christian stylite or dendrite saints. The *akolouthia* of "the celestial man" and "the earthly angel," (Foundoulis 1992) St. Simeon the Stylite, for instance, similarly invokes mortality salience. It does so by reminding the faithful of the association of the mortification of the flesh and the passions by means of living on a pole (i.e. at an altitude) with the words: "In your most fervour faith, wise Father, and in contempt of all mundane matters you followed Christ with the force of the Holy Spirit, you melted your body in self-containment, most holy, foreseeing the celestial glory; hence, you invented a pole with a ladder for divine ascent…" (*Kathisma* in Tone 5). It is also worthy of noting that one of the Vespers' service *troparia* likens the saint's pole to Christ's Cross (Foundoulis 1992).

Often, a pilgrimage's *topos* is in itself either a tomb or reminiscent of a tomb. The Orthodox pilgrimage of Pecherskaya Lavra in Kiev, Ukraine, is a prime example of a pilgrimage whose *topos* is comprised of tombs in underground caves, themselves also being reminiscent of tombs. Underneath the monastery's 18th century complex, there is a network of caves and cavities, some natural, others painstakingly carved by monks. They were used as hand-carved chapels, hermit cells, and death caves containing dozens of coffins with the incorrupt relics of saintly monks. (Louth 2007, 287-9) Having argued about the association of caves with tombs, there are many cases in which such caves at an altitude were used as cells of anchorite monks later turning to pilgrimage destinations. We could mention here the pilgrimage site at the Monastery of the Holy Trinity on Mount Sagmata, Theva, Greece, in one of whose natural cavities St. Clement of Sagmata "went to the high edge of a mountain considered terrible by anyone crossing over or climbing it, and, with the help of a pole, positioned and confined himself on top of it, after which he remained until the end of this vain and corrupt life." (Stamatiadis 1896, 22-4). In this "very high and narrow pole (n.b. cave) he remained bravely forbearing the forces of winds and heat and rain in all privation, affliction and anguish, conversing with God despite the harsh glacier and the heat of the sun." (Stamatiadis 1896, 22-4). Cave monasticism which combines with altitude is known throughout the provinces of Epiros and Albania [Figs. 1-3] (Popa 1965; Chouliaras 2015).

Figure 1: Cave Hermitage of Saint Nicholas, southern view, 16th century, stone and mortar, Tranosisht, Lunxhëri - Gjirokastër, Southern Albania.

Figure 2: Cave Hermitage, 14th century, Kosharisht, Librazhd, central Albania.

Figure 3: Cave Hermitage of Saint George, western view, 12th century, stone and mortar, Dhivër, Saranda, Southern Albania.

MOUNTAINOUS PILGRIMAGE IN ALBANIA: CHRISTIAN AND BEKTASHI

In section two of this chapter we discussed the history and sacred traditions of the notion that the divine dwells in the heavens or near the summit of mountains and that the religious concept of sacrifice or the sensation of nearness to death were conducive to the sensation of proximity to the spiritual or the divine while encouraging group cohesion and continuity. In the third we documented that, on the one hand, fear of death enhances in-group solidarity and, on the other, that the Christian Church was empirically aware of this property of death remembrance utilizing it to enhance spirituality and a move away from the material. In this section, we contextualize the findings of the previous sections with four religious mountainous pilgrimage sites from Albania, all of which invoke death salience in relation to altitude.

In previous works, K. Giakoumis demonstrated the importance of authority (political, economic, or ecclesiastical) in making and sustaining pilgrimages (2013 and 2014).The following cases demonstrate that the authorities involved in the making and sustaining of mountainous pilgrimages empirically and intuitively understood that death nearness at their pilgrimage sites was very important for the sustainability of these sites, as it enhances the in-group solidarity of their pilgrims.

THE PILGRIMAGE DATA

The objective of this section is to contextualize findings in the previous sections, i.e. the relation between mountains with religion and spirituality, the association of mountains with the feeling of nearness to death, as well as with how such a feeling enhances in-group solidarity. This contextualization will be done with reference to four concrete case-studies from Albania. The following pilgrimage data were collected by K. Giakoumis on the basis of bibliographic research as well as twelve expeditions to the very pilgrimage sites presented herein for the purpose of participating in various pilgrimages organized in these sites over a period of six years. The festivities at Monastery of Saint Anthony of Padua in Laç were visited four times; the Monastery of the Holy Trinity in Pepel, Gjirokastra, was visited twice; the *Teke* of Sarı Saltık, Kruja, was also visited twice; and the *Teke* and *Türbe* of Abbas Ali on Mount Tomorr were visited three times.

Participant observation fieldwork was selected as a method of getting close to pilgrims to observe and record information about their pilgrimage experience without reaction. This method permits the collection of a number of qualitative data: field notes, photographs, as well as video and audio recordings. Fieldwork involved three different roles: **A) Complete participant**, as a member of pilgrimage groups well-known to the researcher and his activity before the actual fieldwork. **B.1) Observing participant,** as a member of a group participating in pilgrimage activities while recording the attitudes of other members of the group; **B.2) Participating observer**, as an outsider participating in some aspects of life in the surrounding and recording what is possible. **C) Complete observer**, following people around and recording their pilgrimage behaviour with little, if any, interaction. This method (Bernard 2006, 342-86) has been considered as appropriate for the study of pilgrimage, while multiple visits and alternate roles in observing were selected for the purpose of combining random and non-random samples and time, thereby enhancing the internal and external validity of findings. Table No. 1 indicates the methodological roles the researcher employed in each of the field visits:

Table 1: The methodological roles of the researcher

#	Site	Date	Role	Notes
1	St. Anthony, Laç	15.06.2010	B.2	
2	Sarı Saltık Teke, Kruja	21.04.2013	B.2	
3	Monastery at Pepel	27.07.2013	B.2	
4	Mount Tomorr	22-23.08.2014	B.1	Participant in a group of four pilgrims of mixed nationalities.
5	St. Anthony, Laç	17.03.2015	B.1	Participant in a group of three international pilgrims.
6	St. Anthony, Laç	12.05.2015	B.2	
7	Mount Tomorr	23.05.2015	B.2	In part with C. Lockwood.
8	Sarı Saltık Teke, Kruja	31.05.2015	C	With C. Lockwood.
9	Monastery at Pepel	01.06.2015	B.2	
10	Mount Tomorr	17.09.2015	A	Along with four friends from Skrapar, wider Tomorr region.
11	St. Anthony, Laç	31.01.2016	C	

The Pilgrimage of Saint Anthony of Padua in Laç

Located to the east of the city of Laç, ca. 250m above sea level, the church and cave of St. Anthony of Padua lies on a mountainous, once densely forested location, access to which is made through a steep pathway [Fig. 4] on a winding slope with karst cavities, the largest of which forms a cave [Fig. 5] – several meters long, 2-3 meters high and 1-4 m wide. This pilgrimage is one of the largest such events in modern-day Albania (Giakoumis 2013, 270-3; Prelaj and Kurti 2013, 100-1). The shrine's historical background interweaves the stories of two different saints, St. Blaise (Gk. Vlasios) of Sebastea and St. Anthony of Padua. The ruins close to the pilgrimage have been attributed to the City of Sebaste, a city synonymous with the ancient Sebastea (modern Şivas, Turkey) and a location associated with various early 4th-century martyrs such as Saint Blaise and the Forty Martyrs. Hence, the cave of the pilgrimage was associated with the location of Saint Blaise' life; the spot was thus named "the Cave of Saint Blaise." (Giakoumis 2013).The cave was believed to be the spot where Saint Blaise was arrested before being martyred in Durrës (Prelaj and Kurti 2013, 14). Death salience must have manifested itself more intensely in previous periods, as it was reported by Mark Skuraj on December 20th 1641 [Zamputi 1965, 243-5] that the monastery and the cave of Saint Blaise were situated next to a cemetery. For thirteen Tuesdays before the saint's feast day (June 13), pilgrims amass at the site in participation of "the Thirteen Tuesdays of St. Anthony" (Prelaj and Kurti 2013, 96-8). From June 11th until the feast-day of the church on June 13th, hundreds of Catholics, Muslims and Orthodox toil together up the stony path. Some of these pilgrims are barefoot and wedge their feet into cracks among the rocks believed to have healing attributes, while others are prompted to lie on a rock dent where the saint is believed to have lied to rest, light candles on the slope's crevices [Fig. 6], touch and kiss stones, or to collect five white stones on their way and to whisper to each one before laying them once again on the ground.

Figure 4: The steep pathway from Laç city to the convent of ShnaNdout.

Figure 5: *Cave Hermitage of Saint Blaise*, North-eastern view, ShnaNdou Convent, Laç, Northern Albania.

The pilgrimage thrived during the course of the 20th century, until June 1966, when it was declared a "military zone." Its visitation was then banned, while both the Church of St. Anthony and St. Blaise's cave were blown up with explosives. Despite this, faithful pilgrimages to the site continued throughout the period of communist rule (Giakoumis 2013, 272), the shrine was completely reconstructed soon after the fall of the communist regime and a new, 4 km-long asphalted road from the city of Laç was built in 1992, the result of which was a drastic proliferation in the number of pilgrims. Currently, the site attracts thousands of pilgrims throughout the year, and particularly on the shrine's feast day of June 13. Many pilgrims amass at the site beginning on June 11 for a three-day-long pilgrimage (De Rapper 2012, 29) in order to plea for the saints' protection and to offer devotional objects for miraculous healing and good health.

Some pilgrims pledging the saint's support opt to start their pilgrimage at the footsteps of St. Blaise from the cemetery at the outskirts of the Laç towards the monastery. T.P. from Puka, aged 61 in May 2015, was together with her daughter and granddaughter on May 12, went all the way up to the monastery barefoot. This was the sixth annual pilgrimage of hers; she had pledged the saint for the health of one of her sons who was left paralyzed by a car accident a few years before. Her son visits the monastery by car and the family meets at the monastery. The ascent from the cemetery to the monastery requires some strenuous seventy minutes' walk over a stony 2.0-2.5-km-long path which was recently widened at the expenses of the monastery for its security of pilgrims wishing to ascend it as part of their pilgrimage penitential activities. T.P. carries this journey without a word, contrary to her daughter and granddaughter who are constantly chatting on their way. As we approach the monastery's hill T.P. gets increasingly frown and falls onto her knees crossing herself at the monastery's entrance. She then lights candles at the candle caverns [Fig. 6], whispers "for healing the sick" and heads to the cave of St. Blaise. She later joins her family at the monastery's church, where her son on a wheel-chair can also attend. After a certain degree of familiarization, when asked why she performs this painful penitential ritual she responds "këtu gjejmë derman për sëmundjet tona" (here we find comfort for our illnesses).

Figure 6: On the way to the convent of Shna Ndou in Laç, hordes of pilgrims climb up the stony path and light candles in the slope's cavities.

The visitation to the cave of saint Blaise is indeed one of the culminant points of the pilgrimage. At the day of the monastery's feast, a special service is conducted after mass at the very early hours of June 13. The cave is situated ca. 150 m below the monastery at a steep rocky mountainside, access to which is facilitated by a stony staircase. The sight from the cave to the mountain slope below is both spectacular and creepy, but the existence of metal banister nowadays significantly eases the challenge. At the cave of the saint, some pilgrims leave their own clothes, those of relatives or those of others in need of help. Other pilgrims lie in the church, while all pilgrims cross themselves and touch or kiss the saint's statue at the site of the church. The invocation of the saint's help is also called by young couples, some of which, when unnoticed by the monastery's guards outside the cave, either carve or simply write their names on the cross of the door preventing pilgrims from entering to the far-edge of the cave, even carve their names on the cave's rock [Fig. 5] and, on occasion, get a piece of the cave's rock "për të mirën" (for the good). "The cave helps those with mental problems, as well as those with problems at the upper parts of their body" stated a pilgrim in a March 2015 expedition. Especially those with such problems place their head in a cavity of the ceiling of the cave [Fig. 5]. Indeed, several people with disabilities are to be found at the pilgrimage site, as I experienced all four times of my visit. In addition, several young couples with babies visit St. Blaise's cave, the babies being taken for blessing to the far-edge of the cave, normally visited only upon permission of the monastic community typically in cases of terminal illnesses and only at the presence of a guardian. In my June 2010 expedition I had the opportunity to discuss with Ç.D., a 20-years-old male pilgrim, about his experience. When asked about the sort of messages his pilgrimage inspired him to give to his fellow-youth, his response was stunning: "Jetoni këtë jetë se nuk e kemi më (live your life, because we no longer have it)."

The Pilgrimage of the Monastery of the Holy Trinity at Pepel, Gjirokastër

The monastery of the Holy Trinity at Pepel, Gjirokastër [Map 1], is situated high upon a once forested hill currently occupied by an olive-grove at the summit of the village of Pepel, Upper Dropull (Southern Dropull). It was once one of the biggest monasteries of Upper Dropull, as evidenced by its buildings and ruins (Thomo 1998, 135-9). The monastery was reconstructed in 1750 and painted in 1754 (Popa 1998, 241[Nos. 583 and 584]; Giakoumis 1994, 24-5). Legend has it that at one time the hill on which the monastery was constructed was densely forested and inhabited by spirits of the forested mountains. According to one version of its foundational story, local inhabitants (Baras 1966, 209; T.L. n.d.), or hermits living in nearby huts, repeatedly saw (Pappa 86-7) a light emanating from the arbutus and yew forest throughout the day or overnight, which frightened them a great deal. When they rushed there, they found an icon of the Holy Trinity, which they transferred to the parish church (or, according to another version, an oak cavity). The following day or night, however, the icon returned to the spot where it was originally found and continued to illuminate the forest. It was there – according to the legend – that a church was initially built and then later transformed into a convent (Baras 1966, 209; Pappa 2009, 85-6). Baras' source (1966, 209) is not mentioned; however, the life-span of the author (1887-1964), the *post-mortem* publication date of his book and the fact that he started collecting notes and publishing materials at an age of less than 20 years old (Vranousis 1966, 3-12), may provide some hints about the date of his source. Considering that Pappa (2009, 86 and n. 150) quotes an oral account of a local inhabitant very similar to the one recorded by Baras, it appears that the foundational story should be dated sometime around the end of the 19th century at the earliest.

Map 1: The location of the Holy Trinity Monastery at Pepel, Dropull, Gjirokastër, Southern Albania.

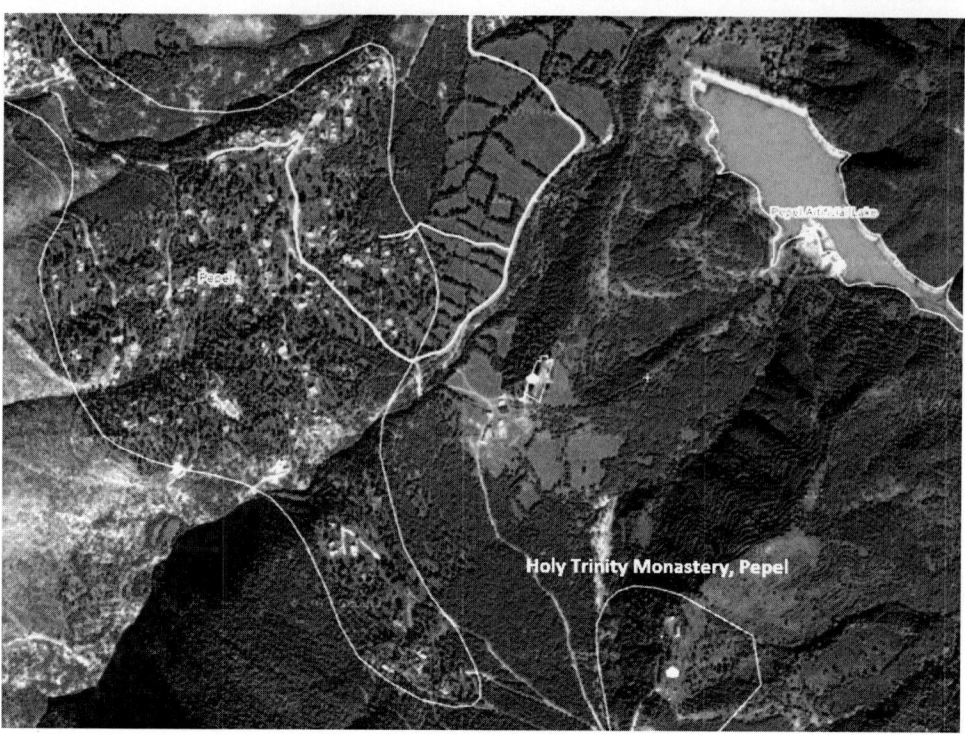

The element of fear in this foundational story, both in terms of the dense forest, as well as the myth of the inexplicable light illuminating it, for whose appeasement the chapel and the very monastery were allegedly constructed, is noteworthy. This is especially the case given the empirical understanding by the Church that death salience enhances in-group solidarity and therefore supports structures of authority. There is little doubt that the foundational story of the monastery is mere fiction, first because the sole inscription of an icon of the Holy Trinity that was preserved dates to 1815 and well after the monastery's (re)establishment (Popa 1998, 267, Inscription No. 686). Secondly, the miraculous finding of the icon (whose light scared local inhabitants) is not recorded in an earlier account of the monastery's foundation by its very abbot. This written account, dated February 1, 1837, was copied in a codex compiled mostly likely in 1874 (*Property Register* f. 27^r). Finding no reason why a monastery's abbot would forget to record a miracle that sparked the (re)establishment of the monastery, we suggest the myth was added at a later stage to sustain and appease the element of fear towards the spot of the monastery, as well as to enhance its reputation as a pilgrimage site. Such practices, after all, are sufficiently known both in the Orthodox East (Chrysochoidis 2007, xxix-xxxvi) as well as in the Catholic West (Menuge 2000; Hoffmann 2014, 101-8).

The monastery turned into an important pilgrimage and social centre for the wider region as it was situated on a travel route. Because it was well-funded with endowments, donations and other funds, it once sustained a considerable income (Giakoumis 2002, 412, 422; Pappa 2009, 85-90) and engaged in a wide range of social services, operating as a primitive lunatic asylum, nursing home, workhouse and nursery of illegitimate infants who were brought up with the hope of adoption by childless families. This is how Mammopoulos experienced the pilgrimage to the monastery back in the 1920s (1980, 29-31):

> At the shadowy, most respectable monastery, at the idyllic place surrounded by oak, olive and yew trees there was a Childcare Nursery, rudimentary as it may, yet perhaps unique in the East, at the time when beneficence had not been crystallized to modern standards.[It hosted] infants whose mothers could not attend to them, illegitimate infants – seeds of the sin of women whose husbands had long immigrated abroad and who went astray. Mothers and babies found recourse to the mercy of the Holy Trinity. How could they live in a society whose laws they violated? Thanks to the Monastery of Pepel the perpetrators of these societal norms found divine mercy. The illegitimate children of the Childcare Nursery were taken by women for adoption by the childless families of Pogon which asked for them. It is not only the Childcare Nursery that make us wonder, but also the rudimentary penitentiary, lunatic asylum.
>
> [...] Popular medicine was completely powerless in cases of "psychic illness." What could these naïve "doctors" know from the mystery of the human's world of soul? It is noteworthy, though, that they noticed two issues. Mental disorders leave the dark human forces unmanaged and the man can be dangerous to his fellow human beings; thus, these forces had to be contained or appeased. Christians and Turks [i.e. Muslims], converted Christians preferred Saint Nicholas at Cepo [i.e. another monastery with a rudimentary lunatic asylum], brought patients to Pepel from all over the places, especially those suffering from schizophrenia or dangerous maniacs, those who the love of relatives could not manage.
>
> "Quiet" patients, men and women, dwelled in separate designated cells. Every morning they would go to church where special prayers would be read for them. As for maniacs, [...] they threw them in the domed basements and kept them there tied on logs crying or laughing! Their groans would vanish in the depths of these basements... What were Pepel's logs? A crude and heavy log down on the floor of the cell of the basement, with two notches, one at each end at a distance of one meter. The shins of the patient would be placed through these notches, close to the ankles. On the top of this log another log was adjusted with grommets, hands likewise

tied to its notches. And thus the patient would lay motionless on his back for 10-15 days, only in bread and water, often in a pile of human wastes to the day that a monastery's servant would clean up…

On its feast day of the Holy Trinity (Pentecost Monday), the monastery once hosted one of the largest religious and commercial fairs, as well as cattle markets of the region (Evangelidis 1919, 107). Its fair started on the Saturday evening of Pentecost and lasted until Monday, the feast of the Holy Spirit. Before 1944, when it was set on fire by German occupation forces, the monastery is reported to have hosted no less than 50 pilgrims on any given day of the year. On the monastery's feast-day, thousands of pilgrims – Christian and Muslim, Greek, Vlach and Albanian alike – gathered at the monastery from the regions of Dropull, Pogon, and Delvinë, including pilgrims from villages currently situated in Greece. Every village had its own threshing floor, also used for dancing, and musicians. Food was provided by the monastery thanks to donations offered by pilgrims who were enrolled at the donors register compiled annually at the monastery's feast-day. The Vespers and the Holy Liturgy were solemnly celebrated at the monastery with the presence of many priests from the neighbouring villages. Cattle dealers and merchants had their own space, while retailers and peddlers announced their merchandise (Gikas 2015; T.L. n.d.).

The monastery is no longer home to a monastic community. On its feast day the local Metropolis of Gjirokastra, at the request of locals might dispatch a priest for the service. Hence, the monastery and its feast is but a shadow of its past. Yet, people would still gather and celebrate with instruments and dances, many of whom return from the places of their immigration on this occasion; yet, the number of pilgrims is nowhere close to the monastery's past number of pilgrims. Very few pilgrims would now go on foot, for the additional reason that "the path has been damaged in parts," as a respondent stated in June 2015. In the diaries of 2013's expedition, however, Giakoumis recorded traces of the crosses and landmarks placed by the monastery at the most dangerous spots of the path, whose traces indicate a basement where once an icon would be placed. On both expeditions in the monastery it was noted that pilgrims systematically avoided visiting the terrible monastic basements, which once housed the lunatic asylum, where one can still see the relics of the inhumane treatment of patients. Giakoumis twice attempted to ask pilgrims whether they knew what the basement used to be and why they did not visit it. Respondents were all aware of what the place was, but the rest of their response indicated they found the question obtrusive and they went back to the music and dances.

The *Teke* of Sarı Saltık, Kruja

The pilgrimage of Sarı Saltık's *teke* in Kruja is essentially a conferment of honours to tombs at a spot where there was once a cave-cult. The funerary complex where the *teke* is located just below the top of the Kruja Mount, 1176 m above sea level and roughly 550 m above the city's altitude. Access to it is made either through a stone path 35-45 minutes' walk from the city of Kruja, or via an asphalted road completed in the summer of 2011. The complex consists of the *teke* [Fig. 7], the place for bloody sacrifices (*kurban*) [Fig. 9] and the *türbe* of Sarı Saltık in a 20-meter-deep cave below the *teke* [Fig. 10]. Due to the limited surface available at the surface of the complex, the *teke* lodge [Fig. 7] is structured in three rooms, one operating as the guardians' room, library and kitchen, another as a guest room [Fig. 8] and the third for storage.

Figure 7: The Teke of Sarı Saltık, Lodge's Exterior, 1992, stone with mortar and lime, Kruja, Central Albania.

Figure 8: The Teke of Sarı Saltık, Lodge's Interior, 1992, stone with mortar and lime, Kruja, Central Albania.

Figure 9: The Teke of Sarı Saltık, Kurban place, 1991, Kruja, Central Albania.

Figure 10: The Teke of Sarı Saltık, the Funerary Cave, 1991, Kruja, Central Albania.

The *teke* and *türbe* complex honours the figure of Sarı Saltık. Existing on the fringes of history and legend, he is believed to be either a disciple of Hadji Bektash Veli (1247-1338/1341), or a dervish from the court of Sultan Orhan (1326-1360); more likely, he is or is subsumed to be an early Balkan figure, often beclouded with such Christian saints as St. Nicholas or Symeon the Stylite, whose legends were first recorded by Ibn Battuta, a 14th century voyager and geographer, and widely spread throughout the Balkans in the 16th century. The saint is believed to have died in Corfu as St. Spyridon, much venerated by Albanian Bektashi believers (Elsie 2001, 225-9; Elsie 2010, 396-8; Kołczyńska 2013, 54-5). Sarı Saltık's tomb is held to be in three places: Corfu, where he is believed to be subsumed within the figure of St. Spyridon, at the monastery of St. Naoum in Ohrid, or on the top of Mount Pashtrik. The festival on Mount Pashtrik is celebrated by Catholics and Muslims alike on August 2 or 22. This is undoubtedly the case of a spot also contested by Catholic (celebrating the Dormition and Assumption of Mary on August 15) and Orthodox (Orthodox of Prizren place the tomb of St. Panteleimon there, celebrating there over the summer as well) Christians (Elsie 2001, 201, 227).

The cult of Sarı Saltık in Kruja subsumed local Christian religious practices. While it is believed that the site of the *türbe* was once used for the church of St. Alexander (Tirta 1976) or St. Spyridon, (Kaleshi 1971, 821) the Albanian version of the legend of Sarı Saltık involves his rescuing a Christian princess from a hydra (kulshedra), which devoured a man or a woman every day in the fashion of St. George. Apparently a foundational story for Bektashism's spread over Christianity in the Kruja region (Degrand 1901, 236-43). After Harry Norris, "[s]uch a sequence of conversion is the norm in Albania on summits of mountains and in forests, in groves near lakes and by sacred springs" (1993, 156). Sarı Saltık was later threatened by locals and was forced to leave the cave in which he lived as a hermit. When he did so, he made three strides marked by a *teke* and a footprint at each step (Norris 1993, 156), one of which was later enclosed in a shrine at Kruja [Fig. 11]. The first mention of the pilgrimage to the tomb of Sarı Saltık dates to 1567/8 (Kiel 1995), while in his expedition to the region Franz Babinger found a Turkish inscription dated 1104 H (1692/3) (Clayer 1990, 336-9). Sarı Saltık's feast day is celebrated on August 22, when thousands of pilgrims gather to confer honours upon him (Kołczyńska 2013, 51-71).

There is currently an asphalted road from which the second expedition was conducted; the steep stony path to the *teke* which was chosen for the first expedition (April 21st 2013), however, is much more rewarding in terms of view, although physically strenuous and in parts quite dangerous on account of the land-slides. The local guide, Xhavit, told the stony path had significantly deteriorated in the course of winter and also all the more pilgrims abandon the path road. The *teke* is just below the mountain and is not obvious from the path, as is placed behind huge rocks. Xhavit mentioned that a number of pilgrims fell from the path and injured themselves, for which reason the *teke* custodians had to repair and widen it in order to reduce, yet not eliminate, the risk of danger. Upon ascent with the local guide, the researcher closely followed a group of four pilgrims, one old man, a couple and a young boy (their age groups indicating three different generations) in their pilgrimage ritual, in which they engaged altogether as a group. The observations of the pilgrimage ritual were also confirmed in another visit and casual observations to the same pilgrimage site conducted two years later. They had already purchased a ram from the *teke* vendor and brought it to the *kurban* place with its hooves-tied and its horns decorated with a ribbon. At the sacrificial place the ram was given water to drink and then was laid down, facing left, at the lowest edge of the platform [Fig. 9]; before slitting the neck of the *kurban* animal, the pilgrim who slaughtered it spelt out "me të mbarë Sari Salltiku" (for the sake of good we invoke Sarı Saltık); two other pilgrims of his company approached the slaughtered animals and placed some of its blood on their foreheads. They then flayed the animal, left a portion to the *teke* and then placed the rest in plastic bags.

Figure 11: The Shrine of Sarı Saltık's Footstep, Kruja, Central Albania.

They then proceeded to the *teke*. Before entering the cave shrine, they removed their shoes and entered with great respect kissing the column to the right of the entrance three times. Then, they lit several candles whispering prayers for family members and left clothes of relatives who were, as they shrine is believed to have healing attributes. Afterwards, they altogether passed from the mausoleum of the dervishes buried in the *türbe* touching their graves and rubbing some of the clothes they held together onto the graves. They then moved to the lowest edge of the cave, where they drank water from the spring placed there, washed their face and head, filled some plastic bottles with water and soaked the clothes they carried with them. At the end of their veneration they exited the *türbe* and went to the *teke*'s guest-rooms for coffee and a candy. Then, they moved to their car taking the plastic bags of meat from the ram they slaughtered and the clothes they left in the cave with them. The small group of pilgrims was happy to respond to few questions addressed by the researcher. When asked on the purpose of taking the life of the sheep, the old man said that the spilt blood of the sacrificial animal is offered to God for the sake of the good health of pilgrims and their relatives. When asked what the attraction was of a place at such a high altitude and with so many tombs, they stated that this was a holy place; however, none of them stated readiness to come on his or her own on a solitary pilgrimage to this site.

The *Teke* And *Türbe* Of Abbas Ali on Mount Tomorr

Mount Tomorr (2416 m) is home to the footprint shrine, the *teke* and the *türbe* of Abbas Ali. This Muslim holy man, whose veneration on Mount Tomorr subsumed the veneration of the Prophet Elijah (Norris 1993, 98; Elsie 2001, 3, 84), is said, according to one legend, to have been half-brother to Hasan and Husein, who visited Tomorr on his way to Mount Olympus. Another Bektashi tradition maintains that Hadji Bektash Veli (1247-1338/1341), the legendary founder of Bektashism, aiming at subsuming the Christian pilgrimage to the top of the mountain on August 15, the feast of the Dormition of the Mother of God, to Bektashi religious practices, exhumed a bone from the grave of Abbas Ali in Karbala, Iraq, to re-consecrate Mount Tomorr as Abbas Ali's second grave (Elsie 2001, 3; Elsie 2010, 446). Every year, on August 20-25, hordes of pilgrims gather at all sites associated with the cult of Abbas Ali on the Mount of Tomorr. Local hear-says hold that more than a quarter of a million pilgrims visited the sites in 2015. Many pilgrims conduct a three-day-long trip to Mount Tomorr, spending one day at each of the three aforementioned sites associated with the pilgrimage.

K. Giakoumis visited the site both on a mule traversing the traditional 12-hour-long pathway (August 22, 2014), as well as with car (May 31, 2015 and September 19, 2015). In my second visit, I also had to abandon my car until the following day, when locals with the help of shovels and other cars pulled my car out of the snow, so that I visit the *türbe* at the mountain's top; fear of being blocked in the high snowy mountain compelled some fellow pilgrims to abort this part of the expedition. The third visit was conducted in a group as a complete participant.

The pilgrimage is comprised of three principal stops and several other intermittent stops to minor "holy places" of Mount Tomorr, where one may still find old fibres of cloth. In modern times, access to the shrine is made either through a half-day-long path from the nearest village or through a non-paved road. The construction of the road has significantly increased the number of pilgrims travelling by car and almost eliminated pilgrims ascending the mountain on foot. On the way to the *teke*, the pilgrim first encounters the recently built shrine containing Abbas Ali's footstep [Fig. 12], a circular building with perimetrical windows surrounded by a court, entry to which is made through an arch. This is the first principal stop of the pilgrimage, a small *teke* housing a horse's footprint, believed to be the place from which baba Abbas Ali passed mounted on his horse. On the first and third expedition we stopped there to light a candle in the *teke*, although numerous labels forbid this. The 45-year-old guide of the first journey narrated that "at the time of Enver the *teke* was not destroyed. The excavator went three times there to demolish the *teke*'s walls, but on the third the excavator was burnt away. They [i.e. the communists] never managed to demolish the holy place and left it without ever engaging in this again."

Figure 12: The Shrine of Abbas Ali's Footstep, Mount Tomorr, Southern Albania.

The second and more visited spot is the *teke* of Abbas Ali. The *teke* of Abbas Ali is on the spot of the southern elevation of Mount Tomorr, called Kulmak, 2173 m above sea level. The *teke*'s complex is comprised of a sacrificial place (*kurban*) [Fig. 13], a section with the tombs of a number of deceased dervishes [Fig. 14], initially built in 1924 and rebuilt in 1994, a big lodge for the guardians, prominent Bektashi members and pilgrims [Fig. 15], as well as a spot for camping. Before entering, pilgrims light candles or oil lamps, enter the site whispering prayers, and go around of every tomb of deceased dervish kissing it, leaving coins to the special box of contributions [Fig. 14]. On occasion they leave personal items such as piece of clothes or photographs [Fig. 17] in order to plead for the miraculous intervention of the saint.

Figure 13: The Sacrificial Place, Teke of Abbas Ali at Kulmak, Mount Tomorr, Southern Albania.

Figure 14: Tombs of Deceased Dervishes, Teke of Abbas Ali at Kulmak, 1924 (reconstructed in 1994), Mount Tomorr, Southern Albania.

Figure 15: Lodge for the guardians and the Teke Community, Teke of Abbas Ali at Kulmak, Mount Tomorr, Southern Albania.

Figure 16: The Türbe of Abbas Ali on the top of Kulmak, Mount Tomorr, Southern Albania.

In spite of labels warning that trade is prohibited in the shrine, sacrificial animals are on sale almost all days of the year in which the sites are accessible, while at the pilgrimage site itself, retailers and peddlers announce their merchandise. Animals are dumb out of exhaustion, decorated with a ribbon and with their hooves tied. The *teke* guardians are often requested to slaughter the animals. After the traditions associated with *kurban*, a portion of the carcass is offered to the *teke*, although increasingly fewer people are doing so, according to what the guardians told us. When asked why, though looking unwealthy, he offered a generous portion of the family's *kurban* to the *teke*, a respondent of an apparently poor family stated that "this holy place has nothing to do with wealth; this is mostly for the recovery of the sick; and we have been concerned with illness but we did not have any health problems. We are all very well. "Only on the heydays of the annual pilgrimage more than 7,000 sacrificial animals are slaughtered for *kurban* and, in spite of the organized way of slaughtering to the particularly designated place, there are complaints that the left-overs of the slaughtered animals litter the environment;[2] indeed, both the spectacle and the atmosphere of the *teke*'s *kurban* spot is disturbing, especially for inhabitants of the cities, unaccustomed to animal slaughtering as they might be. The *teke* has arranged a special place for roasting the *kurban* animals. In the course of my first visit to the site, I observed pilgrims roasting their *kurban* lambs and simultaneously socializing with fellow-pilgrims around them and treating one another.

Finally, Abbas Ali's cenotaph *türbe* is located on the peak of the mountain [Fig. 16], along with the tombs of two deceased dervishes. On my very first trip to Mount Tomorr the teke's guard explained why people leave photographs under the tomb-mark of the deceased dervishes [Fig. 17]: "In order to have good luck you should visit this place three times. You should worship, make a sacrifice (kurban), donate money, and, if you have sick relatives that you cannot bring with you, you should bring a piece of their cloth without fail and place it on one of the tombs there or get a photograph and place it close to the tombs." On my third trip I participated in a group of four young pilgrims from Skrapar (central Albania), aged 27-45, who had pulled my car out of the snow during my second trip and with whom we maintained contact. They went to the *türbe* on the peak of the mountain to sacrifice a sheep. "There are many people who are cured here that were not healed by other means, including doctors," says the eldest of them. "This is a saintly, good place. It is even better if you make a sacrifice (*kurban*)." The sheep was placed just below the elevation of the *türbe*, with its feet tied, and one of the pilgrims slaughtered it, while another invoked for Abbas Ali's help: "ajde mbarë Abbas Aliu" (may Abbas Ali make matters good). The ritual involves applying blood from the sacrificed animal on the foreheads of those who offered it.[3] Then, the carcass is excoriated, its soles being kept at home as

---

[2] "A1 Report - Tomor, bagëtitë theren në natyrë mbetjet lihen në ambiente të hapura." Accessed at https://www.youtube.com/watch?v=m2xTG73VuqA, on January 21, 2016.

[3] "Në Tomor, 17.09.2015." Accessed at https://www.youtube.com/watch?v=g95XpfeAehE, on January 21, 2016.

phylactery; the carcass' shoulders are kept by those who offered the *kurban*, while the rest is given to relatives or close friends, by which act the blessing of the *kurban* in this saintly place is believed to be transferred to those who receive the other parts of the sacrificed animal.

Figure 17: Capital of a Funerary Stele from the Türbe of Abbas Ali with a photograph underneath. Top of Kulmak, Mount Tomorr, Southern Albania.

Two types of pilgrims were observed: a religious fervour type, driven by piety, and a curiosity type, driven by the appeal of something unknown. Both types enjoy documenting themselves at the shrine with photographs. Rich in kind and in-cash donations by pilgrims not only significantly sustains the local economy, but also contributes generously to the central Bektashi authorities. The first type of pilgrims tend also to get pieces of stone or earth from the *teke* and *türbe* of Abbas Ali, on Mount Tomorr to invoke the protection of the saintly man.

ANALYSIS

All four pilgrimages described above are situated in high altitude; death salience in these pilgrimages is projected in various ways. These ways are related to the very pilgrimage site, sites associated with and in close proximity to it, contacts with sick people or people with serious mental or other disabilities, as well as sacrificial rituals.

E. Turner (2012, 164-5), in her construct of the *communitas* of nature has argued that the experience and recognition of energy in nature has "something to do with religion. At this stage, the soul comes creeping back, with facts about healing, the *communitas* of the land, and our undeniable relationship with the animals and plants as well as with each other." Situated in high places, undergoing a penitential pilgrimage to the pilgrimage sites under study involves not only contact with the energy in nature, but also a perilous and painstaking walk to stony paths. The intervention of the pilgrimage's centre to repair (Krujë), widen (Laç) or otherwise provide spiritual comfort to pilgrims (Pepel) is evidence of recognition of the journey's perils by the centre; in recognition that the pathways with their dangers limit the number of pilgrimages, access to the pilgrimage centres was also made through asphalted (Kruja and Laçi) or stone roads (Tomorr), suitable for cars. The destruction of the infrastructure to ease the perils of Pepel's pilgrimage journey indicates the vital role of a community running the pilgrimage centre. Both the construction and the deconstruction of infrastructure point to the temporalization of landscape, a fundamental element in the apprehension of landscape in the dwelling perspective (Ingold 1993).While forests are known for filling those passing them with trepidation (Giakoumis 2014, 103-4), two of the pilgrimage sites are or used to be in forested areas (Laç, Pepel). Moreover, two of our sites were at or contained caves (Laç, Krujë). Turner's belief that caves represented "both birth and death, womb and tomb" (Turner 1986, 42; Turner 1987, 25-6), informed by extensive research by John Pfeiffer (1982, 174-90) to prove that caves were once ritual theatres (Schechner 1985, 361), seems to gain support by the message invoking life and death by the young pilgrim in Laç. After all, the association of death and life with caves is also biblical, as noted by the nativity of Christ (Protevangelium of James 18:1) burial and resurrection of Lazarus (John 11:38) and Jesus (Mt. 27:60) in caves (cf. Taylor 1993, 157-206).

The use of paths that saintly figures once walked, together with the veneration and rituals at locations used by these same figures, as well as the souvenirs sold at these locations, are all important in the way pilgrims imagine the past in landscape. The rock dent where St. Blaise is supposed to have rested on his way to his cave at Laç, or the footprints of Sari Satlik in Kruja and of Abbas Ali on Mount Tomorr, are spots in which pilgrims perform a *materializing* mode of imagining the past in the sacred landscape, which "turns the past into an object of memory, to be displayed and consumed as heritage" (Ingold 2012, 8). The process of walking along the sacred path forges memories "of redrawing the lines and pathways" of saintly activity; this is what Tim Ingold classifies as *gestural* mode of imagining the past in landscape (Ingold 2012, 8; cf. Vergunst 2012, 36). Last, souvenirs sold at these pilgrimages offer a *quotidian* mode, whereby the souvenir recreates "what remains from the past and provides a basis for carrying on" (Ingold 2012, 8).

The association of our pilgrimages with deserted, dead sites or tombs also seems to evoke death salience. The pilgrimage of St. Anthony of Padua in Laç is not only close to the deserted city of Sebaste and thus helped pacify popular fears of deserted places being haunted (Giakoumis 2014, 104); but was once next to a cemetery (Zamputi 1965, 243-5). The *türbe*/tombs of Bektashi saints (Sari Satlik and Abbas Ali) or tombs of deceased dervishes in the *teke*s of Kruja and Mount Tomorr; the cemetery from which the pilgrimage at Laç starts and the pilgrims with physical and mental disabilities one can encounter there; and legends of people with mental disorders tied on logs in the "depths" of Pepel Monastery's "basements," who were thus tortured to death invoke echoes of death to pilgrims. Last but not least, the very act of bloody sacrifice (Krujë, Tomorr) is in itself salient of death, as it removes life from a living sacrificial animal in order to invoke the help of a saint in preserving life. There is a dialectic relation between sacrifice/death and life (Esposito 2010, 33): "Sacrificing life to its preservation is the only way of containing the threat that menaces life. Yet this is the equivalent of preserving and perpetuating as well life's capacity to be sacrificed; to 'normalize' the possibility if not the reality, of its sacrifice."

We would argue that the collection of various phylacteries from such pilgrimage places which in various ways invoke fear of death, not least on account of their site on high altitudes, demonstrates that there is a binary association between 'fear of death' and 'preserving life;' fear is never alone; it comes with hope: "Hobbes admits as much when in *De homine* he explains that hope is born from conceiving an evil together with a way of avoiding it, while fear consists, once a good is in view, in imagining a way of losing it. From this we read his conclusion, which sounds like a substantial identification between fear and hope: And so it is manifest that *hope* and *fear* so alternate with each other that almost no time is so short that it cannot encompass their interchange. "Isn't it hope that pushes men to trust in themselves, carrying them right up to the edge of the abyss?" (Esposito 2010, 21-2)

Group solidarity in the pilgrimages sites under consideration is evidenced by the rarity of solitary pilgrimage in the sites under study and experienced through the observation of multiple *communitas*. The term was extensively used by Turner to denote "a relational quality of full, unmediated communication, even communion, between people of definite and determinate identity, which arises spontaneously in all kinds of groups, situations, and circumstances" (Turner 2004, 97). David and Edith Turner argued that pilgrimage is an activity in which *communitas* flowers (*op. cit.*, 99), as…

> … [f]riends are made and a sense of sacredness grows as the days of travel go by. The religion and the forward urging of the people, often in collective prayer, together produce an elated sense of sisterhood among all, something that draws pilgrims to come again year after year.

Considering that "the pilgrimage situation does not eliminate structural divisions" (*op. cit.*), we suggest that there is no single *communitas* developed in a single pilgrimage situation, but rather multiple, of different constitution and not rarely in conflict to each other, as indicated by the Abbas Ali *teke*'s administration vs. vendors' clash. The existence of multiple *communitas* in a pilgrimage site is also implied by Nataša Gregorič-Bon (2014, 145), when she refers to pilgrimage to Stravridi Monastery, Himarra (South Albania), where "pilgrims redefine their identity through their links or 'meetings' with other people." Thus, the suggestions of multiple *communitas* with occasionally contending interests or agendas is in line with John Eade and Michael Sallnow's critique (1991, reprint 2013) of endemic conflict in pilgrimage, which permit religious power hierarchies to decide the major outcome of pilgrimage. In the field we distinguished twelve different types of *communitas* (**Annex 1**):

> **1. Penitential Route to Pilgrimage *Communitas*:** This involves the sort of bond developed between people who undertake the long, tiring and dangerous pathway to a mountainous pilgrimage, which enabled K. Giakoumis to develop a degree of familiarity that enabled the observation of valuable insights regarding the Laç, Krujë and Tomorr pilgrimages.
> **2. Pilgrims in Danger & Locals *Communitas*:** This *communitas* is constructed between pilgrims who face the dangers of the route to a pilgrimage site and local inhabitants who run to their help. The intimacy developed between the local inhabitants of Tomorr with K. Giakoumis as they helped him pull his car out of the snow made a third expedition possible.
> **3. Non-Penitential Route to Pilgrimage *Communitas*:** This refers to bonds developed between those who simultaneously undertake pilgrimage to the same destination by public or private transport (i.e. with transport other than family cars).
> **4. Extended Family Members, Present or Non-Present *Communitas*:** Pilgrims at the pilgrimage sites of Laç, Krujë and Tomorr in their prayers or *kurban*s commemorated all members of the extended family, whether present or not in the pilgrimage. Such bonds also involved communication prior to the pilgrimage undertaking, so that photographs or pieces of cloth be taken; as well as after the pilgrimage, once these items or other phylacteries taken from the pilgrimage sites are handed to family members not present in the pilgrimage.
> **5. Village Festivity Spot *Communitas*:** On the Pepel Monastery's feast day every neighboring village was reported to have its own threshing floor for dancing. This type of *communitas* therefore refers to bonds developed in the course of common participation to the pilgrimage's festivities.
> **6. Fellow Youth *Communitas*:** This type refers to the sort of bond developed between young people, present or not in a pilgrimage site. The 20-years-old pilgrim at the monastery of St. Anthony in Laç who enjoined his fellow-youth to live their lives because life is short is good evidence of such bonds. By extension, it is assumed that such type of *communitas* can also develop amongst people of other age-groups.
> **7. Religious Services' *Communitas*:** This regards the sort of relations developed by people participating in common liminal activities, such as various religious services.

8. Groups of Pilgrims with a Pilgrimage Site's Guide *Communitas*: This is the relational quality of communication and communion between various groups of pilgrims with the pilgrimage site's guides; such a *communitas* develops only in pilgrimage sites with a community running them.

9. Vendors and Buyers *Communitas*: Vendors often develop relations with their buyers beyond the limits of a transaction, such as when they are called to slaughter a sacrificial animal, or when asked on the rituals to be performed at a pilgrimage site.

10. Healthy Pilgrims with People with Problems, Present or not, *Communitas*: This type can be real or imagined and is manifested in the prayers of people for relatives or others with mental or other sorts of problems observed in such pilgrimage sites, as is Laç, Krujë and Tomorr.

11. *Kurban* Rituals' *Communitas*: People contributing to a *kurban*, present or not in a pilgrimage site, are linked with a bond of unity manifested by the consummation of the same *kurban*; they are often in communion to relatives, poor people or the pilgrimage's people, as a portion of the *kurban* is given to them. Such relations also develop between persons called to slaughter the *kurbans* (Krujë, Tomorr), or persons who roast their *kurbans* simultaneously (Tomorr).

12. *Communitas* of People Sleeping at the Same Pilgrimage Place: Pilgrims with overnight sojourn in a pilgrimage site often develop relations with fellow pilgrims sleeping at the same place or close to it.

Annex 1 contextualizes these types of *communitas* with observations made at the pilgrimage sites under study in this chapter.

CONCLUSIONS

In this essay we have presented evidence that high-altitude and mountainous pilgrimage carries a direct connection with nearness to death and consequently enhances both spirituality and the feeling of communion with God (a "higher state of being") as well as the greater transcendent understanding of the religious community. We have therefore endeavoured to show that the feeling of nearness to death, or "remembrance of death": 1) bears a direct relationship with altitude and mountainous terrain; 2) increases in-group solidarity; and 3) enhances the experience of religious pilgrimage, as it facilitates a direct connection with the transcendent spiritual realm beyond the earth. As such, remembrance of death – enhanced by the ascetic practice of ascending away from the lower and heavier realm of the "earth" towards the more spiritual and areal realm of "heaven" – together with a desire to maintain spiritual continuity and contact with the divine, enhances in-group solidarity to the various *communitas* established in the course of pilgrimage (Gregorič-Bon 2014, 145). These conclusions emerged in the context of studying four mountainous pilgrimage sites from Albania (<u>Orthodox Christian Pilgrimages</u>: the Monastery of the Holy Trinity in Pepel, Gjirokastër; <u>Catholic Christian</u>: Saint Anthony of Padua, Laç; <u>Bektashi</u>: The Tomb of Sari Satlik, Krujë) as well as one site which attracts both Christian (Feast of the Dormition of the Virgin, August 15) and Bektashi pilgrims (*Teke* and *Türbe* of Abbas Ali, August 20-25) throughout different days of August.

In-group solidarity achieved in close rapport with the actual pilgrimage site is also indicated by the multiple visits of pilgrims to the same locations. The provisions made by the pilgrimage centres to facilitate both the pathway and destination of pilgrimage, as well as to moderate, yet, not eliminate fear of death, constitute cases in which a pilgrimage centre intervenes and modifies natural landscapes. The link between the feeling of nearness to death and in-group solidarity seems to support a structuralist interpretation of pilgrimage in mountainous sites – that is, as supporting social order. However, the diversity of representations of such pilgrimage by different actors within and outside the cultic constituency challenges positivist premises of phenomenological approaches.

Annex 1: Table of the types of Communitas encountered in each Pilgrimage Site.

Pilgrimage Sites	Types of *Communitas*											
	1. Penitential Route to Pilgrimage	2. Pilgrim(s) in Danger & Locals	3. Non-Penitential Route to Pilgrimage	4. Extended Family (Present & Non-Present)	5. Village Festivity Spot	6. Fellow Youth (Present or Imagined)	7. Religious Services	8. Groups of Pilgrims with a Pilgrimage Site's Guide	9. Vendors & Buyers	10. Healthy Pilgrims & People with Problems (Present or not)	11. *Kurban* Rituals	12. Pilgrims sleeping at the same place.
1. St. Anthony of Padua in Laç	X		X			X	X	X	X	X	X	
2. Holy Trinity Monastery, Pepel	X		X	X	X		X		X			
3. Teke of Sarı Satlık, Krujë	X	X	X	X			X	X	X	X	X	
4. Teke and Türbe of Abbas Ali, Tomorr Mountain	X	X	X	X			X	X	X	X	X	X

REFERENCES

Ahrensdorf, Peter J. 2000. "The Fear of Death and the Longing of Immortality: Hobbes and Thucydides on Human Nature and the Problem of Anarchy." *American Political Science Review* 94: 579-93.

Baras, Vasileios. 1966. *Το Δέλβινο της Βορείου Ηπείρου και οι Γειτονικές του Περιοχές Αργυροκάστρου, Χειμάρρας, Πωγωνίου, Φιλιατών, Παραμυθίας, κλπ*.Athens.

Becker, Ernest. 1971. *The Birth and Death of Meaning*, 2nd edition. New York: Free Press.

Becker, Ernest. 1973. *The Denial of Death*. New York: Academic Press.

Becker, Ernest. 1975. *Escape from Evil*, 2nd edition. New York: Academic Press.

Bernard, Russell H. 2006. *Research Methods in Anthropology. Qualitative and Quantitative Approaches*, 4th edition. Lanham, New York, Toronto, Oxford: Altamira Press.

Blasi, Anthony. 2002. "Visitation to Disaster Sites." In *From Medieval Pilgrimage to Religious Tourism*, edited by William H. Swatos and Luigi Tomasi, 159-80. Westport, CT: Praeger.

Carpenter, Eugene E. and Comfort, Philip W. 2000. *Holman Treasury of Key Bible Words*. Nashville: Holman Reference.

Chouliaras, Ioannis. 2015. "ΤοΑσκηταριότων «Αγιών» στηνΠεριοχήΔελβινακίουΙωαννίνων. Πρώτες Παρατηρήσεις σε Ένα Άγνωστο Βυζαντινό Σύνολο." In *Αφιέρωμα στον Ακαδημαϊκό Παναγιώτη Λ. Βοκοτόπουλο*. Edited by Vasilis Katsaros and Anastasia Tourta, 377-87. Athens: Kapon.

Chrysochoidis, Kriton. 2007. Introduction to *Έντυπες Ακολουθίες Αγίων. Συλλογή Ντόρης Παπαστράτου*, by Dimosthenis Stratigopoulos, xiii-xlviii. Athens: National Hellenic Research Foundation.

Claval, Paul. 2007. "Changing Conceptions of Heritage and Landscape." In *Heritage, Memory and the Politics of Identity. New Perspectives on the Cultural Landscape*, edited by Niamh Moore and Yvonne Whelan, 85-93. Aldershot and Burlington: Ashgate.

Clayer, Nathalie. 1990. *L'Albanie, Pays des Derviches: Les Ordres Mystiques Musulmans en Albanie à l'Époque Post-Ottomane (1912–1967)*. Berlin and Wiesbaden: Otto Harrassowitz.

Coleman, Simon and Eade, John. 2004. *Reframing Pilgrimage. Cultures in Motion*. London and New York: Routledge.

Degrand, Jules Alexandre Théodore. 1901. *Souvenirs de la Haute-Albanie*. Paris: Welter.

De Rapper, Gilles, 2012. "The *Vakëf:* Sharing Religious Space in Albania." In *Sharing Sacred Spaces in the Mediterranean. Christians, Muslims and Jews at Shrines and Sanctuaries*, edited by Diogene Albera and Maria Couroucli, 29-50. Bloomington and Indianapolis: Indiana University Press.

Dezutter, Jessie, Soenens, Bart, and Hutsebaut, Dirk. 2006. "Religiosity and

Mental Health: A Further Exploration of the Relative Importance of Religious Behaviors versus Religious Attitudes." *Personality and Individual Differences* 40/4: 807-818.

Eade, John and Sallnow, Michael J. (Eds.). 2013. *Contesting the sacred: The anthropology of Christian pilgrimage*. Eugene, OR: Wipf and Stock Publishers.

Eliade, Mircea. 1959. *The Sacred and the Profane: The Nature of Religion*, trans. Willard R. Trask. New York: Harvest.

Elsie, Robert. 2001. *A Dictionary of Albanian Religion, Mythology, and Folk Culture*. New York: New York University Press.

Elsie, Robert. 2010. *Historical Dictionary of Albania*. Lanham: The Scarecrow Press.

Encyclopaedia Britannica Online, s. v. "high place", accessed January 21, 2016, http://www.britannica.com/topic/high-place.

Esposito, Roberto. 2010. *Communitas. The Origin and Destiny of the Community*, trans. Timothy Campbell. Stanford: Stanford University Press.

Evangelidis, Dimitrios, 1919. *Η Βόρειος Ήπειρος*. Athens: Σύλλογος προς Διάδοσιν Ωφελίμων Βιβλίων.

Fortner, Barry V. and Neimeyer, Robert A. 1999. "Death Anxiety in Older Adults: A Quantitative Review." *Death Studies* 23:387-411.

Foundoulis, Ioannis. 1992. "'Όσιος Συμεών ὁ Στυλίτης." *O Poimen (Ὁ Ποιμήν)* 57: 223□227.

Gennep, Arnold van. 2004. *The Rites of Passage*, reprint. London: Routledge.

Gesser, Gina, Wong, Paul T.P., and Reker, Gary T. 1987-88. "Death Attitudes across the Life-Span: The Development and Validation of the Death Attitude Profile." *OMEGA – Journal of Death and Dying* 18/2:113-28.

Giakoumis, Georgios. 1994. *Μνημεία Ορθοδοξίας στην Αλβανία*. Athens: Doukas Publ.

Giakoumis, Konstantinos. 2002. "The Monasteries of Jorgucat and Vanishtë in Dropull and of Spelaio in Lunxhëri as Monuments and Institutions During the Ottoman Period in Albania (16th-19th Centuries)." Ph.D. diss. The University of Birmingham.

Giakoumis, Konstantinos. 2008-2012. "Dialectics of Pragmatism in Ottoman Domestic Interreligious Affairs. Reflections on the Ottoman Legal Framework of Church Confiscation and Construction and a 1741 Firman for Ardenicë Monastery." *Balkan Studies* 47: 73-132, 238-9.

Giakoumis, Konstantinos. 2013. "An Enquiry Into the Construction, Deconstruction, Transubstantiation and Reconstruction of Christian Pilgrimages in Modern-Day Albania." *Ηπειρωτικό Ημερολόγιο* 32: 267-318.

Giakoumis, Konstantinos. 2014. "From Religious to Secular and Back Again: Christian Pilgrimage Space in Albania." In *Pilgrimage, Politics and Place-Making in Eastern Europe: Crossing the Borders*, edited by John Eade and Mario Katić, 103-18. London: Ashgate.

Giakoumis, Konstantinos, and Egro, Dritan. 2010. "Ottoman Pragmatism in Domestic Inter-Religious Affairs: The Legal Framework of Church

Construction in the Ottoman Empire and the 1741 Firman of Ardenicë Monastery." *ΗπειρωτικάΧρονικά*44: 73-127.

Giakoumis, Konstantinos, and Lockwood, Christopher. 2015. "Pilgrimage Centered at Text and Memory: The Lapidar in Qukës–Pishkash." *Lapidari*, edited by Vincent van Gervain Oei, vol. 1, 89-96 (Albanian translation, 97-104). Brooklyn NY: Punctum Books.

Gikas, Photis. Jan. 15, 2015. "Τα σπουδαιότερα πανηγύρια της Δρόπολης πριν την απαγόρευση της θρησκείας – Αγία Τριάδα Πέπελης και Παναγία Επισκοπής." Accessed January 25, 2016. https://vorioipirotes.com/2015/01/15/%CF%84%CE%B1-%CF%83%CF%80%CE%BF%CF%85%CE%B4%CE%B1%CE%B9%CF%8C%CF%84%CE%B5%CF%81%CE%B1-%CF%80%CE%B1%CE%BD%CE%B7%CE%B3%CF%8D%CF%81%CE%B9%CE%B1%CF%84%CE%B7%CF%82-%CE%B4%CF%81%CF%8C%CF%80%CE%BF%CE%BB/

Greenberg, Jeff, and Arndt, Jamie. 2012. "Terror Management Theory." In *Handbook of Theories of Social Psychology*, edited by Paul A.M. Van Lange, Arie W. Kruglanski, and E. Torry Higgins, 398-415. London: Sage.

Greenberg, Jeff, Koole, Sander L., Pyszczynski, Tom. 2004. *Handbook of Experimental Existentialist Psychology*. New York: The Guilford Press.

Greenberg, Jeff, Pyszczynski, Tom, Solomon, Sheldon, Rosenblatt, Abram, Veeder, Mitchell, Kirkland, Shari, and Lyon, Deborah. 1990. "Evidence for Terror Management Theory II: The Effects of Mortality Salience on Reactions to those who Threaten or Bolster the Cultural Worldview." *Journal of Personality and Social Psychology* 58/2: 308-318.

Greenberg, Jeff, Solomon, Sheldon, and Arndt, Jamie. 2008. "A Uniquely Human Motivation: Terror Management." In *Handbook of Motivation Science*, edited by James Y. Shah and Wendi L. Gardner, 113-34. New York: Guilford.

Greenberg, Jeff, Pyszczynski, Tom, and Solomon, Sheldon. 1986. "The Causes and Consequences of a Need for Self-Esteem: A Terror Management Theory". In *Public Self and Private Self*, edited by Roy F. Baumeister, 189-212. New York: Springer-Verlag.

Gregorič-Bon, Nataša. 2014. "Secular Journeys, Sacred Places: Pilgrimage and Home-Making in the Himarë/Himara Area of Southern Albania." In *Pilgrimage, Politics and Place-Making in Eastern Europe: Crossing the Borders*, edited by John Eade and Mario Katić, 135-49. London: Ashgate.

Hirsch, Emily G. 1906. "High Place." *The Jewish Encyclopedia*, vol. 6, 387-9. New York: Ktav.

Hirsch, Eric. 1995. "Introduction. Landscape: Between Place and Space." In *The Anthropology of Landscape. Perspectives on Place and Space*, edited by Eric Hirsch and Michael O'Hanlon, 1-30. London: Clarendon Press.

Hoffmann, Richard C. 2014. *An Environmental History of Medieval Europe*. Cambridge: Cambridge University Press.

Ingold, Tim. 1993. "The Temporality of the Landscape." *World Archaeology*,

vol. 25/2: 152-174.
Ingold, Tim. 2011. *Being Alive. Essays on Movement, Knowledge and Description.* London and New York: Routledge.
Ingold, Tim. 2012. "Introduction." In *Imagining Landscapes. Past, Present and Future*, edited by Monica Janowski and Tim Ingold, 1-18. Farnham & Burlington: Ashgate.
John, Climacus, Saint. 1959. *The Ladder of Divine Ascent.* Translated by Archimandrite Lazarus Moore. London: Harper and Brothers.
Kaleshi, Hasan. 1971. "Albanische Legenden um Sari Saltuk." In *Actes du Premier Congrès International des Études Balkaniques et Sud-Est Européennes* 7: 815-28.
Kearl, Michael. 2009. "Death, Sociological Perspectives". In *Encyclopedia of Death & Human Experience*, edited by Clifton D. Bryant and Denis L. Peck, 291-6. London: Sage.
Kiel, Machiel. 1995. "A Note on the Date of the Establishment of the Bektashi Order in Albania: The Cult of Sarı Saltık Dede in Kruja attested in 1567-1568." In *Bektachiyya, Études sur l'Ordre Mystique des Bektachis et les Groupes Relevant de Hadji Bektach*, edited by Alexandre Popovic and Gilles Veinstein, 169-76. Istanbul: Isis Press.
Kołczyńska, Marta. 2013. "On the Asphalt Path to Divinity. Contemporary Transformations in Albanian Bektashism: The Case of Sari Saltik *Teke* in Kruja." *Anthropological Journal of European Cultures* 22/2: 51-71.
Legat, Allice. 2008. "Walking Stories; Leaving Footprints." In *Ways of Walking. Ethnography and Practice on Foot*, edited by Tim Ingold and Jo Lee Vergunst, 35-49. Aldershot and Burlington: Ashgate.
Louth, Andrew. 2007. *Greek East and Latin West: The Church, AD 681-1071.* New York: St Vladimir's Seminary Press.
Lucian of Samostata. 1913. *De Syria Dea (The Syrian Goddess).* Translated by Herbert A. Strong and John Garstang. London: Constable.
Lee, Dorothy. 2004. "On the Holy Mountain: The Transfiguration in Scripture and Tradition." *Colloquium* 36/2 (2004): 143-59.
Lund, Katrín. 2008. "Listen to the Sound of Time: Walking with Saints in an Andalusian Village." In *Ways of Walking. Ethnography and Practice on Foot*, edited by Tim Ingold and Jo Lee Vergunst, 93-103. Aldershot and Burlington: Ashgate.
Mammopoulos, Alexandros. 1980. "Στην Αγία Τριάδα της Πέπελης." In *Η Δρόπολις Β. Ηπείρου*. Edited by Alexandros Mammopoulos. Athens: O Drinos.
Meistermann, Barnabas. "Transfiguration." *The Catholic Encyclopedia*. Vol. 15. New York: Robert Appleton Company, 1912. Accessed January 29 2016. http://www.newadvent.org/cathen/15019a.htm.
Menuge, Noël James. 2000. "The Foundation Myth: Some Yorkshire Monasteries and the Landscape Agenda." *Landscapes* 1/1: 22-37.
Morinis, Alan, 1992. "Introduction: The Territory of the Anthropology of Pilgrimage." In *Sacred Journeys. The Anthropology of Pilgrimage*, edited by Alan Morinis, 1-27. Westport, CT: Greenwood Press.

Neimeyer, Robert A. 1994. *Death Anxiety Handbook: Research, Instrumentation, and Application.* Washington D.C.: Taylor and Francis.

Neimeyer, Robert A., Wittkowski, Joachim, and Moser, Richard P. 2004. "Psychological Research on Death Attitudes: An Overview and Evaluation." *Death Studies* 28:309-40.

Norris, Harry T. 1993. *Islam in the Balkans: Religion and Society between Europe and the Arab World.* London: Hurst & Company.

Oei, Vincent van Gervain, ed. 2015. *Lapidari*, 3 vols. Brooklyn NY: Punctum Books.

Osmani, Edlira. "God in the Eagle's Country: The Bektashi Order." *Quaderns de la Mediterrània* 17 (2012): 107-16.

Pappa, Eutychia. 2009. "Η Επαρχία Δρυϊνουπόλεως της Β. Ηπείρου κατά τη Νεώτερη Περίοδο (Τουρκοκρατία, 20ός Αιώνας.)"Ph.D. diss., Aristotle University of Thessaloniki.

Pfeiffer, John E. 1982. *The Creative Explosion: An Inquiry into the Origins of Art and Religion.* Ithaca, NY: Cornell University Press.

Popa, Theofan. 1965. "Piktura e shpellave eremite ne Shqipni." *Studime Historike*19 (3): 69-101.

Popa, Theofan. 1998. *Mbishkrime të kishave në Shqipëri.* Edited by Nestor Nepravishta and Kostandin Gjakumis. Tirana: Akademia e Shkencave - Instituti i Historisë.

Prelaj, Marjan, and Kurti, Donat. 2013. *Histori e Vogël mbi Shenjtorën e Shna Ndout në Sebaste*, Shkodra: Botime Françeskane.

Preston, James J. 1992. "Spiritual Magnetism: An Organising Principle for the Study of Pilgrimage." In *Sacred Journeys. The Anthropology of Pilgrimage*, edited by Alan Morinis, 31-46. Westport, CT: Greenwood Press.

Property Register of Monasteries in the Metropolis of Dryinoupolis and Argyrokastron, Central Archives of the State, Tirana F. 137, D. 2 (1868-1873).

Reinhard, Johan, and Ceruti, Constanza. 2005. "Sacred Mountains, Ceremonial Sites, and Human Sacrifice Among the Incas." *Archaeoastronomy*19:1-43.

Rossi, Pjetro. 2013. *Shna Ndou i Padovës. Shenjti i Gjithë Botës.* Translated by Tefe Krroqi. Edited by p. Zef Pllumi. Shkodra: Botime Françeskane.

Schama, Simon. 1995. *Landscape and Memory.* New York: Vintage Books.

Schechner, Richard. 1986. "Magnitudes of Performance." In *The Anthropology of Experience.* Edited by Victor W. Turner and Edward M. Bruner, 344-69. Urbana and Chicago: University of Illinois Press.

Shaikh, Fazlur Rehman.2001. *Chronology of Prophetic Events.* London: Ta-Ha, 2001.

Sophrony, Archimandrite. 1991. *Saint Silouan the Athonite*, trans. Rosemary Edmonds. Crestwood: SVS.

Sophrony, Archimandrite. 2006. *We Shall See Him as He Is*, trans. Rosemary Edmonds. Platina: St. Herman of Alaska.

Stamatiadis, Kalliopios, ed. 1896. Ἀκολουθία τοῦ Ὁσίου καὶ Θεοφόρου Πατρὸς ἡμῶν Κλήμεντος Ἀσκήσαντος ἐν τῷ Ὄρει Σαγματᾷ τῆς Βοιωτίας

Ἑορταζομένη τὴν 26 Ἰανουαρίου. Athens: Athanasiadis.
Stravinskas, Peter M.J. 2002. *Catholic Dictionary*. Huntington, IN: Our Sunday Visitor.
Swatos, William H., and Tomasi, Luigi. 2002. "Epilogue: Pilgrimage for a New Millennium." In *From Medieval Pilgrimage to Religious Tourism*, edited by William H. Swatos and Luigi Tomasi, 207-8. Westport, CT: Praeger.
Taylor, Joan E. 1993. *Christians and the Holy Places. The Myth of Jewish-Christian Origins*. Oxford: Clarendon Press.
Tomasi, Luigi. 2002. "Homo Viator: from Pilgrimage to Religious Tourism Via the Journey." In *From Medieval Pilgrimage to Religious Tourism*, edited by William H. Swatos and Luigi Tomasi, 1-24. Westport, CT: Praeger.
Thucydides. 1963. *History*, 2 vols. Edited by Henry Stuart Jones and J. Enoch Powell. Oxford: Clarendon.
Thomo, Pirro. 1998. *Kishat Pasbizantine në Shqipërinë e Jugut*. Tirana: Botim i Kishës Orthodhokse Autoqefale të Shqipërisë.
Tirta, Mark. June 1976. "Survivances Religieuses du Passé dans la Vie du Peuple (Objets et Lieux de Culte)." *Ethnographie Albanaise*, special edition, 49-69. Tirana.
T.L. n.d. "ΤοΜοναστήριτηςΑγίαςΤριάδαςστηνΠέπελη." Accessed in January 17, 2016. http://www.pepeli.gr/%CE%B7-%CE%B1%CE%B3%CE%B9%CE%B1%CF%84%CF%81%CE%B9%CE%B1%CE%B4%CE%B1/
Turner, Edith. 2004. "Communitas, Rites of." In *Encyclopedia of Religious Rites, Rituals and Festivals*, edited by Frank A. Salamone, 97-101. New York: Routledge.
Turner, Edith. 2012. *Communitas. The Anthropology of Collective Joy*. New York: Palgrave-MacMillan.
Turner, Victor. 1969. *The Ritual Process: Structure and Anti-Structure*. Chicago: Aldine.
Turner, Victor, and Turner, Edith. 1978. *Image and Pilgrimage in Christian Culture: Anthropological Perspectives*. New York: Columbia University Press.
Turner, Victor. 1986. "Dewey, Dilthey, and Drama. An Essay in the Anthropology of Experience." In *The Anthropology of Experience*. Edited by Victor W. Turner and Edward M. Bruner, 33-44. Urbana and Chicago: University of Illinois Press.
Vergunst, Jo. 2012. "Seeing Ruins: Imagined and Visible Landscapes in North-East Scotland." In *Imagining Landscapes. Past, Present and Future*, edited by Monica Janowski and Tim Ingold, 19-37. Farnham & Burlington: Ashgate.
Vranousis, Leandros. 1966. "Πρόλογος" and "ΒασίλειοςΜπαράς (1887-1964.)" In Vasileios Baras. 1966. *Το Δέλβινο της Βορείου Ηπείρου και οι Γειτονικές του Περιοχές Αργυροκάστρου, Χειμάρρας, Πωγωνίου, Φιλιατών, Παραμυθίας, κλπ*.Athens.
Wink, Paul, and Scott, Julia. 2005. "Does Religiousness Buffer against the Fear

of Death and Dying in Late Adulthood? Findings from a Longitudinal Study." *Journal of Gerontology: Psychological Sciences* 60B/4:207-14.

Zamputi, Injak. 1965. *Relacione mbi gjendjen e Shqipërisë veriore dhe të mesme në shekullin XVII (1634-1650).* Tirana: Universiteti Shtetëror, Instituti i Historisë dhe i Gjuhësisë.

Zecher, Jonathan L. 2011. "The Symbolics of Death and the Construction of Christian Asceticism: Greek Patristic Voices from the Fourth through Seventh Centuries." Ph.D. diss., Durham University.

Zecher, Jonathan L. 2015. *The Role of Death in the Ladder of Divine Ascent and the Greek Ascetic Tradition.* Oxford: Oxford University Press.

RELIGIOUS LANDSCAPE AT THE BORDER: THE CASE OF THE BORDER REGIONS OF PETRICH, BULGARIA AND STRUMICA, MACEDONIA

Violeta Periklieva
Institute of Ethnology and Folklore Studies with Ethnographic Museum,
Bulgarian Academy of Sciences

INTRODUCTION

Religious landscapes have become a topic of some relevance over the past twenty to thirty years, but there is still neither a common definition of this concept nor a particular coherent approach to the use of the various terms – religious landscapes, sacred spaces, sacred geography, etc. (Horster 2010: 436-437). In order to put the present study in a theoretical framework, this paper introduces a working definition of the concept of a religious landscape. After Lenclud (1995), the landscape is a culturally and socially constructed space, a subjective product and structure of interaction. Thus, the landscape is constructed in accordance with a specific conceptual model (social, cultural, religious etc.) inherent in a particular group of people who are in contact with this space. By means of their ideology, social structure, interrelations and relations with other groups, their customs and rites, these people attach specific meaning and content to the landscape, which differ from those that other groups of people attach to other spaces. Landscape is a space that reflects the social and cultural model of specific community; it is a marker of its identity.

Leaning on this understanding of landscape, we could define a religious landscape as a social and cultural space constructed from interactions with specific religious models. A religious landscape reflects the idea that cults and ritual practices exist only if anchored in the space, continuously or temporarily (Scheid, de Polignac 2010: 431). Thus, the material expressions of religiosity (different types of sanctuaries) constitute the religious armature of the space. At the same time however, religious landscape has an intangible and non-visual character; it includes the religious beliefs and discourses associated with its material and visual side (Valtchinova 2015: 19). Therefore, the present study is based on the understanding that religious activities are not only directly connected to sacred geography[1] but rather they constantly shape it as well. A religious landscape is a mirror of the religious life of a people, set in places that actively shape their environment; it is a sort of map that helps to decipher religious processes on local as well as national levels, and to follow the evolution of religious life of communities in a given area.

By decoding the Orthodox Christian religious landscape, the nature of its shaping and functions, this paper attempts to answer the question of what happens to the religious life of a once politically, socio-economically, and culturally uniform region after the demarcation of a state border. Such is the case of Petrich (Bulgaria) and Strumica (Macedonia). The study is based on the author's research and fieldwork in the two regions which started back in 2012 and continues still today.[2]

REGIONAL HISTORY

Regardless of governance, from the 9th century until its liberation from Ottoman rule in 1912, the region of Petrich (Bulgaria) and Strumica (Macedonia) generally shared a common political fate and was not subject to a divisive state border. In the 19th century, with the decline of the Ottoman Empire, the formation of national self-awareness among the subordinate people, and the emergence of nation states on the Balkan map, the region became a scene of various types of national propaganda and political claims. The aspirations of the newly-emerged nation states in the geographical area of Macedonia led to repeated changes of the political border in the region. After the Balkan War of 1912, the region of Petrich was annexed to Bulgaria and the region of Strumica consecutively became part of the Third Bulgarian Kingdom (until 1919), the Kingdom of Serbs, Croats and Slovenes (1919-1941), the Bulgarian Kingdom once again (1941-1944), socialist Yugoslavia, and the Republic of Macedonia. Despite frequent changes, however, the border was "permeable" until 1948 and the population on both sides was relatively free to move within the bordering region. This meant that for centuries communication between the two spatially adjacent regions of Petrich and Strumica was unhindered, furthering the establishment of close social, economic and cultural relations between their populations. These close contacts and relations were further strengthened by the fact that for centuries the two regions were connected by an important trade road connecting Constantinople and Skopje as well as by another one connecting the

---

[1] Leaving aside the discussion on the use of the various terms related to the concept of religious landscape, for the sake of the linguistic harmony of the text, sacred geography is used here as an alternative to religious landscape.
[2] The study is financed by the Program for career development of young scientists, BAS

western and eastern lands of the geographical region of Macedonia (Пандевски and Стоев 1969: 23-24). The famous Dolyan Fair, which took place annually somewhere within the region of Petrich and Strumica, also played an important role. It was significant for the establishment of traditional trade relations between the Petrich and Strumica regions, as well as for various other forms of contact between their populations. Besides the annual fair, this role was also played by the weekly market days in Strumica, Novo selo, and Petrich, which over the course of time became traditional forces that encouraged contacts between people from the two regions. As a result of these relations and interactions, the region of Petrich and Strumica developed a common local (regional) culture and identity.

After the Tito-Stalin conflict and the resolution of the Cominform Bureau of 1948[3], the state border between Yugoslavia and Bulgaria was closed[4] and became an insuperable obstacle that for decades interrupted almost entirely the relations between the two regions. From the late 1950s and early 1960s, one of the few opportunities for contact between the two regions was the so-called 'border meetings'[5]. Contact was re-established in the beginning of the 1990s until Bulgaria joined the European Union in 2007 and introduced visa requirements with Macedonia. The requirement was revoked in 2009, which further liberated cross-border exchange.

Regarding religious aspects, the region of Petrich and Strumica shared a common course of development until 1919. After the conversion to Christianity in 864 and the decision of the Council of Constantinople of 870 to establish the Bulgarian archbishopric in the lands of the First Bulgarian Kingdom, the development of a church organization began. At first the region of Petrich and Strumica most likely came under the sway of the Diocese of Bregalnitsa

---

[3] Cominform Bureau (Information Bureau of the Communist and Workers' Parties) was an organization of Communist parties founded in September 1947. Its purpose was to coordinate actions between Communist parties under Soviet direction. Josip Broz Tito's emancipation from the Soviet Union and his will to follow Yugoslavia's own interests caused constant conflicts between him and Joseph Stalin. As a result, with a Cominform Resolution of June 28, 1948 the Communist Party of Yugoslavia was accused of departing from Marxism-Leninism and exhibiting an anti-Soviet attitude and Yugoslavia was expelled from the Cominform Bureau. That period of poor relations between Yugoslavia and the Soviet Union lasted until 1955 when after Stalin's death of 1953 Khrushchev reconciled with Tito.

[4] On October 1, 1949 Bulgaria presented the Yugoslavian Embassy in Sofia with a note by means of which all relations and agreements between the two countries were suspended.

[5] After a decade of strictly prohibited border crossing, the border meetings were the first opportunity for the people on both sides of the border to meet. The border meetings were organized once per year and were a form of gathering of people from border regions in Bulgaria and Yugoslavia at a specific place (usually a meadow) on the border. Initially, their aim was to give relatives from neighbouring border regions the chance to meet but in the course of time they transformed into some kind of fairs. The first several years, the border meetings between the population of the regions of Petrich and Strumica were organized on the border but afterwards they were moved to the towns – every year the towns of Petrich and Strumica were alternating at hosting the border meeting.

(Петров and Темелски 2003: 19-26). With the establishment of the Archbishopric of Ohrid in the 11th century, the region entered the Diocese of Strumica (Снегаров 1995: 162). This lasted until 1767 when the Archbishopric of Ohrid was abolished and the two regions came under the authority of the Patriarchate of Constantinople: Petrich became part of the Diocese of Melnik and Strumica became part of the Diocese of Strumica. In the period of the Bulgarian National Revival, the church-national struggle of the Bulgarians led to the establishment in the 1860s of Bulgarian church 'communes' in Petrich and Strumica. With the establishment of the Bulgarian Exarchate in 1870[6] from all Macedonian dioceses, only that of Velesh became part of it. After a long struggle, the majority of the Bulgarians in the region of Petrich went over to the Exarchate in 1892, and in 1897 the Bulgarian Bishopric of Strumica was established (Петров and Темелски 2003: 111-118; Пандевски and Стоев 1969: 128, 170). In 1913, part of the former Diocese of Melnik, including Petrich, joined the Diocese of Strumica. Thus, with respect to religious organization, the spiritual life of the Orthodox Christian population from the two regions was generally, until its final political division, organized by the same ecclesiastical centre, the Diocese of Strumica. Consequently, this arrangement furthered the dissemination of common patterns of religious life and the establishment of common local religiosity in the bordering regions of Petrich and Strumica.

After the Treaty of Neuilly of 1919, in which the region of Strumica was integrated with the Kingdom of Serbs, Croats and Slovenes, the Diocese of Strumica fell under the jurisdiction of the Serbian Orthodox Church (SOC). From 1944, an initiative to establish an independent Macedonian church in the territory of Vardar Macedonia began. Thus, in 1958 the Second Macedonian Church National Council decided to restore the Archbishopric of Ohrid under the name of Macedonian Orthodox Church (MOC). The Council elected a Macedonian bishop, head of MOC. He received the title "Archbishop of Ohrid and Skopje and Bishop of Macedonia". However, the relations of MOC and SOC remained unsettled because the latter did not recognize the independent status of the former. In the late 1960s, the relations between the two churches deteriorated and in 1967 a Third Macedonian Church National Council was summoned in Ohrid, where MOC proclaimed itself autocephalous. However, even

---

[6] After the fall of Bulgaria under Ottoman rule in 1396, the Tarnovo Patriarchate in whose diocese was part of the Bulgarian territory was destroyed and its diocese was subordinated to the Patriarchate of Constantinople. The other Bulgarian religious centre, the Archbishopric of Ohrid, managed to survive a few centuries more but in 1767 its diocese was also placed under the jurisdiction of the Patriarchate of Constantinople. As early as the 1820s, a discontent with the supremacy of the Greek clergy started to rise among the Bulgarian population which subsequently transformed into organized struggle for autonomy from the Patriarchate of Constantinople. At the same time, that was a struggle for further rights of the Bulgarians in the Ottoman Empire. Since Ottomans identified nationality with religion and the Bulgarians were Eastern Orthodox Christian, the Ottomans considered them part of the Roum-Milet, i.e. the Greeks. As a result of several decades of struggle, by a decree (firman) of the Sultan promulgated on February 28, 1870 the Ottoman Empire restored the Bulgarian Patriarchate under the name of Bulgarian Exarchate.

today its autocephaly remains unrecognized by the Patriarchate of Constantinople and the rest of the Orthodox Christian churches (Петров and Темелски 2003: 144-147, 155-165).

Thus, although for centuries the regions of Petrich and Strumica shared a common political fate and developed close social, economic, religious, and more generally cultural patterns of behaviour, the roads of these two regions parted.

THE RELIGIOUS LANDSCAPE IN THE REGION OF PETRICH

After 1944, the new socialist authorities in Bulgaria and the ideologically implanted atheism hindered free religious expression, resulting in a transformation of the nature and intensity of religious life. Under the conditions of "stalking" and "slandering" and under the threat of possible sanctions, churches were rarely visited, and usually only by elderly people, and religious rites were strongly reduced – part of the rituals were "domesticated" while others, such as the village and church festivals with kurbans, ceased. These transformations had an impact on the religious landscape in Bulgaria. For decades, until 1989, construction of religious buildings declined. At the same time, for the most part, Christian shrines lost their religious role and were proclaimed and functioned only as cultural monuments. The region of Petrich is no exception to the common process in the country. Generally, the religious landscape in Petrich, which had developed from the mid-19th century to the 1940s, remained unchanged until 1989.[7]

After the fall of socialism in Bulgaria in 1989, processes of transformation of religious life and of intensification of the religious practices began. Throughout Bulgaria there were tendencies toward strengthening the position and role of religion in the public sphere, toward resumption of many Christian practices, and toward an increase in religious activity. These processes are most visible in the religious landscape. An intense phase of building and renovation of old churches seized the country. Thus, one of the basic characteristics of postsocialist religiosity in Bulgaria is in fact its material expression. In the years following 1989, a boom in religious building also occurred in the region of Petrich. It is most tangible in the last 10-15 years and has drastically transformed the religious landscape in the region.

---

[7] After the fall of the region under Ottoman rule in 1395, most Christian shrines were destroyed, and in their place Muslim religious buildings appeared. Other destroyed churches became consecrated grounds where the Christians deprived of religious buildings attended divine services. The resumption of the Christian religious building in the region began in the mid-19th century but reached its culmination after the liberation of Ottoman rule in 1912. Precisely in the period 1912-1944, the religious landscape in Petrich obtained the shape it had almost until the end of the 20th century.

Map 1: Petrich – Strumica map

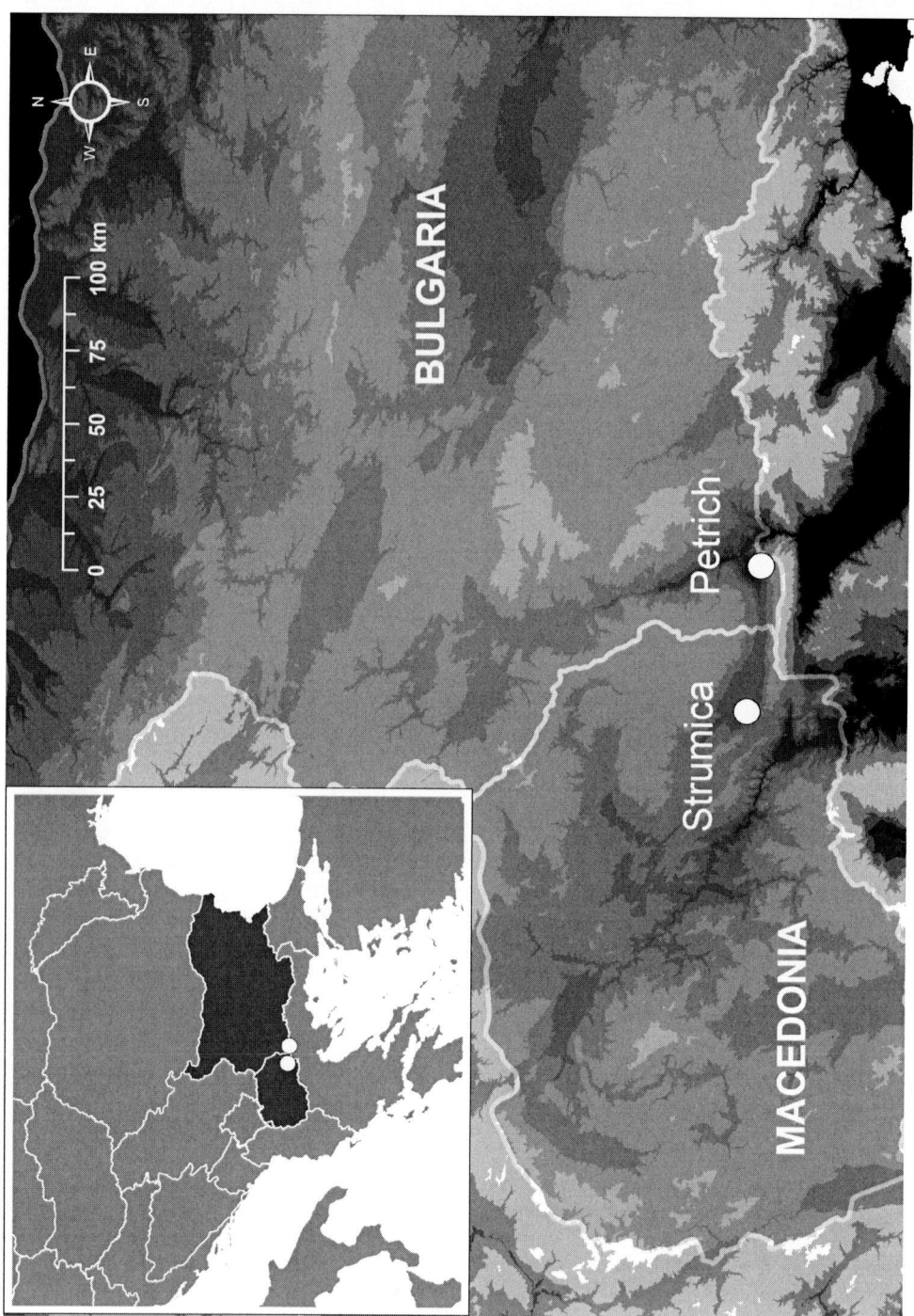

One of the basic characteristics of the transformation of the religious landscape in the region of Petrich in the post-socialist period is the phase of intense building of religious structures in the villages. Until 1944, the concentration of churches was predominantly in the town where almost every old neighbourhood had a church and/or chapel within its territory. During that time, most villages contained only one shrine for people. However, things have changed in the last 15 years. Despite the process of rapid depopulation of villages in the region on one hand, and the expansion of the town on the other, changes in the religious landscape have primarily affected villages. In the town of Petrich during the post-socialist period, only one Christian shrine has been constructed, the Chapel of St. Kyriaki (2005). At the same time, many of the villages whose population does not exceed 1000-2000 people erected several churches and chapels each. This is the case of the village of Skrat with 1007 inhabitants (by 2015) in which today function one church (The Ascension of Jesus Christ) and four chapels (St. Demetrius, St. Elias, St. Theodore, and St. Archangels). Similarly, the inhabitants (1989 in number) of Kolarovo village have three churches (St. Demetrius, St. Menas, and St. Kyriaki) and one chapel (St. Elias).

The significance of this phenomenon is most pronounced in the cases of deserted or nearly deserted villages. Thus, for example, the village of Bogoroditsa, with its 19 inhabitants, has one church (St. Elias) and is surrounded by the ruins of 7 old chapels (St. Elias, St. Paraskevi, St. Spas/Ascension of Jesus Christ, St. Athanasius, St. Kyriaki, St. Menas, and The Blessed Virgin Mary). Foundations of the chapels are still partially visible, and the few inhabitants as well as those who migrated to the town and neighbouring villages, gather there and make kurban for the feast of the respective saint[8]. In the last several years, these old chapels are being rebuilt one after another following the initiative of former inhabitants of the village. Thus, the village received the name "Bulgarian Mount Athos". Even more impressive is the case of the village of Tonsko Dabe, which is completely depopulated. Despite a lack of residents, a new chapel (The Blessed Virgin Mary) was inaugurated in 2012, built with the financial support of a resident of Karnalovo village, who originates from Tonsko Dabe.

---

[8] Every Orthodox Christian religious building is dedicated to some particular saint and celebrates the church feast of its patron saint as a feast of the respective parochial community. The main components of the celebration are the divine service, the kurban and the collective table. In the morning of the patron saint's day the priest holds a service after which he blesses the traditional kurban for the feast. In Bulgarian, the word "kurban" denotes the sacrificial animal and the meal prepared from it as well as the entire ritual complex related to the blood sacrifice. In Western Europe (the Catholic and Protestant world) as well as in the East-European Orthodox world (Russia, Ukraine, Belorussia) the ritual of the blood sacrifice had been eradicated long ago with the help of the church institution and had been replaced with the Christian bloodless sacrifice (the Eucharist). However, in the Balkans and in Bulgaria in particular it is still alive and performed by Orthodox Christians as well as Muslims. On the feast of the patron saint of the churches and chapels, after the priest blesses the sacrificial animal and then the meal prepared of it, usually people sit down to a collective table in the church yard.

Another basic characteristic of the transformation of the religious landscape in the region is its extraecclesiastical nature. Primary changes in sacred geography are initiated, financed, and realized by local people, and in most cases the decisions to build a shrine are not coordinated with the church institution. However, this does not create conflicts, and the Church gladly consecrates the new religious buildings, and the parish priests hold services and bless the kurbans on the feasts of the patron saints.

One of the main forms of initiating changes in the sacred geography of the region "from below", that is, from the people themselves, is 'dreaming'. 'Dreaming' is an ancient and widespread tradition in the Christian Orthodox church in the Balkans that refers to receiving directions from on high, and of announcing and legitimating particular religious initiatives. Usually, it is the Virgin Mary or some other saint who appears in a dream and gives instructions for the building of a church. In other cases, one could dream some unusual phenomenon or certain sacred object (cross, icon etc.). The dreamer understands that if he or she digs in a certain place in the village, he or she would find an icon, a cross, an incense-burner, or some other evidence for the sacredness of a place and the necessity of building a shrine. In the region of Petrich, 'dreaming' as a form of initiating the building of a church could be registered as early as the mid-19th century. As religious activity, 'dreaming' existed also in the socialist period, but as a mechanism for the emergence of sacred buildings, it was revived in the years after 1989. Thus, in some cases, one "received information" in a dream about the necessity of building a shrine as early as the socialist period but the realization of the "command" itself happened only after the fall of the regime that hindered public religious activities. An example for this is the building of the Chapel of St. Elias in the vicinity of the above-mentioned village of Bogoroditsa. As a young girl, Zoya from Bogoroditsa, who is now in her 70s, had an unusual dream. She was at the place of the today's chapel where at the time were the ruins of an old shrine. Suddenly, a dark cloud appeared, swirled around her and disappeared in the ruins. Zoya told the story to baba Vanga,[9] who explained that St. Elias from the old shrine was looking for a new home and that one day she must build it. Decades later, in 2012, Zoya finally finished the building of the Chapel of St. Elias.

In the last 10-15 years, 'dreaming' has enjoyed wide dissemination in the region of Petrich. Many cases of local people dreaming saints has led to the emergence of new churches in the villages or to the restoration of old ones. Thus, we come to the second most popular form of initiating changes in the religious landscape in the region – the restoration of old shrines. The cultural memory of the inhabitants of almost all villages of the region keeps "recollections" of sacred places where there were once shrines. Some of these places function even today, where local people gather for certain feasts and make kurbans. Other places are only known to be sacred, but they are not visited. In both cases, however, the tendency to restore old religious buildings has gained more and more popularity.

---

[9] The figure of the prophetess Vanga is discussed in the text further below.

Usually, the money for their restoration (mainly in the form of small chapels) is donated by particular person or family, but there are also many cases when the inhabitants of the village collect them together. The restoration of a shrine could be just a conscious religious initiative of a person or a group, but it could also be suggested "in a dream".

When speaking of the forms of initiating change in the religious landscape and of legitimating such changes, it is imperative to mention the so-called prophetess Vanga. She fits the notion of an alternative religious specialist, i.e. a mediator between humans and the divine, who perceives herself and is perceived by different social groups or communities as such, but as a rule lies outside the institution that has a monopoly on this mediation, that is, the Church (Valchinova 2002: 91-92). Although most of her life and activities are related to the region of Petrich in South-western Bulgaria, Vanga (Vangelia Gushterova) was born in 1911 in Strumica and initially received her "gift" in this very region. In 1923, Vanga and her father moved from Strumica to the village of Novo selo, Macedonia. Here, she was lifted up by a whirlwind and as a result lost her sight. The accident was a turning point, after which her "gift" was gradually unlocked. Her "career" as an alternative religious specialist began with the onset of World War II when a great number of people from the Strumica region turned to Vanga in order to find out the destiny of their relatives participating in the war. In 1942, Vanga married a man from the region of Petrich and moved with him to the town of Petrich. Here, prophetess's activities gained her popularity, which very soon extended beyond Bulgaria and the Balkans. Despite moving to neighbouring Bulgaria and the closing of the Bulgarian-Yugoslavian border for a long period of time, Vanga remained the most popular alternative for the people of the Strumica region seeking help, crowding in front of her house in Petrich until her death (1996).

As early as the socialist period, Vanga, as well as her houses in Petrich and in nearby Rupite, became part of the religious landscape of the region. At the same time, during her life and after death she has remained a specific trigger for changes in the sacred geography of the area. This is largely due to the fact that while she was still alive she was regarded as a mediator between the people and the divine, while after her death she became a 'living saint', a subject of mass homage, and a cult. Before her death, Vanga initiated the construction of the Church of St. Paraskevi in Rupite; after her death, a large complex was built around the church. The process of sacralisation of the space had an impact on the house of Vanga in Petrich as well; today, it functions as a museum. But beside the fact that the places related to Vanga's activity become part of the religious landscape in the region, her figure legitimizes the emergence of other shrines as well, such as the above-mentioned case of Zoya's dream in the village of Bogoroditsa.

THE RELIGIOUS LANDSCAPE IN THE REGION OF STRUMICA

After 1945, religious life in socialist Yugoslavia did not differ significantly from that of socialist Bulgaria. A purposeful atheistic policy hindered free religious expression, pushed religion out of the public sphere, and "domesticated" it. This policy had an impact on the development of the religious landscape as well; the development ceased and the religious landscape remained generally unchanged in relation to the previous, pre-socialist period.

Similar to Petrich, the pre-socialist religious landscape in Strumica was shaped mainly after the middle of the 19th century and most intensively after the liberation of the region from Ottoman rule in 1912. However, unlike Petrich, the region of Strumica is characterized by a plurality of religious communities, whose active religious life has shaped the sacred geography of the area. In this area, different types of Christian and Islamic denominations coexist. Since the late 14th century, when the area of Strumica was conquered by the Ottoman Empire, Islam has persisted in the region and has deeply impacted the religious landscape. Many Christian shrines were destroyed, with Islamic structures erected in their place. This trend was reversed after the Liberation and the emancipation of this area from Ottoman rule. A major segment of the local Muslim population left for the Ottoman Empire during and after the Balkan Wars (1912-1913) and the First World War. Many Muslim houses of prayer were destroyed by local Christians, mainly Orthodox, who relied on local legends of churches being converted into mosques to claim the latter's transformation back into churches. However, a considerable number of Muslims – Turks as well as Roma – still remain in the area of Strumica.

The vast majority of the Christian population in the region of Strumica is Orthodox, but there are also small communities of Greek Catholics, followers of the Evangelic Methodist Church, and of the Adventist Church, as well as (since the 1990s) Jehovah's Witnesses. The Christian religious minorities in the region of Strumica are relatively recent: the most ancient, the Catholics and a few Protestant denominations, can be easily traced back to the mid-19th or the early 20th century.

After the dissolution of Yugoslavia and the proclamation of Macedonia's independence, changes in religious life also occurred in the country. Apart from tendencies to strengthen the position of religion in the public sphere, resume religious practices, and increase free religious expression (all typical of the whole post-socialist space), a major characteristics of the so-called 'religious revival' in Macedonia was the 're-traditionalization' of religion and the increasing number of so-called 'traditional believers' for whom this 'revival' is related to a return to traditional religious rites and ritual practices (see Matevski 2008). Unlike them, the so-called 'true believers' are observing the dogma more strictly. At the same time, another characteristic of post-socialist religious life in Macedonia is the strengthening of the position and role of the church in the country, as well as its aspiration for full control over religious life. These tendencies have an impact on the development of the religious landscape in Macedonia; with the Strumica region being a prime example.

One of the most striking examples of the impact of the so-called 're-traditionalization' of Strumica's sacred geography is the case of Angelci village. In the last 25 years, a complex of eleven chapels built by local people gradually sprang up in the surroundings of Angelci. All these shrines are erected by people who believe that they are 'enslaved' and 'tortured' by a Christian male or female saint who appears in a 'dream' and gives instructions of where and how to build a shrine. Usually, after a smaller or a larger chapel is built, the 'torture' or possession stops for a shorter or a longer period of time, then the saint reappears to request something else from the person. This began in the mid-1980s, when a local man named Simo went to the town of Petrich to seek help from Vanga. The latter predicted that one day there would be a very special holy place near Angelci, with numerous shrines. After Simo told the story of his visit to Vanga in the village, local people began 'dreaming' and hearing saints' voices intimating them to build shrines in the locality specified by Vanga. Consequently, shrine after shrine emerged, and the wave of 'dreams' continues into the present.[10]

Vanga's prophecy unlocked the already-mentioned practice of building shrines after a 'dream' and by a saint's 'request'. It was well known in the village of Angelci, where in the absence of a formal parish church, a similar shrine was assigned to this function. The shrine was built in 1943 after a woman from the village had a repetitive dream of St. John Chrysostom. The saint told her that the family house is built on the land of a monastery and that they should move away or they will die. People started to die, and the family finally decided to move away. They raised funds from the villagers and built a chapel dedicated to St. John Chrysostom.

However, the result of the re-emergence of this traditional form of religious activity was that people confront the Church. The Bishopric of Strumica continues its refusal to consecrate the chapels in the village. The refusal is grounded on doctrinal as well as practical considerations. The Macedonian Orthodox Church denies 'dreaming' as a justification of lay people's initiative, 'dreams' being part of the so-called traditional faith that the institution fights: the 'dreamers' who initiate such buildings are stigmatized as seers and sorcerers. On the other hand, the Church refuses to consecrate the chapels before assuming full possession of them. Thus, a second main characteristic of the development of the religious landscape surrounding Strumica is the institutionalization of the initiative for building or restoring shrines. The wish of the Bishopric of Strumica to fully control and manage the religious life in the region hinders personal initiatives for building churches. Everyone who wants to make a donation should donate directly to the Church, which will in turn decide the best way to spend the money. At the time being, everyone in Angelci keeps the key to his "own" shrine and takes care of it. This is also the case with the Chapel of St. John Chrysostom, which functions as a parish church. It is very likely that this fact

---

[10] For more on constructing chapels after "dreams" in Angelci, see Periklieva 2016.

provoked the Bishopric of Strumica to start in 2010 the construction of a church in Angelci and thus lay the beginnings of a "proper ecclesiastical, spiritual life" in the village.

Although somewhat restricted, there are enough initiatives for restoration or construction of new churches in the region of Strumica. However, in order to bring them to fruition, the whole process, from beginning to end, should be managed by the Church. Thus, regardless of original initiator, the Church should assume institutional control, and all members of the community would be urged to make donations. The biggest project in the region of Strumica today is the building of the Cathedral church of the Assumption of the Virgin Mary in the centre of the town. The initiative belongs to the mayor of Strumica, Zoran Zaev. The foundations of the church were laid fourteen years ago, but the project was not approved by the Bishop of Strumica and the construction works were ceased. Six or seven years ago, Zaev once again took the initiative, and after long negotiations and disputes with the Bishop, the construction works were renewed on Easter 2012. The Municipality and the Bishopric saw symbolism in the year of construction renewal. It was announced that the church will be the biggest one in the Balkans, and that its building is on the occasion of the 1650th anniversary of the death of the Holy Fifteen Tiberiopolis Martyrs, the 100th anniversary of the Church of Sts. Cyril and Methodius in Strumica, and the 45th anniversary of the autocephalous status of the Macedonian Orthodox Church. Thus, from the very beginning, the new church is being constructed as a symbol of local identity by relating its construction to the anniversaries of the cathedral church and the patron saints of Strumica. However, it also symbolizes national identity by relating it to the anniversary of the autocephalous status of the Macedonian Orthodox Church. All the inhabitants of the Strumica region could make a "religious investment". They receive donation blanks with their monthly water bills on which they only have to write in the amount of their donation.

The clash between the institution of the church and the so-called 're-traditionalization' manifests itself also in relation to the role of Vanga in the religious life of the region of Strumica. Although, in contrast to Petrich, Vanga did not become an object of mass religious worship in this region, while still alive she was a popular alternative for those people who needed help. Today, after her death, she continues to be an object of gratefulness and homage. Moreover, as we saw in the case of Angelci, she is a sort of device for shaping the religious landscape and for its legitimation. At the same time, the Church stigmatizes such type of religious specialists and proclaims Vanga's gift to be "from the Devil". This clash is very well illustrated with the case of the village of Novo selo. Following the example of Petrich, some enterprising people from the region of Strumica became aware of the potential the region could have for the development of tourism, given Vanga's childhood there. Thus, the former mayor of the village of Novo selo came up with the idea of building a memorial park of Vanga at the place of the fountain called Anska cheshma. From the time she was thirteen years old until her marriage Vanga lived in that village. It was in that village where she was lifted by the whirlwind and became blind. Local people associate Vanga's blinding and unusual gift precisely with the Anska cheshma fountain. She was thrown there by the whirlwind and subsequently began hearing a voice, which was telling her to wash her eyes in the fountain in order to get back her sight. Instead, she received her gift. The project proposed to reconstruct the old Anska cheshma, build a memorial park of Vanga around it, and mark places in the village related to moments of Vanga's life and the process of her transformation into a seer. Initially, there was an idea of making a small chapel near the fountain but since the mayor didn't want to start an argument with the Bishopric, he renounced it. However, the Municipality found a way not only to reckon with the Church, but also to attach sacred symbolism to the place. Instead of building a real chapel, the fountain is covered by a big penthouse that resembles church architecture. Within a niche in the fountain sits an icon of the Virgin Mary.

RELIGIOUS LANDSCAPES AND CONTEXT

After the Ottomans conquered the old-time Bulgarian lands, including the regions of Petrich and Strumica, the Church became the main pillar of the Bulgarian ethnicity since Christianity, that is the confessional discrimination functioned also as ethnic differentiation between Bulgarians and Ottomans. The main goal of the Church under conditions of Ottoman rule was to preserve Christian faith, Bulgarian identity, and culture, even if it meant to become reconciled with the pagan elements in the ideology of the people, which in that period were even more vital. The struggle against pagan practices and superstitions was put aside, and clergymen not only tolerated rituals of pagan nature, but even took part in them. Since the 19th century, the Orthodox churches, under whose jurisdiction in different periods was the geographical region of Macedonia (the Patriarchate of Constantinople, the Bulgarian Exarchate and the Serbian Orthodox Church), tried to realize the so-called 'evangelization' or the eradication of pagan remnants in the religious life of the Orthodox population. Those attempts were mostly oriented toward collective village rituals with blood sacrifice (kurban). Despite the efforts, the Church's initiative was not very successful. Thus, until the liberation of the regions of Petrich and Strumica in 1912, religious life in the area remained poorly connected with the Church while preserving numerous local religious elements typical of the pagan ideology.

After the Liberation of Ottoman rule, in the 1920s and the 1930s the region of Pirin Macedonia, part of which is the region of Petrich, fell under the authority of the International Macedonian Revolutionary Organization (IMRO). Thus, for a certain period of time there was no actual official Bulgarian state authority and the structures of IMRO turned the area into a "state within the state". During the "rule" of IMRO in Pirin Macedonia the functioning of official institutions was hindered. To a great extent this also applied to the Church. The regime of IMRO relied on tradition, which in addition to the lack of a properly functioning church organization, furthered the preservation of many forms of local religiosity that otherwise died out faster in other places because of modernization and the influence of the Church. The trauma from the Balkan Wars, two World Wars, local antifascist resistance, change of authority after 1944, and the frequent shifts in the state policy in relation to the Macedonian identity in the region led to a sense of insecurity among local people. The need of a vent for the pressure, such as religiosity, became more and more tangible. Religiosity, however, became a taboo in the socialist period during which state authorities were promoting atheism. All this created conditions for the development of a religious life that became "domesticated" and distanced from the Church. This also created suitable ground for the preservation and affirmation of typical elements of local religiosity as well as of alternative forms for contact with the divine.

The religious 'revival' in the post-socialist period did not lead to significant changes in the traditionally poor authority of the Bulgarian Orthodox Church (BOC). Undoubtedly, the institutional discords and the schism in the Church, whose culmination was the dissent in the Bulgarian Orthodox Church in 1992 and the functioning of Alternative Synod between 1996 and 2012, also exercised an influence in this respect. The BOC does not succeed in establishing itself as a factor in the social life of the country and engaging in activities among the Orthodox population. The institutional weakness of the BOC shows in the sporadic visits to the churches and in the results of a number of sociological studies, according to which only 15% of those queried declared to be "deeply religious" (Bogomilova 1998: 355-357). But the clearest expression of this weakness is the nature of the Bulgarian 'religious revival', which in terms of organization begins "from below". Religious studies in post-socialist Bulgaria show that, locally, the 'religious revival' is initiated by the ordinary believers and not by clerics or the church institution as official mediator between the earthly life and the divine. As a rule, the Church intervenes in this process when the initiatives for religious revival are already locally established and proved their vitality. The traditionally weak position of the church institution is at the root of the low level of religious literacy of the people. The Church keeps alive numerous local religious practices, which from an ethical perspective, have non-Christian, non-canonical, and even pagan characteristics. This fact explains the domination of concrete-visual over abstract thinking that still exists. This becomes particularly visible in the context of the main characteristic of the Bulgarian 'religious revival' – its material expression, the building of new, and the restoration of old shrines. As we saw, these basic processes in the post-socialist religious life in Bulgaria are visible in the sacred geography and its development in the region of Petrich: intense building of new churches and their concentration in small and even depopulated villages, which speaks to a lack of strictly practical preconditions for their emergence; initiation "from below," which acquires an official form by the Church only at its completion; the main trigger for changes in the religious landscape are the traditional ancient non-canonical practices and alternative religious forms, such as 'dreaming' and the figure of Vanga. Namely the figures of the so-called prophetesses and clairvoyants are a good example for the vitality of non-canonical religious practices and for their acceptance by the BOC, or at least its ambiguous attitude toward them. We find such an example in the region of Petrich, where the vicar Angel Kochev is one of the main supporters of the idea for Vanga's canonization, as well as one of the eager supporters of the cult of Reverend Stoyna[11] whose icons appear in every church where father Kochev is allocated to serve.

Shortly after the liberation in 1912, the region of Strumica became part of the diocese of the Serbian Orthodox Church, which held significant control over religious life in its territory and implemented much more successfully the so-called 'evangelization'. Yet, the condition of religiosity in Macedonia from the previous period did not change dramatically. However, the contact with the religious authority of traditionally stronger church institutions inevitably had an impact and probably "inspired" the emancipated new Macedonian Orthodox Church (MOC) to keep a tight rein on religious life. However, this process began only in the 1990s, since during the socialist period Yugoslavia also carried out an atheistic policy. Yet, it should be noted that the religious tolerance of the Yugoslavian state authorities was much greater compared to other countries from the Eastern Bloc, like Bulgaria, for example.

These developments had an impact on religious life in Macedonia after the disintegration of Yugoslavia. An additional factor is the new political context – the striving for the affirmation of the independent Macedonian state, of the Macedonian ethnic affiliation and identity. Under these conditions, compared to Bulgaria, religious life in post-socialist Macedonia started along a different road, where it became more and more institutionalized. MOC not only had more control in the religious sphere, but it played a significant role in the process of constructing and approving Macedonian identity. We could say that the process of the so-called 'antiquization' also became part of the church policy. Since its very establishment, MOC has searched for its roots in the early medieval period, proclaiming itself inheritor of the Archbishopric of Ohrid. In the last twenty odd years, its efforts have been directed toward the search for even older symbols, from the eras of Antiquity and early Christianity. At the same time, there are attempts for the eradication of traditional religious practices, which are considered to be not only non-canonical but "ethnically" alien. The region of Strumica offers illustrative examples of these processes. Apart from examples previously discussed, the so-called 'tables of love' were introduced by the Bishop of Strumica in order to replace the blood sacrifice (kurban) during the festivals of the patron saints of the churches and to give the joint meal related to them the early-Christian form of '*agapi*'. The strive to find a connection to the distant Christian past has impacted the sacred geography of the region. In 2002, the Church of

---

[11] Reverend Stoyna (1883-1933) is an alternative religious specialist from the village of Sushitsa, the region of Petrich. A long time before Vanga, she became a folk/living saint and a cult of her developed in the region. For more details see Измирлиева и Иванов 1990.

St. Gregory Palamas and St. Demetrius was built in Strumica. Its architecture is of typical Byzantine style. Meanwhile, the Bishopric of Strumica makes every endeavour to eliminate all religious practices that are considered to be contrary to the church canon. Changes in the diocese began with the arrival in 1995 of Bishop Naum, who attempted to gradually eradicate religious customs in the region he considered to be incompatible with Orthodox faith or Macedonian nationalistic policy. For example, such is the case with his efforts to eradicate the custom of '*badnikovo drvce*'[12] within the framework of the Bishopric of Strumica, which is considered to be Serbian by the Bishop and the priests. The peculiar forms of 'antiquization' in MOC speak, on the one hand, to its aspirations to prove its right of existence before the Orthodox Churches, which does not recognize its roots in ancient history and the purity of Christianity that it tries to impose. On the other hand, religious 'antiquization' is indicative of the relation of MOC to the state policy of construction of Macedonian national identity. Thus, one of the typical features of the religious life in post-socialist Macedonia is the process of politicization of religion, i.e. establishment of close relations between the political and religious elites in Macedonia (see Земон 2007).

Despite the attempts of MOC to keep a tight rein on the religious life in Macedonia and to bring it into line, as we already mentioned, there is a parallel process of 're-traditionalization'. People find ways to evade or oppose the imposition of church rules and to continue to observe, in one way or another, the traditional religious rites and ritual practices. An example from the region of Strumica is the village of Drazhevo. It has an annual village kurban on St. Michael's Day. In 2012 the feast was on Wednesday, the day on which according to the church canon is lenten. Despite that, the people of Drazhevo were explicit that the ritual of the blood sacrifice had to be observed. According to them, once established on a specific date, the kurban could not be changed or replaced by a lenten one since this may cause misfortunes. Since the local priest refused to participate in a kurban on a lenten day, his role was taken by the sexton of the local church who performed the ritual of the blessing of the kurban and the ritual breads.

CONCLUSION

A review of the religious landscapes of Petrich and Strumica reveals, on the one hand, changes that occurred in the religious life of the two countries in the post-socialist period, and on the other, the different roads these once culturally uniform regions followed. Sacred geography in the region of Petrich is

---

[21] In brief, 'badnikovo drvce' is part of a tree trunk (the type of tree differs according to the local tradition), ritually cut and brought home on Christmas Eve. The log is ritually consecrated and laid on the fire. This or similar types of the custom are recorded among different Christian denominations in the Balkans as well as in various parts of Europe.

developing in the context of weak institutional control, initiation "from below", and vital and unhindered local religious practices. In contrast, the development of the religious landscape in the Strumica region is taking place under the conditions of stronger religious control executed by the Diocese and MOC under a policy of eradication of traditional local practices and institutionalization of religious initiatives. This shows the impact of the official (central) policy of the BOC and the MOC on the religious life of the respective regions. If in the region of Petrich such policy is hardly visible, it is quite obvious in the region of Strumica and represents part of the overall policy for construction of a Macedonian identity. At the same time, we notice that people in Strumica find a way to evade or adapt to the official policy imposed by MOC. Thus, despite everything, an initiative "from below" and the maintenance of traditional religious mechanisms created new churches in the region. In fact, this shows the clash between the interests on a national (state) level and on a local (non-institutional) level. If the interests on the state level aim at constructing and approving the national identity, those on the local level are directed to the local identity. Religious life in Petrich does not reveal the presence of centralized policy of national identity construction but there are obvious processes of local identity confirmation, especially at the level of the village. This is clearly represented by the cases of intensive building of shrines in depopulated villages by their former inhabitants and the naming of chapel concentrations "Bulgarian Mount Athos". Undoubtedly, one of the reasons for this process is the strong internal migration (from the villages to the cities) as well as the more and more intensive external migration (to various European countries). To a greater extent, external migration influences the processes of local self-identification in the region of Strumica. Yet, another significant reason is the religiously mixed population of the region. On one hand, it stimulates the official religious policy. Certainly, the traditional local religious practices are the point of interaction of the various confessions in the region: Catholics participate and even organize kurbans together with the Orthodox Christians, and Muslims light up candles in Christian chapels and seek help from their patron saints. On the other hand, the presence of different confessions, especially Islam, determines the significant role of religiosity in local self-identification and the religious symbolization of the space by sacred buildings. It can't be a coincidence that the complex with the numerous chapels in Angelci emerged precisely in a village that is divided from the neighbouring Muslim settlement of Gradoshorci by a single street.

This study shows how a changed political situation led to significant changes in the religious life of a once culturally uniform region. These changes are determined by the development of the regions within different states, by the different current needs of these states, and the policies related to them. However, at the same time, the development of religious life is also dependent on the concrete local interests of the regions, which are a precondition for the preservation of a number of common religious elements. Such elements (religious as well as cultural), which are "non-institutional" by nature, could be grounds for the maintenance of eventual communal unity and identity of the two regions. This, however, is a topic of another study.

REFERENCES

Bogomilova, Nonka. 1998. "Religion und sozialer Wandel in Bulgarien." In *Religiöser Wandel in den postkommunistischen Ländern Ost- und Mitteleuropas*, edited by Detlef Pollack, Irena Borowik, Wolfgang Jagodzinski, 347-69. Würzburg: Ergon Verlag.

Horster, Marietta. 2010. "Religious Landscape and Sacred Ground: Relationships between Space and Cult in the Greek World." *Revue de l'histoire des religions*, 4, 435-458.

Lenclud, Gérard. 1995. "L'ethnologie et le paysage? Questions sans réponses." In *Paysage au pluriel. Pour une approche anthropologique des paysages*, 3-17. Paris: MSH.

Matevski, Zoran. 2008. "The challenges of Sociology of religion in Macedonia after 1991." In *The Sociology of Religion in the Former Yugoslav Republics*, edited by Dragoljub Đorđević, 41-56. Niš: YSSSR.

Periklieva, Violeta. 2016. "'Dreaming' saints and building chapels in times of crisis (The case of Angelci, Macedonia)." *Ethnologia Balkanica*, 18, 204-213.

Scheid, John, et François de Polignac. 2010. "Qu'est-ce qu'un « paysage religieux"? Représentations cultuelles de l'espace dans les sociétés anciennes." *Revue de l'histoire des religions*, 4, 427-434.

Valtchinova, Galina. 2002. "Orthodoxie et communisme dans les Balkans: réflexions sur le cas bulgare." *Archives des Sciences Sociales des Religions*, 119, 79-97.

Valtchinova, Galina. 2015. "Introduction." *Études Balkaniques: Cahiers Pierre Belon*, 18, 13-28.

Земон, Рубин. 2007. "Ролята на религията и религиозните институции в новите обществени, политически и етнически промени в Република Македония." In *"Завръщане" на религиозността*. София, 168-177.

Измирлиева, Валентина, и Петко Иванов. 1990. "Сушишката светица Стойна. 1. Житие." *Български фолклор*, 3, 75-94.

Пандевски, Манол, и Ѓорѓи Стоев. 1969. *Струмица и Струмичко низ историјата*. Струмица.

Петров, Петър, и Христо Темелски. 2003. *Църква и църковен живот в Македония*. София: Македонски научен институт.

Снегаров, Иван. 1995. *История на Охридската архиепископия*. Т.1, София: АИ "Марин Дринов".

SITES OF MEMORY AND SOCIAL CHANGE IN CROATIA: A CASE STUDY OF THE *SEAGULL'S WINGS* MONUMENT

Marko Mustapić and Benjamin Perasović
Institute of Social Sciences *Ivo Pilar*

INTRODUCTION

Political power is clearly revealed in rituals and symbols, including monuments and commemorations of historical events. Indeed, commemorative activities are extremely important for the construction and renewal of collective memory. Memory is rooted in the particular – in space, in a gesture, an image or an object – which explains the importance of sites of memory, and especially monuments. Since the fall of socialism and the beginning of the transition to democracy in Croatia, numerous socialist monuments have been damaged or torn down.

Podgora is a settlement in the Makarska Riviera, 60 km to the southeast of Split.[1] The Makarska Riviera is one of the focal points of the antifascist uprising in Croatia during World War II. The Yugoslav Navy was also founded along the Riviera in 1942. In 1962, in honour of the 20th anniversary of the establishment of the Yugoslav Navy, the monument *Seagull's Wings*, by the sculptor Rajko Radović, was erected in Podgora. The monument measures 33 m high and is located on the hill above the sea. As its name suggests, it reflects the form of a seagull with one wing held high in salute to the victory over fascism, and the other, a broken wing, representing the fallen sailors. An 800-seat amphitheatre was also built as part of the monument. The goal of this paper is to examine theoretical determinants of collective memory and reinterpretation of the meaning of the monument. It also evaluates commemorative practices surrounding

---

[1] According to the official censuses, the population of Podgora in the past 100 years varied between 2,101 (1910) and 1,268 (2011). A great number of participants and casualties in World War II relative to the small population would later have strong impact on the collective memory and commemorative practices in the local community.

the *Seagull's Wings* in the context of social changes that have occurred since the monument was built. For this purpose, this paper focuses on the political and historical context of the monument at the local and national level in Croatia, and it introduces basic determinants of collective memory.

Figure 1: The Seagull's Wings Monument, dedicated to the Establishment of the Yugoslav Navy in Podgora, 1942

Source: own research

SOME ASPECTS OF CROATIAN HISTORICAL AND POLITICAL CONTEXT

In order to interpret the findings of our research on sites of memory and social change in Croatia, it is crucial to provide the context surrounding the establishment and ultimate breakup of Socialist Yugoslavia, particularly as they related to World War II (1941-1945) and the Homeland War (1991-1995), respectively. Within the Kingdom of Yugoslavia, World War II formally commenced on April 6, 1941, with the attack of German, Italian and Hungarian military forces. On April 17, just twelve days later, the Kingdom of Yugoslavia capitulated. The Axis Powers divided the Kingdom of Yugoslavia into territories under the direct rule of Italy, Hungary, Bulgaria and Romania. The Axis Powers then installed Ante Pavelić, the leader of the fascist Ustasha[2] movement, to create a puppet state referred to as *Nezavisna država Hrvatska* (NDH), or the Independent State of Croatia. The NDH was proclaimed on April 10, 1941, after German forces entered Zagreb. The government was totalitarian, and a personality cult formed around its absolute leader, Ante Pavelić. This puppet state covered most of the territory of today's Croatia and Bosnia and Herzegovina, as well as some parts of Vojvodina. It was a quisling regime that was enforcing Nazi race laws and is therefore responsible for the prosecution of Serbs, Jews and Roma, as well as the Croatians that were deemed to be the enemies of the regime. In Serbia and other areas where the Serbian population was a majority, military groups known as Chetniks were established. They were founded by the members of a pre-war Chetnik movement and the officers of the defeated Yugoslav Army. Since the fall of 1941, the Chetniks were reduced to a mere collaborationist paramilitary force, dependent on the collaboration and logistics of Germany and Italy, while their main goal became the destruction of the Partisan forces. The Chetnik movement was active in the south and east parts of the NDH as well, where it was led by the former Yugoslav officer Draža Mihailović. Ideologies of the Ustashas and the Chetniks were based on the ethnic exceptionalism and the idea of an ethnically 'clean state'. The only real resistance against the fascist occupants and their local collaborators in Yugoslavia from 1941 to 1945 were the Partisans, organized by the *Komunistička partija Jugoslavije* (KPJ), or Communist Party of Yugoslavia, and led by Josip Broz Tito. The Partisans and the KPJ promoted the idea of 'a new socialist society' and 'brotherhood and unity' between the Yugoslav nations. In Yugoslavia, World War II ended on May 15, 1945. After a tremendous loss of lives, Tito, the KPJ and the Partisans ended World War II as a part of global antifascist coalition. A recent study by Žerjavić (1993) estimates the total number of war related deaths in Yugoslavia to have been 1,027,000, which includes 237,000 Partisans. The number of civilian victims was 581,000, including 57,000 Jews. In late spring of 1945, the Axis powers and the collaborationist military forces in Yugoslavia were defeated, in which tens of thousands of so-called *class enemies*, soldiers of the defeated armies and their civilian sympathizers, were killed at numerous execution sites such as Bleiburg, Kočevski Rog, Tezno, Žumberak etc. In his research of the number of the victims from the defeated collaboration armies, Žerjavić (1992) establishes that about 50,000 people were killed in those operations. Bleiburg is a small town in Austria close to the Slovenian border. Due to that fact, commemorations of victims couldn't be stopped by Yugoslav socialist authorities and those commemorations gained continuity. That's the main reason why Bleiburg has become a symbol and a metaphor for all the suffering of the Croatian Communist winner in 1945, but only a minority of soldiers and civilians have been killed in the Bleiburg and around. The casualties of war have caused both family and collective traumas that continue to exert a powerful influence on the social and political processes in Croatia. For the time Yugoslavia existed it was allowed to

---

[2] Ustasha – Croatian Revolutionary Movement is Croatian fascist and terrorist organisation founded by Ante Pavelić in 1929 in Italy, with the goal of creating independent state of Croatia. They acted mainly in emigration. In 1934 they participated in preparing and executing the assassination of Yugoslavian King Aleksandar in Marseilles. After the proclamation of the NDH, Ustashas become the key element of the armed forces of NDH. After the end of WW2, the term Ustasha acquired negative connotations because of war crimes and other atrocities.

publicly speak or write exclusively about the fascist and collaborationist crimes. Only since 1989 have Partisan crimes and the mass murders of civilians and collaborationists that followed immediately after World War II ended been a matter of public discussion in Croatia and Yugoslavia. In the first post-war years in Yugoslavia, the Soviet model of building a socialist society was implemented. The victory of the Partisans in World War II ('*Partisans cult*') and Tito's 'personality cult' were the central points of the new Yugoslav collective identity and its *official memory*. The political oppression of the totalitarian communist regime was known for its violent persecutions and assassinations of political opponents, both within Yugoslavia and beyond'. Political taboos and bans were numerous. "This symbiotic connection turned out to be counterproductive in the 1980s and the 1990s. The war as the central social 'experience' provided legitimacy and meaning, but, in the long run, it did not suffice in shaping the present and the future" (Sundhaussen 2006, 243).

Marshal Josip Broz Tito died in 1980. In the years following his death, changes in the federal republic's practices of cultural memory of World War II became apparent both in mass media and popular culture, which is also true of Croatia (for details, see Ramet 1996, Thompson 1999). The economic and political crisis intensified, and the subsequent democratic transitions of East European countries affected the events in Yugoslavia. Peaceful democratic development of Yugoslavian republics was opposed by the centralistic and hegemonic Serbian communist politics under the leadership of Slobodan Milošević. The *Hrvatska demokratska zajednica* (HDZ), or Croatian Democratic Union, was a Croatian nationalistic political party founded at the assembly on June 17, 1989. The key political aim of HDZ was the breakup of the Yugoslav Federation and construction of an independent and internationally recognized Republic of Croatia. Ultimately, the establishment of a multiparty system and the subsequent victory of the Croatian Democratic Union, led by Franjo Tuđman in the spring elections of 1990, along with similar political developments in other parts of the country, led to the breakup of Yugoslavia. The inevitable breakdown of totalitarianism in Yugoslavia enabled various national interpretations of historical events, which were formerly supressed and largely opposed. The *Srpska demokratska stranka* (SDS), or Serbian Democratic Party, organized meetings in support of Milošević's politics since the beginning of 1990, mostly in the rural parts of Croatia with a Serbian majority (e.g., North Dalmatia, Lika, Kordun, Banija). That is to say, the majority of local Serbian politicians are siding with the Greater Serbia politics of Milošević. This later led to the Knin rebellion - an insurrection of Serbs in Knin against the new democratic government of Croatia in August of 1990. In the spring of 1991, part of the Serbian population in Croatia started an open military rebellion against the newly established state, with the help of the Yugoslav People's Army and assistance from Serbia and Montenegro. This started the conflict later referred to in Croatian historiography as the *Homeland War (Domovinski rat)*. In June of 1991, the Constitutional Decision on the Sovereignty and Independence of the Republic of Croatia was passed. It was the final breakdown of Yugoslavia, and by the following January,

Croatia was internationally recognized as an independent country. In August of 1995, *Operation Storm* liberated the occupied territory, except for a small part in eastern Slavonia. During and after Operation Storm, approximately 250,000 Serbs fled the previously occupied territory of Croatia, mostly to Serbia and Bosnia and Herzegovina. Direct demographic losses in the Croatian Homeland War (1991–1995) counted 22,192 people (Živić and Pokos 2004, 737). The years of war operations, 700,000 people who were forcibly displaced (Goldstein 2008), as well as the damage worth billions of dollars, additionally exacerbated the necessary processes of economic consolidation and democratization of the Croatian society. In short, after almost half a century of various collective memories and practices of commemoration of the casualties of World War II a new war broke out in Croatia, bringing new casualties and new commemorative practices. Considering that certain Yugoslav symbols (such as red star) were also used by the aggressors during the Homeland War, the attitude towards the commemoration of World War II in Croatia changed significantly. Here we will present how the attitude of the small local community towards the monument to the establishment of the Yugoslav Navy changed over time.

LOCAL COMMUNITY AND SOCIAL CHANGE IN CROATIA

Numerous sociologists agree upon the importance of community for the functioning of society as integrated system. Tönnies 1887 (*Gemeinschaft und Gesellschaft*) and Durkheim 1897 (*Le suicide - Etude de sociologie*) already addressed its extreme importance in their classical sociological studies. Durkheim stresses that a functional community is a necessary precondition of society, for without it, an individual would be estranged from the state, and society as an integrated system would fall apart. According to Pusić (1963), people and space are dominant characteristics of the local community. Since people act in a certain area in order to fulfil various needs, Ajduković (2003) deems that local community should be understood as a process. Ajduković (2003, 25) concludes that such a state "represents a basis for the process of creating and changing numerous institutions and organisations, ideas and values, the process which includes cooperation and conflict in a continuous exchange of peaceful periods and sudden changes." The continuity of development of modern civic society in Croatia is that of modernization discontinuities. This syntagm summarizes the radical social and political conflicts and changes that are typical of the modernization of Croatian society. Each new stage in this modernization involved a dramatic institutional, cultural, symbolic and discursive break-up with the legacy of the previous period. In the past two centuries or so, the modernization discontinuities in Croatian society have not favoured the development of democratic values. Quite the opposite, authoritarian values, institutions and norms, as well as the social climate, favoured various forms of personality cults, the hero code, and loyalty to a party or a nation. Placing Croatia in the European geopolitical and historical context, Rogić (2000, 613) claims the following is central: "Croatia is on Europe's periphery, in a system of state formations that are themselves a European modernization periphery." Rogić (2000) believes that the modernization of Croatian society took place in three major periods. The achievements of the first stage of modernization (1868–1945) were very modest. The second stage of modernization in Croatia (1945–1990) was that of a typical socialist totalitarianism. Geopolitical and territorial mapping followed the outcome of the war and post-war events after 1945. The disintegration or collapse of the communist regimes in Europe was a logical result of the unsuccessful communist modernization model. The third stage of modernization in Croatia (1991–present day) is transitional. "Transition" denotes certain processes that serve as agents of change, or a transition from one political and/or social system to another. In Croatia, this term denotes a transition from a totalitarian to a democratic society, that is, a transition from planned economy to a capitalistic economic system, as well as the sociocultural processes that the two transitions cover. The continuing economic and social crisis is additionally worsened by the social memories of historical events, which manifests in the understanding and commemoration of the crucial events of Croatian history from World War II to today.

METHODS AND THEORETICAL FRAMEWORK

The aim of this paper is to determine the ways in which the local community in Podgora interpreted the meaning of the Seagull's Wings monument since it was built, and how it has constructed the memory of antifascists that fell as victims in World War II. There are several reasons why we deem that case study is the most appropriate method for this research: this specific case is convenient for examining the existent theoretical determinants; it is important for understanding the relationship of local communities in Croatia to cultural memory; it is suitable for chronological analysis. In the empirical part of this paper, we present historical events and social changes in the area of Podgora and the Makarska Riviera since World War II, after which we present our results by using qualitative analysis of historical monographs, archival entries and newspaper articles about Podgora. We also use semi-structured interviews with Podgora citizens (eight respondents between the ages of 24 and 75; interviews were conducted during June and December 2015), in order to gain information on respondents' interpretations of contemporary commemorative and social activities around the monument in Podgora.

Figure 2: Map of the Makarska Riviera

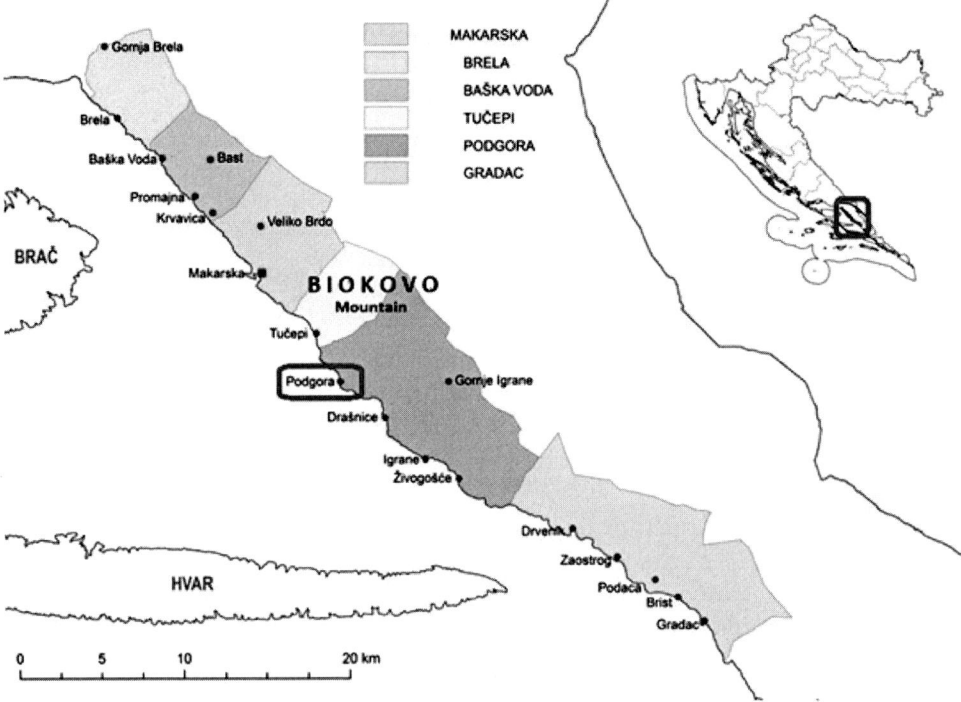

Source: own research

Halbwachs (1992) conceptualized the term *collective memory* as a selective adoption of the past from the perspective of the present. The central thesis that Halbwachs advocated in his work concerns the social determination of memory. He defined the term of social frameworks (*cadres sociaux*) as 'establishing and stabilizing memory'. The subject of memory is always an individual, depending on the social frameworks that organize their memory. Therefore, memorizing is a psychological process, while memory is a constant or sporadic renewal of a notion about the past. In the past three decades, a powerful research faction focused on the 'construction of collective memory' was established within the framework of the interdisciplinary approach to the phenomenon (Janeković Römer 2001). Assmann (2006) emphasizes that collective memory represents a group of memories shared by a community, and since it is tied to a community, collective memory is a fragile fruit of a momentary consensus within the community.

This is especially true of political communities.

"The notions of space and time in collective memory are vitally connected to the forms of communication within a group, connection which is affective and based on values. There is another characteristic of collective memory that most closely relates to being tied to a group, which is the reconstruction potential. Therefore, remembering has a reconstruction effect. It cannot preserve the past as it is. It is rather continuously reorganized through the changeable relational framework of the present moving forward." (Assmann 2006, 55-6). Therefore, collective memory adapts to social and political change. As collective identities and their meanings are changeable, so are the 'memories' and values on which these identities are based (Sundhaussen, 2006). The subject of *cultural memory* is 'the memory that makes a community'.

Assmann (2006, 65) emphasizes:

"It is not factual history that is important for cultural memory but only remembered history. One may also say that, in cultural memory, factual history is transformed into remembered history, and thus into myth. Myth is a founding history, a history that is retold in order to shed light on the present from the position of the source."

Memories are operationalized as objects of cultural significance with a tangible existence. They are monuments, museum exhibits, media reports, books and publications, commemorative rituals, and similar objectified memories (Nora 1996, Assmann 2006, Olick 2007). Of special importance for this text is also the *official memory* (Olick, 2007), a type of memory that is brought about by institutional production, that is, under a direct supervision of the authorities of a certain social and political system. However, as Meusburger, Heffernan and Wunder (2011, 8) point out, "But memory is always elusive. Most historical narratives are provisional: continually reshaped by new experiences and new knowledge and positioned within shifting centres and asymmetries of power. Narratives are contingent and depend on particular cultural systems of meaning that vary in space and time." As opposed to a series of rituals, myths, specific language, authority and everything that represents criteria of belonging, identification and loyalty to the Socialist Yugoslavia, there are alternative narratives of memory, both individual and group, preserved primarily by the oral tradition within the family, and sometimes within certain local communities and their particular collective memories. Considering that socialisation is an interactive process in which information is received through communication with others, but is also thought through and used to make life-changing decisions of individuals and society in general, these 'family narratives' permanently form the attitudes of a certain portion of the post-war generations in both Yugoslavia and Croatia. Birin (2005, 35) stresses that in Socialist Yugoslavia many subjects of contemporary history, especially in the period from 1941 to 1945, had to fit the politico-ideological frameworks imposed by the Communist Party and the state, which is why "historiographical interpretation of these historic events – which was, thanks to the possibility of using sources, masked as scientific – represented, naturally, a coarser of finer copy of the 'official' attitude of the Party and state." In other words, the crimes committed by the Partisans during and after World War II were covered up (e.g., Bleiburg, the Way of the Cross, murders of Catholic priests, collective expulsion of politically 'unsuitable' ethnic groups as Germans or Italians, murders of the Croatian political emigrants abroad). During the last two decades, following the breakdown of Communism, there have been various reinterpretations of historical events, organizations and persons, and primarily those associated with the events in World War II within the territory of the former Yugoslavia. What was once the official and institutionalized communist interpretation of World War II is now being pushed back by various narratives of the formerly suppressed personal and group memories - interpretations that were, in the former regime, most frequently punishable by law. During socialism, Croatian society was under totalitarian control of the ruling Communist Party of Yugoslavia. In that context, numerous 'forbidden narratives' and traumas that many families suffered are now being shared quite openly and publicly. Furthermore, street names that were once part of the communist narrative have been massively changed (Marjanović 2007, Markovina 2012), while many monuments and memorials have been destroyed. Delač and Šimunković (2013) confirmed that out of 937 monuments around the city of Zagreb, only one third has been preserved. Robionek, Müller and Vulesica (2010) reached a similar conclusion for the county of Split-Dalmatia, noting that out of 620 monuments, only one third has been preserved.

THE SEAGULL'S WINGS AND COLLECTIVE MEMORY IN PODGORA

HISTORY OF WORLD WAR II IN PODGORA

After the Roman Treaty between the Independent State of Croatia and the Kingdom of Italy was signed on May 18, 1941, the majority of the Croatian coast was lost to Italy. Italy annexed almost the entire coast. Those parts of the coast not directly annexed were put under Italian rule as part of a so-called demilitarized zone in which institutions of NDH were subordinate to the Italian Army. This included the Makarska Riviera. The Italian Army entered Makarska on April 20, 1941. Freivogel and Rastelli (2014, 116) inform us that the first Partisan camps in Biokovo Mountain were organised at the end of 1941.[3] At this time, Partisan activity in the area was mostly restricted to maintaining illegal sea traffic between the islands and the mainland. Biokovo soon became the centre of Partisan uprising in Dalmatia, and it remained so until the capitulation of Italy in September of 1943. Incessant Partisan actions from Biokovo led to the great Italian army operation *Albia* (12 – 21 August 1942) in which both Ustasha

---

[3] According to Anić (2005, 52), at the end of 1941 there were 7,000 Partisans in Croatia. By 1944 their numbers grew to 165,000, the entire Yugoslavia counting 550,000 Partisans.

and Chetniks were included. According to Anić (2005), the *Albia* operation turned into revenge against the population of the Makarska Riviera and the area surrounding the Cetina and Neretva rivers. One thousand and eight civilians and fourteen Partisans were killed. Even though most of the Partisans from Biokovo had retreated into Bosnia by that time, one Partisans battalion (*Vid Mihaljević*) remained in the area. On September 10, 1942, the First Naval Platoon was established in Podgora in order to impede Italian sea traffic. After the war ended, this event was to be celebrated as the Day of the Establishment of the Yugoslav Navy. Freivogel and Rastelli (2014, 480) stress that seventy eight Partisan diversions and attacks were inflicted upon Italian sea traffic in the East Adriatic from April of 1941 until the Italian capitulation on September 8, 1943. Thirty of those attacks were in the area of the Makarska Riviera. The population of the Makarska Riviera suffered great losses during World War II. The greatest losses occurred during the *Battle of Sutjeska* (May 15 – June 16, 1943), when the Axis Powers' offensive launched with a goal of breaking Partisan forces in Yugoslavia. The offensive failed, but numerous Partisans fell in the battle that was a turning point in the course of war in Yugoslavia. Anić (2005, 142-3) stresses that 127,000 soldiers of the Axis Powers were confronted by 22,000 Partisans (out of which 6,000 were from Dalmatia). 7,500 Partisans were killed in the Battle of Sutjeska, almost half of them from Dalmatia, with most of them being from Split (five hundred and fifty eight), Šibenik (five hundred and thirty five), Trogir (two hundred and twenty eight) and Sinj (hundred and twenty) (Anić 2005:144). Four hundred and two Partisans from the Makarska Riviera participated in the battle, and hundred and eighty eight of them were killed. Thirty nine Partisans from Podgora fell in the battle. In comparison, five Partisans from Zagreb and twenty one from Beograd were killed in the same battle.

THE SEAGULL'S WINGS UNTIL AND AFTER 1990: THE CONSTRUCTION OF MEMORY OF THE YUGOSLAV AND CROATIAN NAVY AND NEW TENDENCIES AMONG LOCAL YOUTH

In 1948, Ivan Mirković erected a monument in Podgora to the Partisans and civilians that fell in World War II. It was a statue of a Partisan defending a wounded sailor. The artistic concept of the monument *Seagull's Wings*, erected in memory of the establishment of the Yugoslav Navy, is completely different. This monument contains no star or similar ideological symbols. The right side of the monument holds a single marble plaque inscribed with the verses of Croatian poet Jure Kaštelan: "*Stop and listen living legend of freedom, the sea whispers below the rocks of Biokovo, sea tireless sea, deep sea.*" After a naval parade, the monument was inaugurated on September 10, 1962, by the then President Tito on the occasion of the 20th anniversary of the establishment of the Yugoslav Navy. It was a first-class political and media event which included the entire

Yugoslavian leadership and foreign military attachés and ambassadors. Until the dissolution of Yugoslavia, the monument was a central memorial site in the Makarska Riviera: key events of World War II were commemorated there, as well as political manifestations of Pioneers and the Socialist Youth League of Yugoslavia. Many respondents confirm this in our semi-structured interviews with citizens of Podgora. One respondent (49) recalls:

"During World War II, people of Podgora were mostly Partisans, like my parental granddad. My mother's uncle died in the Battle of Sutjeska. These sacrifices were greatly appreciated when I was a child, people admired them. The Day of Yugoslav Navy was the greatest celebration of the year; ships full of sailors would arrive, there'd be an orchestra, children wouldn't go to school, everyone would walk to the monument in procession, it was beautiful."

Since 1991 and the beginning of the Homeland War, those commemorative practices ceased to exist.

The change of the monument's function and related commemorative practices in the local community is also noticeable in the posters (Figure 3) which show that various social actors adopted the symbolism of the monument in certain periods of time. In the 1980s that is the socialist narrative of the establishment of the Yugoslav Navy, in the 1990s that changes into the Croatian narrative of the establishment of the Croatian Navy, and in the 2000s the monument is adopted by youth, in this particular case by the supporters of the Hajduk Football Club which invite the audience to the rock concert held in the vicinity of the monument.

Figure 3: Posters; 40th anniversary of the Establishment of the Yugoslav Navy (1982); the first celebration of the Day of the Croatian Navy (1993); concert and the celebration of Torcida Podgora (2013)

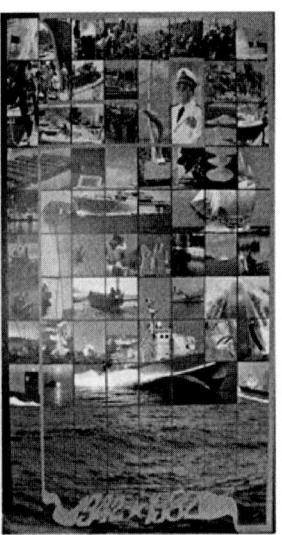

Source: Makarska Municipal Museum

Uncoordinated struggles of the Yugoslav People's Army and rebellious Serbs against Croatian police forces in central Croatia during April and May of 1991 escalated into a war that spread through Croatia. According to the 1991 population census, the Makarska Riviera had 21,041 citizens, 1,452 of those living in Podgora. At the beginning of August of 1991, a battalion of volunteers was formed in Makarska (Croatian National Guard – *Zbor narodne garde*). On December 21, 1991, the 156th brigade of the Croatian Army was established, counting approximately 700 soldiers. The beginning of the war in the summer of 1991 also demonstrated superiority of the Yugoslav Navy, for Croatian forces did not have enough army vessels until they took over the ships from the military port in Šibenik in November of 1991. The solemn session of the municipal assembly that used to mark Navy Day in Podgora was never held. The members of the Assembly of Makarska held a working session on September 9, 1991, from which a telegram was sent to the Yugoslav Navy in Split: "*In the name of piety and memory of the antifascists of this area – the founders of the Yugoslav Navy – the members of the Assembly of Makarska deny the right of the present Navy to consider themselves the inheritors of the Yugoslav Navy which was created in Podgora in 1942. Because of the military actions that the Yugoslav Navy has taken against the Republic of Croatia we also deny them the right to commemorate the anniversary of the Establishment of the Yugoslav Navy as their own.*" (Morović 1991, 1) The pride of the citizens of Podgora and the memory of the fallen Partisans and sailors suddenly became a part of the historical turning point and symbolic fuss. The local monthly newspaper (Morović 1991, 1) writes about the demonstrations of the citizens of Podgora against the 'invading navy', holding banners reading: AGRESSORS, STOP – THIS IS CROATIA! Since the beginning of the war, locals apparently started to distance themselves from the Yugoslav Navy and build their own identity on the idea of the Croatian Navy. According to Raguž (2012, 412-42), eleven soldiers from the Makarska Riviera died in the Homeland War, none of them from Podgora. Since the beginning of the Homeland war, there was a tendency to tear down or damage Partisan (Yugoslav) monuments in Croatia – and something similar happened with *Seagull's Wings*. A powerful explosion surprised the citizens of Podgora on March 26, 1992, when an anonymous culprit attempted to blow up the monument. The act provoked bitterness of the local community, which led to peaceful demonstrations by the citizens of Makarska on March 27 and citizens of Podgora on March 28, 1992. All political actors of the Makarska Riviera (self-government, political parties, Croatia's Association of Antifascist Veterans, etc.) condemned this "barbaric act" in the local monthly newspaper (Kuluz 1992, 1). The Presidency of the Assembly of Makarska issued an announcement that stated:

"…the attempt of tearing down the monument Seagull's Wings in Podgora is nothing but a political primitivism and callousness, for this monument is ideologically unmarked. It shows courage and manliness of the peasants and fishermen of Podgora and all the other Croatian sailors which fought for the freedom of their homeland and Croatian Adriatic. This monument has become a symbol of Podgora, a town which always knew how to appreciate the freedom of its people and its sea, which is why it denied the right of the Yugoslav Navy to consider the monument as their own on 10th of September 1991. By this act, the monument ceased to be a monument of Yugoslav Navy and became what it always was – a symbol of Croatian sailors fighting for freedom!..."

Franjo Tuđman, then president of the Republic of Croatia, soon adopted a decision on commemoration of the *Day of the Croatian Navy*. The date – September 18, 1993 – was chosen in memory of the first victory of the Croatian Navy over Venice in the Battle of Makarska in the year 887, and in accordance with new political and historical narratives based on the idea of a *thousand year old dream of an independent Croatian state*. Therefore, within the framework of the *new official memory*, since November 18, 1993, the monument *Seagull's Wings* has been used as a site to commemorate an event over eleven centuries old. One of the respondents (1974) describes this when talking about the 'new' Navy Day in Podgora: "*It's completely different; today, the Day of Croatian Navy, 18th September, is almost irrelevant to the people here, they do not see the connection of Podgora with the battle of Venice a thousand years ago. The Croatian Navy officers come here, there's a wreath laying ceremony, some speech, and that's that.*" Furthermore, since the beginning of the millennia, two anniversaries are celebrated because the reinterpreted Croatian antifascist version of the establishment of the Yugoslav Army has been resurrected. A respondent (1979) describes it thusly: "*There are a few old people in Podgora, perhaps twenty or thirty of them, who celebrate 10th of September, but that's all. To the young the date means nothing, and it all goes to show that September, 18 will remain the anniversary to be celebrated, but no one talks much about it in Podgora.*" The other respondents from Podgora describe the situation similarly. For example, the central celebration of the anniversary of the Croatian Navy was held in 2012 in Podgora and it was attended by the Croatian president Ivo Josipović and military and diplomatic representatives of numerous countries. On that occasion, the Croatian president said:

"The tradition of freedom that is nurtured in this area, inherited by the Croatian Navy, is one of the important characteristics of hard-working and capable men. What marks the Croatian Navy the most is the engagement in the Homeland War – which is why we must remember all the participants in the Homeland War which have sacrificed their lives for freedom. Next to the Croatian flag, here is a historical flag of antifascists, which together with this beautiful monument speaks about a generation which has risen to defend the homeland, freedom and their lives. Two generations, that of the Homeland War and that of our fathers and grandfathers, are examples to generations to come. We extend them our gratitude!" (Dragičević 2012, 12).

For the past two decades, the foundation of the Yugoslav Navy has been commemorated quite differently than before. For example, on September 10, 2014, the commemoration in Podgora was attended only by the leaders of the self-government of the Makarska Riviera, the leaders of local 'left' political parties, and a small number of elderly participants of the World War II and antifascist associations. The attendants were greeted by the municipal head of Podgora and the president of the Antifascist Association of Makarska, the latter of whom emphasizes the role of the Makarska Riviera and Podgora in World War II:

"We are standing in front of the grand monument to the Partisan sailors, which bears testimony to the courage and pride of the people with hearts of steel, peasants and fishermen who dared to attack the steel enemy ships in small wooden boats and chase them away from the Croatian coast. Just like during World War II, the youth of Podgora gathered in 1991 on these stairs to join the 156th brigade of the Croatian Navy and participate in the liberation of our country from the enemies" (Franić 2014, 2).

Even in the celebration of the old date there is a new discourse that combines memories of World War II and the Homeland War. The past two decades brought other changes as well: there are touristic and cultural manifestations such as concerts, plays, and a celebration of St. Vincent, the patron saint of Podgora. This commercialisation of the monument is attractive to the youth who seek 'nights out' and parties. A respondent (1976) commented on this turn of events:

"Oh, that's ok. It would be a pity for the monument to crumble, to die away. This way it's being maintained, restored, taken care of, and it attracts youth which otherwise wouldn't come. I think the monument has become a sort of tourist attraction as well, which is why the municipality grants concessions to caterers when there are concerts and such."

The Seagull's Wings is also an emblem of municipality and certain local firms, but its meaning is understood differently than that of the symbol of antifascist fight. This refers in particular to the youth – especially when we consider some of the problems we are facing in Croatia, such as the lasting controversy about historical revisionism (Goldstein 2008) and weak interest of youth in history (Mustapić, 2015). In accordance with the recent social changes, the practice of school trips to antifascist sites of memory has stopped. On the other hand, the youth sees the monument in Podgora primarily as a *place for practicing hedonism*. The monument is known far and wide as a place where pop-concerts are held in summer; even the municipality organises certain celebrations at the site. A lot of couples see the site as a good place for romance, as is confirmed by one respondent (1976): "*There's nothing better than the Seagull's Wings for summer flings with foreign girls. You've got to know, there's no place to go at night other than the beach and the monument – be it in a car, or even better, on that marble of the monument which is still warm from the summer sun, it's a dream…*" Besides, marihuana consumers of the Makarska Riviera see the monument as a popular place for smoking 'weed', as a respondent (1989) vividly describes: "*The atmosphere is ideal for smoking, especially at night, the way it is illuminated, there's a nice feel to it, you play some good music and goof around with a bunch of friends, it really gets crazy good…*"

CONCLUSION

The role of the monument *Seagull's Wings* in official memory has been transformed: where the initial concept was linked to the Yugoslav Navy, the new one is linked to the Croatian Navy. The commemorative date of celebrating the establishment of the Navy was changed from September 10, (1942) to September 18, (887) – in short, the Partisan narrative has been exchanged for the narrative of an independent Croatian state. Likewise, since the democratisation of Croatia in the 1990s, schools do not organise trips to the monument. As a result, the memory of the local community, which suffered great casualties in the struggle against fascism, started to be transferred almost exclusively within families. The transformation of memory in the sphere of politics was followed by twofold transformation in the local community of the Makarska Riviera and Podgora: one within institutions and one among the local people. Transformation within institutions refers to the fact that local institutions eagerly follow the new (Croatian) official memory and the leadership of state institutions. However, the response of the local population to the commemoration of September 18 is weak. On the other hand, local institutions still commemorate September 10 and the antifascist narrative about the establishment of the Yugoslav Navy. However, this commemoration is no longer supported by state institutions in any significant way. Furthermore, the Yugoslav Navy is now interpreted to be a forerunner to the Croatian Navy and its role in the Homeland War. In other words, the new interpretation of the monument is a certain crossover from the Yugoslav (antifascist) to the Croatian (nation-building) memory. Citizens of Podgora no longer feel the strong connection to the commemoration of September 18th as they did to the commemoration of September 10th. The latter commemoration is, nowadays, attended by only a small number of citizens of Podgora and the Makarska Riviera, and they consist mostly of the participants in World War II and their families. The youth of Podgora has less and less knowledge and interest in the culture of memory and the original function of the monument. Therefore, it is not surprising that more and more young people see the monument as a "cool" place in which they can have fun during the summer months. Besides, the local community is aware of the commercial potential of the monument, which has become an increasingly popular tourist attraction. This study shows that collective memory is a process with various actors, each of them creating their own discourses and interpretations of the monument in accordance with official and local (and sometimes alternative) narratives – the youth accepting its past almost exclusively from a present day perspective.

REFERENCES

Ajduković, Dean. 2003. „Socijalna rekonstrukcija zajednice." In *Socijalna rekonstrukcija zajednice: psihološki procesi, rješavanja sukoba i socijalna akcija*, edited by Dean Ajduković, 11-39. Zagreb: Društvo za psihološku pomoć.

Anić, Nikola. 2005. *Antifašistička Hrvatska – Narodnooslobodilačka vojska Hrvatske 1941 – 1945.* Zagreb: Multigraf marketing.

Assmann, Jan. 2006. „Kultura sjećanja." In *Kultura pamćenja i historija*, edited by Maja Brkljačić and Sandra Prlenda, 45-78. Zagreb: Golden marketing – Tehnička knjiga.

Birin, Ante. 2005. „Ideološke politizacije i najnovija hrvatska historiografija (1989.-2002.)" In *Hrvatska historiografija XX. stoljeća: između znanstvenih paradigmi i ideoloških zahtjeva*, edited by Srećko Lipovčan and Ljiljana Dobrovšak, 33-55. Zagreb: Institut društvenih znanosti Ivo Pilar.

Dragičević, Ana. 2012. "Josipović na 21. obljetnici HRM-a: Dvije generacije su primjer onima koji dolaze!" *Slobodna Dalmacija*, September 15.

Delač, Domagoj, and Šimunković, Mario. 2013. *Sjećanje je borba - spomen obilježja Narodnooslobodilačke borbe i revolucionarnog pokreta na području grada Zagreba.* Zagreb: Savez antifašističkih boraca i antifašista Hrvatske.

Durkheim, Émile. 1897. *Le Suicide: Étude de sociologie.* Paris: Félix Alcan.

Franić, Ozren. 2014. "Obilježena 72. godišnjica osnutka Partizanske mornarice." *Makarsko primorje*, September 10.

Freivogel, Zvonimir. and Rastelli, Achille. 2014. *Pomorski rat na Jadranu 1941-1945.* Zagreb: Despot infinitus.

Goldstein, Ivo. 2008. *Hrvatska 1918. - 2008.* Zagreb: Novi Liber Europapress holding.

Halbwachs, Maaurice.1992. *On collective memory.* Chicago: The University of Chicago Press.

Janeković Römer, Zdenka. 2001. „Povijesna spoznaja i metodologija povijesti u postmoderni." In *Radovi – Zavod za hrvatsku povijest 32-33*, edited by Ivo Goldestein, Marijan Maticka and Mario Strecha, 203-220. Zagreb: Zavod za hrvatsku povijest Filozofskog fakulteta Sveučilišta u Zagrebu.

Kuluz, Željko. 1992. "Bezumni čin." *Makarska rivijera*, April 1.

Marjanović, Bojan. 2007. „Promjena vlasti, promjena ulica." *Diskrepancija* 8:105-27.

Markovina, Dragan. 2012. „Kultura sjećanja u Splitu: Fenomen dvadesetog stoljeća." *Kulturna baština* 38:65-88.

Meusburger, Peter. Heffernan, Michael. and Wunder, Edgar. 2011. „Cultural Memories: An Introduction." In *Cultural Memories: The Geographical Point of View*, edited by Peter Meusburger, Michael Heffernan and Edgar Wunder, 3-14. Heidelberg: Springer.

Morović, Jasna. 1991. "Okupatorska mornarica." *Makarska rivijera*, October 10.
Mustapić, Marko. 2015. „Interes za povijest i kultura sjećanja mladih u Zagrebu: "hmm...povijest...pa zanima me, ali ...me i ne zanima..."In *Demokratski potencijal mladih u Hrvatskoj*, edited by Vlasta Ilišin, anja Gvozdanović and Dunja Potočnik, 99-123. Zagreb: IDIZ I CDP Miko Tripalo.
Nora, Pierre. 1996. „General Introduction: Between Memory and History." In *Realms of Memory: Rethinking the French Past* 1, edited by Pierre Nora, 1-20. New York: Columbia University Press.
Olick, Jeffrey K. 2007. *The Politics of Regret: On Collective Memory and Historical Responsibility*. London: Routledge.
Pusić, Eugen. 1963. *Lokalna zajednica: prilog proučavanju odnosa lokalnih samoupravnih jedinica i teritorijalnih društvenih grupa*. Zagreb: Narodne novine.
Raguž, Jakša. 2012. „U Konavoskim brdima" – prilog poznavanju ratnog puta 156. makarsko-vrgoračke brigade/domobranske pukovnije HV-a." In *Makarsko primorje danas: Makarsko primorje od kraja Drugog svjetskog rata do 2011*, edited by Marko Mustapić and Ivan Hrstić, 409-444. Zagreb: Grad Makarska, Institut društvenih znanosti Ivo Pilar.
Ramet, Sabrina P. 1996. „Rock Music." In *Balkan Babel. The Disintegration of Yugoslavia from the Death of Tito to Ethnic War*, edited by Sabrina P. Ramet, 127-150. Boulder: Westview Press Place of publication.
Robionek, Bernd. Müller, Nils. and Vulesica, Maja. 2010. *Erinnerungskultur in Dalmatien: Vom Partisanenkult zur Repräsentation der Nationalstaatlichkeit*. Berlin: OEZ-Berlin Verlag.
Rogić, Ivan. 2000. *Tehnika i samostalnost: Okvir za sliku treće hrvatske modernizacije*. Zagreb: Hrvatska sveučilišna naklada.
Sundhaussen, Holm. 2006. „Jugoslavija i njene države sljednice. Konstrukcija, destrukcija i nova konstrukcija 'sjećanja' i mitova." In *Kultura pamćenja i historija*, edited by Maja Brkljačić and Sandra Prlenda, 239-284. Zagreb: Golden marketing – Tehnička knjiga.
Thompson, Mark. 1999. *Forging war. The Media in Serbia, Croatia and Bosnia-Herzegovina*. Luton: University of Luton Press.
Tönnies, Ferdinand. 1887. *Gemeinschaft und Gesellschaft*. Leipzig: Fues's Verlag.
Žerjavić, Vladimir. 1992. *Opsesije i megalomanije oko Jasenovca i Bleiburga. Gubici stanovništva Jugoslavije u drugom svjetskom ratu*. Zagreb: Globus.
Žerjavić, Vladimir. 1993. *Yugoslavia – manipulations with the number of second World War victims*. Zagreb: Croatian Information Centre.
Živić, Dražen and Pokos, Nenad. 2004. „Demografski gubitci tijekom domovinskog rata kao odrednica depopulacije Hrvatske (1991.-2001.)." *Društvena istraživanja* 13:727-50.

CONCLUDING THOUGHTS: (CULTURAL) LANDSCAPES IN SOUTHEASTERN EUROPE

Gregory Zaro
University of Maine, Department of Anthropology

INTRODUCTION

The intent of this volume is to explore the concept of landscape and the methodological underpinnings of its investigation from an array of disciplinary fields. A number of the chapter contributions were formulated from presentations and discussions at the conference "Movements, Narratives, and Landscapes," which took place at the University of Zadar, Croatia, in the summer of 2015. Other contributions were solicited after the conference. Authors come from a number of disciplinary backgrounds, including cultural anthropology, archaeology, folklore, geography, and history. As the introductory chapter of the volume notes, the lack of specific guidance or direction given to the participants in advance was purposeful and intended to allow authors the freedom to explore the concept of landscape within their own unique disciplinary backgrounds, professional training, and interests. Authors were simply directed to address their study on landscapes in the geographic context of Southeastern Europe and permitted to go on about their work.

This approach creates both opportunities and challenges when seeking to understand how landscapes are treated among disciplines. On the one hand, it leaves authors untethered to any specific criteria to which the editorial leaders may subscribe, with the expectation that the resulting papers would reflect the state of landscape studies – or *a* state of landscape studies – within each expert field. On the other hand, without any imposed restrictions, this approach may also elicit a broad and loosely defined array of contributions, which can be problematic when looking to establish comparative baseline information on shared investigative practices and conceptual notions of landscape. In my view, this collection of papers falls somewhere in the middle: they differ considerably in approaches to the concept of landscape and its investigation, but common ground also surfaces on several key points.

DEFINITIONS AND COMMON THREADS

Without clear guidance, the degree to which contributors explicitly offered a definitional stance on landscapes varied considerably. Some used quite explicit terminology, stating both the context and theoretical approach upfront. For example, following Hirsch and O'Hanlon (1995), Galaty and colleagues define landscape as containers that "hold and are bounded by geographical features, such as mountains, lakes, plains, and rivers, but also enable and limit human perceptions and behaviors." Within this framework, they proceed to study prehistoric social change in the Shkodër province of northern Albania, using a mix of archaeological markers across the region. Zaro and Čelhar take a similar approach to their work in the Ravni Kotari region of coastal Croatia, recognizing that landscapes reflect "human engagement with the environment...and link the social and physical worlds into a dynamic mold." Both studies are squarely archaeological and focus on the context of the material record (cultural) within the broader environment (physical and/or anthropogenic).

Giakoumis and Lockwood also take an explicit stance on landscapes in their study of mountain pilgrimages in Albania. Like Galaty and colleagues, they refer to the work of Hirsch (1995) to suggest that landscape is "the meaning imputed by local people to their cultural and physical surroundings." This is not unlike Periklieva's interpretation of specific kinds of landscape, and in her case, the religious landscapes of Bulgaria and Macedonia. In her paper, she defines a religious landscape as "a social and cultural space constructed from interactions with specific religious models." She goes on to write that the "material expressions of religiosity constitute the religious armature of the space" but that such landscapes also include an intangible and non-visual character.

Other contributors remained a bit more vague in their definitional viewpoint on landscapes, or they chose not to offer an explicit position, preferring instead to take a more implicit tactic to the subject matter. For instance, in Glavaš's study of Croatia's Velebit region, she utilizes "archaeological, inscriptive, historical, oral, and landscape data" to reconstruct the territories of indigenous *civitates*. Trained as an archaeologist, Glavaš's work is highly interdisciplinary, drawing on a range of information to reconstruct territories of indigenous communities. She argues that through stories, some landscape features become recognizable and important to archaeologists, and they give the landscape its "spatial and physical identity, which helps preserve [boundary] traditions for the present and future." Her notion of landscape as both physical and cultural is implied in her work, and the lack of definitional criteria may simply be a reflection of the interdisciplinary nature of her research – it remains broad to account for the diverse kinds of methods and questions that fall under the nomenclature of landscape studies in archaeology (see also Horowitz and Fontes 2018). In her case, landscape is not defined in any single manner, but rather is the result of cultural and historical processes inscribed on the physical environment over time.

In a similar manner, Mustapić and Perasović focus their work on the role of commemorative activities in the renewal of collective memory. Using the Seagull's Wings monument in Podgora, Croatia, they demonstrate the changing symbolic value and importance of such "sites of memory" through time. Although not explicitly stated, their work also speaks to the inscription of collective memory across a landscape through monument building, but one that is malleable and available for reinterpretation as historical and cultural contexts change.

Finally, in her historical and geographic study of premodern landscapes in Serbia and Bosnia, Mrgić leaves the concept of landscape somewhat undefined, but suggests that an observer transforms an environment (geographical space) into a landscape by reading its various and ambiguous meanings among its physical and cultural features. Interestingly, she also refers to the notion that society "experiences nature through culture," a point to which I will return later.

In all contributions, whether explicitly defined or not, landscapes are the expression of human experience. Indeed, the general emphasis on landscapes as something fundamentally social and cultural is not terribly surprising given that the majority of contributing authors come from the social sciences and humanities, where people are the object of study. If this exercise had included scholarship stemming more directly from biology, ecology, or the geophysical sciences– other disciplines with strong landscape foci – the final collection of papers may have been much more variable on this point.

INSCRIPTIONS OF CULTURE AND HISTORY

Most of these studies, focused at least in part on material culture, consider landscapes to be spatially defined units where notions of history, identity, politics, religion (i.e., culture) are *inscribed* on the land. Culture and history are thus either tangibly or symbolically sewn into the physical environment, constituting a record of local human experiences. For the archaeologists and historians, this is clearly the case. Galaty and colleagues see landscape as a pallet upon which the processes characterizing the emergence of social inequality are inscribed, while Zaro and Čelhar argue that urbanization across northern Dalmatia is also written into the landscape. Both studies focus on landscape as a way to unravel the human story – one of settlement, domestication, colonization, inequality, and complexity, with the understanding that such cultural processes are inscribed passively or purposefully across a geographic region. Glavaš's focus on boundary walls, inscriptions, and the oral histories that surround them offers an additional example of the long-term human experience codified in the landscape.

Periklieva addresses the religious landscape, which may include both tangible and symbolic components. She argues that a religious landscape is "a mirror of religious life of a people, set in places that actively shape their environment; it is a sort of map that helps to decipher religious processes on local as well as national levels, and to follow the evolution of religious life of communities in a given area." In this sense, meaning is manifested in the physical and symbolic elements of the religious landscape (see also Giakoumis and Lockwood, this volume).

AT THE INTERSECTION OF CULTURE AND NATURE

One of the most common elements to emerge from this exercise is the recognition that landscapes lie at the intersection of culture and nature (or perhaps as Mrgić notes, the manner in which society *experiences* nature). Landscapes are intentionally or systematically transformed entities, or the product of long-entangled relationships between humans and the environments with which they interact. In these contexts, the relationships between humans and their environments, either physically or symbolically, constitute "cultural landscapes." As Rössler (2006: 334) notes, they are at "the interface between nature and culture, tangible and intangible heritage, biological and cultural diversity – they represent a closely woven net of relationships, the essence of culture and people's identities…" Although not explicitly stated in such terms, the concept of landscape is largely used in similar manners throughout most of the current volume. That is, landscape is a cultural concept that reflects the articulation with and co-evolution of human cultures with the non-human biological and geophysical worlds. This is the case with respect to the archaeological landscapes of social inequality (Galaty et al.), urbanization (Zaro and Čelhar), and sociopolitical boundaries (Glavaš). It is also the case with respect to the historical landscapes of Bosnia and Serbia (Mrgić), and the contemporary built landscape, including churches, monuments, and other features (Periklieva). Finally, pilgrimages combine with high elevation mountain environments in interesting ways to create associative cultural landscapes (Giakoumis and Lockwood).

An added challenge to landscape studies, however, is their evolution through time and changing symbolic value in the context of human cultures and societies. Historical events or cultural values may be commemorated with the construction and maintenance of monuments, shrines, churches, and pilgrimage routes, which may also be interpreted in new ways as cultural perceptions and values change. Such landscapes may also vacillate between stages of 'domestication', 'wild', or even 'feral', as cultural landscapes are periodically abandoned and repopulated, rendering them subject to reinterpretation. In nearly all cases, societies inherit past landscapes, often with deep anthropogenic roots, and they assign new symbolic meaning, whether the anthropogenic nature of landscape is recognized or not. In the case of built landscapes (terraces, groves, settlements, civic structures, churches, mosques, and other monuments), continuing or relic symbolic values may be evident. However, in the case of species composition, including forests, groves, prairies, and the many species that inhabit them, the contemporary view of a "wild" landscape may, in fact, be the result of millennial scale processes of human-environment dynamics (hunting, farming, burning, etc.). Nevertheless, the landscape lies at this intersection between human cognition and the environment itself, providing a way for people to engage with and comprehend the natural world.

CULTURAL LANDSCAPES AS HERITAGE

While reflecting upon this collection of papers, I found it to be a useful exercise to review literature concerning landscapes as cultural heritage in the context of UNESCO's criteria for cultural landscapes, including the historical evolution of the concept and applicable criteria for its protection and preservation. Over the course of it becoming recognized as a category of heritage for international consideration and protection, a number of contrasting visions of nature, culture, and landscape emerged. The category of cultural landscapes as World Heritage ultimately came from a negotiating process that involved several key actors in global heritage. Two advisory organizations, the International Council on Monuments and Sites (ICOMOS) and the International Union for the Conservation of Nature (IUCN), have been charged with the evaluation of sites proposed for inclusion on the World Heritage List since 1978 (Gfeller 2013: 488). Cultural landscapes as world heritage includes three categories of outstanding universal value for World Heritage purposes (WHC Operational Guidelines, 1995): (1) Clearly defined landscapes designed and intentionally created; (2) Organically evolved landscapes, which include relict or fossil landscapes with visible features, or continuing landscapes that retain an active social role in contemporary society associated with a traditional way of life; (3) Associative cultural landscapes, which include the powerful religious, artistic or cultural associations of the natural element rather than the material cultural evidence.

Today, the debate over the cultural landscape definition seems much less contested in World Heritage literature than perhaps the debate over criteria for its protection. Taylor and Lennon (2011: 541) note that a link emerges between a Cultural Landscape as an interface between people and nature and a Protected Landscape as "a protected area where the interaction of people and nature over time has produced an area of distinct character with significant ecological, biological, cultural, and scenic value." In the evolving discussion of cultural landscapes in heritage management and world heritage, the criteria for protection is more narrowly focused on outstanding universal value, often intended to protect biodiversity and/or cultural diversity while also promoting generations of human wisdom showcased in a landscape's built environment (Aplin 2007: 440). The idea that cultural landscapes must represent aesthetic beauty, or hot spots of biodiversity long managed by people is, perhaps, criteria for their protection, but not for their inclusion under the broader rubric of cultural landscape.

Overt emphases on either cultural or natural criteria still pose difficulties for the protection of cultural landscapes, but such challenges should be easier to overcome with respect to their basic recognition and interpretation. Protection inherently includes a competition for resources, whereas recognition is simply the identification of cultural landscapes as the interface between people and nature, either physically, intangibly, or both. Although not charged to specifically do so, the collection of papers in this volume find common ground on this fundamental point – that at the heart of human engagement with nature lies the cultural landscape.

REFERENCES

Aplin, G. 2007. World heritage cultural landscapes. *International Journal of Heritage Studies* 13(6): 427-446.

Gfeller, A.E. 2013. Negotiating the meaning of global heritage: 'Cultural landscapes' in the UNESCO World Heritage Convention, 1972-92. *Journal of Global History* 8: 483-503.

Hirsch, E. 1995. Introduction – Landscape: Between Place and Space. In *The Anthropology of Landscape. Perspectives on Place and Space*, edited by E. Hirsch and M. O'Hanlon, pp. 1-30. London: Clarendon Press.

Hirsch, E. and M. O'Hanlon. 1995. *The Anthropology of Landscape: Perspectives on Place and Space.* London: Clarendon Press.

Horowitz, R.A. and L.M. Fontes. 2018. Geography on a human scale: Global case studies exploring landscape archaeology. *Journal of Archaeological Science: Reports* 10.1016/j.jasrep.2018.02.022.

Rössler, M., 2006. World Heritage cultural landscapes. *Landscape Research* 31(4): 333–353.

Taylor, K. and J. Lennon. 2011. Cultural landscapes: A bridge between culture and nature? *International Journal of Heritage Studies* 17(6): 537-554.

WHC. 1995. Operational Guidelines for the Implementation of the World Heritage Convention. Available: http://whc.unesco.org/

INDEX

Albania 35, 98, 100
Animal husbandry 18
Anthropocene 50
Assman, Jan 153, 154

Bosnia 69
Bronze Age 35
Bulgarian Orthodox Church 142

Cameron-Daum, Kate 9
collective memory 15, 44, 147, 153, 154; official 150, 154; cultural 154
Croatia 147, 148, 150, 151, 160, 161

Dalmatia 49
Djurdjevi Stupovi monastery 79
Dolabella, Publius Cornelius 18, 19, 25
Dubrovnik 73

Eade, John 119
Europe 10, 35

Gajtan 39
Giakoumis, Konstantino 98, 99, 106, 111
Gregorič-Bon, Nataša 119

Halbwachs, Maurice 153
Herzeg Stephan Vukčić 80
heterarchy 70, 74
hill top 35, 45, 46, 59
Hirsch, Eric 10, 35, 166
homoarchy 70

Illyricum 15, 19, 92
Ingold, Tim 117
Intangible heritage 168

Jablanac 18, 19

Katić, Mario 81
King Stephan Tvrtko 80
Kodër Boks 38, 45
Kosovo 44

Kruja 106, 107, 109

Landscape 9; cultural 15, 16, 23, 30, 168, 169, 170; archaeological 15, 168; local 16; karst 16, 17; regional 35; studies 35; natural 46; long-term 50, 51; cultivated 50; modern 50; regional 52; changes 61; past 62, 168; hidden 71; lost 71; sacred 79; mountainous 89; religious 129, 133, 136, 137, 139, 140, 144, 145, 166, 167, 168; historical 168; built 168; evolved 169; fossil 169; continuing 169

Macedonia 130, 131, 138, 139, 141, 143, 144
Macedonian Orthodox Church 132, 139, 140, 143
Mali pisani kamen 16, 23
Mediterranean 17, 59, 60
mental maps 74

Nadin 49, 53, 54, 55, 56, 57, 59, 60

O'Hanlon, Michael 10, 35, 166
Oral tradition 15, 16, 22, 25, 30
Orthodox Christian 130, 132, 133, 136, 144, 145
Ortoplini 21, 22, 25, 26, 28
Ottoman 55, 70, 73, 141

Parentini 21, 22, 26, 28, 29
Petrich 130, 131, 132, 135, 136, 137, 139, 140, 141, 143, 144, 145
pilgrimage 89, 90, 96; Bektashi mountainous 90; Christian 93, 111; mountainous 94; orthodox 96
Pisani kamen 16, 21, 23, 24, 26
Podgora 147, 152, 156, 157, 158, 161

Ravni Kotari 49, 53
Roman 15, 19, 56, 70

Sallnow, Michael 119
Seagull Wings (monument) 147, 148, 152, 158, 159, 160, 161, 167
Serbia 69
Serbian Orthodox Church 74, 143
Shkodër 35, 36, 37, 38, 44, 45, 46
Slavs 71
Southeastern Europe 166
St Blaise 102, 103, 117
Strumica 130, 131, 132, 137, 138, 139, 140, 141, 144, 144, 145

Tilley, Christopher 9
Terror Management Theory 94
tumuli 35, 38, 43

Turner, Edith 117, 118

urbanization 49, 51, 52, 62

Vanga 139, 140, 141, 143
Velebit 15, 16, 18, 22

Zadar 49, 52
Zagorë 38, 39, 45

Studies on South East Europe
edited by Univ.-Prof. Dr. Karl Kaser (Graz)

Dominik Gutmeyr
Borderlands Orientalism or How the Savage Lost his Nobility
The Russian Perception of the Caucasus between 1817 and 1878
In Russia's cultural memory, the Caucasus is a potent point of reference, to which many emotions, images, and stereotypes are attached. The book gives a new reading of the development of Russia's perception of its borderlands and presents a complex picture of the encounter between the Russians and the indigenous population of the Caucasus. The study outlines the history of a region standing in between Russian reveries and Russian imperialism.
Bd. 19, 2017, 316 S., 34,90 €, pb., ISBN 3-643-50788-4

Basilius J. Groen
Aufstieg, Kampf und Freiheit
Nikos Kazantzakis, seine *Asketik: Die Retter Gottes* und die griechisch-orthodoxe spirituelle und liturgische Tradition
Das Œuvre des berühmten griechischen Schriftstellers Nikos Kazantzakis (Autor von u. a. *Alexis Sorbas*, *Griechische Passion* und *Die letzte Versuchung*) ist nicht nur äußerst umfangreich, sondern auch sehr religiös. Er wurde in der liturgischen und spirituellen Tradition der griechisch-orthodoxen Kirche erzogen, distanzierte sich aber später von der Kirche seiner Jugend und fand zahlreiche andere spirituelle Wege als die traditionell christlichen. Er versuchte jedoch, von der christlichen Tradition das, was ihm für seine eigenen philosophisch-religiösen Auffassungen nützlich schien, zu bewahren und zu verwenden.
Bd. 18, 2015, 162 S., 29,90 €, br., ISBN 978-3-643-50697-9

Milan Ristović
Schwarzer Peter und die Räuber vom Balkan
Themen über den Balkan und Serbien in satirischen Zeitschriften 1903 – 1918
Dieses Buch zeigt uns, wie bitter, geschmacklos und vor allem heimtückisch Karikaturen, aber auch sonstige Inhalte der humoristischen Presse sein können. Es geht um Themen wie das „Bild des Anderen", in dem auch das „Feindbild" leicht erkennbar ist, jedoch wird die politische Problematik unverkennbar vermengt mit der Sichtweise des Anderen oder mit der Dichotomie von „wir" und „sie" ... Alles erhält eine ganz besondere Dimension, zumal das gesamte Material durchdrungen ist von zivilisierter Arroganz und der Bereitschaft, die Anderen zu diffamieren ... Variationen zum Thema Europa und der Balkan, wozu auch andere bekannte verbale, d.h. psychologische Klischees gehören ...
(Aus der Rezension von Andrej Mitrović)
Bd. 17, 2015, 184 S., 29,90 €, br., ISBN 978-3-643-50648-1

Christian Promitzer; Siegfried Gruber; Harald Heppner (Eds.)
Southeast European Studies in a Globalizing World
vol. 16, 2014, 232 pp., 29,90 €, pb., ISBN 978-3-643-90595-6

Robert Pichler (Ed.)
Legacy and Change
Albanian transformation from multidisciplinary perspectives
vol. 15, 2014, 200 pp., 34,90 €, br., ISBN 978-3-643-90566-6

Mario Katić; Tomislav Klarin; Mike McDonald (Eds.)
Pilgrimage and Sacred Places in Southeast Europe
History, Religious Tourism and Contemporary Trends
vol. 14, 2014, 232 pp., 29,90 €, pb., ISBN 978-3-643-90504-8

Karl Kaser (Ed.)
Household and Family in the Balkans
Two Decades of Historical Family Research at University of Graz
vol. 13, 2012, 632 pp., 79,90 €, pb., ISBN 978-3-643-50406-7

LIT Verlag Berlin – Münster – Wien – Zürich – London
Auslieferung Deutschland / Österreich / Schweiz: siehe Impressumsseite

Karl Kaser
The Balkans And The Near East
Introduction To A Shared History
vol. 12, 2011, 416 pp., 29,90 €, pb., ISBN 978-3-643-50190-5

Aleksandar R. Miletić
Journey under Surveillance
The Overseas Emigration Policy of the Kingdom of Serbs, Croats and Slovenes in Global Context, 1918–1928
vol. 11, 2012, 192 pp., 19,90 €, pb., ISBN 978-3-643-90223-8

Sabine Rutar (Ed.)
Southeast Europe – Comparison, Entanglement, Transfer
Contributions to European Social History of the 19th and 20th Centuries
vol. 10, 2013, 504 pp., 49,90 €, pb., ISBN 978-3-643-10658-2

Andreas Hemming; Gentiana Kera; Enriketa Pandelejmoni (Eds.)
Albania
Family, Society and Culture in the 20th Century
vol. 9, 2012, 224 pp., 29,90 €, pb., ISBN 978-3-643-50144-8

Margit Rohringer
Der jugoslawische Film nach Tito
Konstruktionen von kollektiven Identitäten
Bd. 8, 2008, 344 S., 29,90 €, br., ISBN 978-3-8258-1289-8

Karl Kaser
Patriarchy after Patriarchy
Gender Relations in Turkey and in the Balkans, 1500–2000

Karin Taylor
Let's Twist Again: Youth and Leisure in Socialist Bulgaria

Christian Promitzer; Klaus-Jürgen Hermanik; Eduard Staudinger (eds.)
(Hidden) Minorities
Language and Ethnic Identity between Central Europe and the Balkans
vol. 5, 2009, 304 pp., 29,90 €, pb., ISBN 978-3-643-50096-0

Ulf Brunnbauer (ed.)
(Re)Writing History. Historiography in Southeast Europe after Socialism
vol. 4, 2004, 384 pp., 29,90 €, pb., ISBN 3-8258-7365-x

Miroslav Jovanović; Slobodan Naumović (Eds.)
Gender Relations in South Eastern Europe
Historical Perspectives on Womanhood and Manhood in 19th and 20th Century
vol. 3, 2004, 416 pp., 29,90 €, pb., ISBN 3-8258-6440-5

Slobodan Naumović; Miroslav Jovanović (Eds.)
Childhood in South East Europe
Historical Perspectives on Growing Up in the 19th and 20th Century
vol. 2, 2004, 304 pp., 29,90 €, br., ISBN 3-8258-6439-1

Miroslav Jovanović ; Karl Kaser; Slobodan Naumović (Eds.)
Between the archives and the field
A dialogue on historical anthropology of the Balkans
vol. 1, 2004, 280 pp., 29,90 €, br., ISBN 3-8258-6438-3

LIT Verlag Berlin – Münster – Wien – Zürich – London
Auslieferung Deutschland / Österreich / Schweiz: siehe Impressumsseite